WHAT PEOPLE ARE SAYING ABOUT *FIGHT LIKE HEAVEN*...

Fight Like Heaven! A Cultural Guide to Living on Guard was so much more than expected from the title. It's a barometer of the cultural WAR through the eyes of the church and history. Make no mistake; we are in WAR, good versus evil. Drenda describes the seven mountains of influence and our climb in a way that is fresh, unique, and inspirational. You begin to understand that God made us all to climb and to conquer the seven mountains of influence. We are to "occupy till He comes" (Luke 19:13).

You will gain an in-depth knowledge of the definition, history, and direction of what needs to happen for the church to take her rightful place in this WAR. We will win against the forces of evil. We guarantee you that you are going to have trouble putting this book down. This book is filled with a wealth of information concerning the current battlefronts we face. You will come out more educated, equipped, and motivated to take your position in this WAR and conquer the enemy. You are about to embark on the trek and the climb of your life and stake your territory for Christ. We must have "All hands on deck!" Well done, Drenda, well done! This is now going to be added to the recommended reading list for the Flashpoint Army!

—Gene (*Flashpoint* Host) and Teri Bailey

Drenda is bold, courageous, and unapologetic as she tackles some of the toughest issues facing the church today. Without compromise, she touches on those issues that are near and dear to the heart of God! It's time for the church to stand up and fight like Heaven.

—Joni Lamb, Co-founder of Daystar, Host of *Joni Table Talk*

I've had the privilege of knowing Drenda Keesee for over a decade. Drenda is a Proverbs 31 woman brimming over with talents and rich fruit. Her latest book is an example of the abundance of rich fruit she continues to produce. Fight Like Heaven! is a personal journey for Drenda and can and should be a personal journey for each of us. We all benefit from a well ordered society built on God's principles and favor. Conversely, we all suffer when His principles are ignored or worse, mocked. This is an uplifting book that inspires us all to draw closer to the One who made us and to the One who will never abandon us and Who declares His banner over us is Love!

—Michele Bachmann, Dean, Regent University, Former member, U.S. Congress

---

INFORMATION + HOPE + ACTION

Again Drenda steps out, and she gives us critically needed information in this upside-down world. The information found in this book will push you out of your comfort zone!

Keep reading… Drenda infuses her book with answers for hope and the courage to boldly follow God's call for us. She give us guidance for answering our call to action.

Thank you, Drenda, for a much needed book in these times.

—Jean Pilla, Instructor

As I sat reading this book, Fight Like Heaven!, by Drenda Keesee, not only was it an honor to write something about it, but I applaud her boldness and courage to stand against the modern-day Pharisees and write the truth in love!! Drenda states we are in a war culturally, spiritually, and personally. I personally feel like the line has been drawn as to who is on the Lord's side!! And when you read the information that is laid out with no fear, you will see why we "Fight like Heaven"!!

—Pastor Robin Bullock

Wow! Everyone on the planet should read this book! Drenda Keesee is one of the most courageous women we know and is a serious force in the Kingdom. This book is bold and truthful. Drenda fearlessly shines light on evil's agendas, urging readers to discern the day in which we are living and to recognize the significant part we play. This powerful work stirs us to Fight Like Heaven during this vital time in history—especially for the sake of the next generation!

—Tom & Kathy Toney, Founders, KUEST Student Leadership, KUEST.org

Pastor Drenda points out the obvious hubris that has grown in our society as a decreased desire for relationship with the God of Abraham, Isaac, and Jacob has led sycophants like Harari and others who have programmed influence in today's society.

Pride comes before a fall, and the trend is to boast with little information based on external data only. Those who choose to lack wisdom will always misconstrue the exact purpose and meaning of the facts set before them without using the lens of God.

We are tripart beings created in God's image and likeness. These individuals have rejected complete knowledge.

This book is chock full of wisdom based on Kingdom principles that make it a must read to prepare ourselves for the current cultural, societal, and personal challenges that we are facing.

As a neurosurgeon, I am confronted with a perception of the facts presented to me on a daily basis, especially when I encounter life-threatening events requiring emergent surgery. Pastor Drenda brings a fresh view of our weapons of warfare and their application to life's threatening events.

Pastor Drenda guides our focus to the answer by highlighting our view and use of Glory, Goodness, Agreement, and Faith. We must take an active role in this process in order to realize our victory.

This treatise is a must have in everyone's armamentarium as we live and fight the good fight of faith!

—Dr. Avery Jackson, Neurosurgeon

It took courage and boldness to write this book! The enemy will fight like hell to keep it from being released. In the military intelligence community, we gather information from many different sources. No matter where we acquire the information, it is put through a stringent process to determine if it is accurate (vetted) and if we can launch a successful operation against the enemy with the information. (Is it actionable?) This book is both vetted and actionable. Drenda exposes the true schemes of the enemy and who they are using to bring destruction and disorder to godly countries and the body of Christ.

Drenda also explains how Christians can and should engage in combat with the enemy. If you love freedom and righteousness, stop being distracted by cable news stations and read Fight Like Heaven! A Cultural Guide to Living on Guard. After spending decades in government intelligence and now in full-time ministry, I am surprised how most Christians allow the enemy to distract them with propaganda while they implement their destructive strategies. Well, not anymore. Thank you, Drenda Keesee for providing us with this unprecedented view of our Commanding Officer's (God's) orders to defeat the enemy.

One of my favorite insights from Fight Like Heaven! is: "We are called to love people but not to placate the devil and the spirits that attempt to operate against us or others. Has the church vacated areas of influence as the devil moved into them instead of taking a firm, respectful stand for right versus wrong? When we surrender these areas, they are taken over by dark forces. We have forfeited our influence and let the enemy occupy. For the last decade, we have heard so much about tolerance that we have allowed evil actions, especially against children, to go unchecked."

—Aaron Ward, Retired Senior Anti-terrorism Specialist with Naval Special Warfare, NATO Combat Advisor, and Author of Building Your KINGDOM FIRETEAM

I cannot think of a better, more qualified person to write this book, Fight Like Heaven, than my good friend and fellow minister Pastor Drenda Keesee. Why? Because Drenda has both borne and produced good fruit in her marriage, family, ministry, and local church, along with her character and personality that not only talk the walk but also walk the talk.

In taking on the "Goliaths" of today, Drenda exposes the very battle that the church, God's righteous army, is fighting and the forces that God's faithful saints are up against.

Many may dismiss some of this book as more "conspiracy theories"; some may just not want to know, burying their heads in the sand; while others will "wake up and strengthen that which remains" (Revelation 3:2) and fight the good fight alongside Drenda and Gary.

It is clear that Fight Like Heaven! has been well researched, well thought out, and well written in a way that once you start, you will not want to put it down. One would be blind and very naive not to see that the seven mountains of society are definitely being infiltrated by the "powers of darkness." Drenda exposes this truth and gives practical, biblical keys for living out today.

There is so much material in this book that one would be wise to read it through then read it again.

—Pastor Peter Mortlock, Senior and Founding Pastor of City Impact Churches International

In my opinion, there's no one on the face of this planet who cares more about promoting righteousness and helping you live a life founded on what God says than my Mom, Drenda Keesee. She has always been and continues to be passionate about helping people in the areas of their faith, their freedom, their health, and their family. In this, her most ambitious and comprehensive book to date, she tackles the lies Satan has tried to sell people while she also brings God's Truths to shed light. Her prophetic voice and her insight will galvanize and fuel your boldness, giving you courage and practical answers to some of the toughest questions we face today.

There's nothing like having an "aha moment" in an area within where you've been struggling. I know you will have many of those moments throughout this book! You won't be able to put it down—I know I couldn't.

—Amy Keesee Freudiger, Author of *Healed Overnight* and *The 30-Day Healing Dare*

Drenda Keesee boldly and skillfully wields the sword of the Spirit as she goes toe-to-toe with the devil himself in Fight Like Heaven! Having a shrewd, even scholarly understanding of current events, world history, and constitutional law, Drenda lights a fire under the American church to wake up, reclaim our government, stand on our God-given rights, and resist the political schemes of Satan, who she aptly describes as the "First Tyrant." This book is a must read for every Christian who is ready to battle against the powers of darkness and spiritual forces of evil but doesn't know how. For those tried and tested soldiers for Christ, this book will reignite the fight of faith to war for the Kingdom of God until Jesus returns!

—Amanda Prebble Lenhart, Attorney

"As John Adams said, 'Facts are stubborn things; and whatever may be our wishes, our inclinations, or the dictates of our passions, they cannot alter the state of facts and evidence.' What Drenda presents in *Fight Like Heaven*—however hard it may be to accept and however unbelievable it may seem—are hard facts. To ignore them is foolish and dangerous. To believe they don't exist is childish and self-destructive. It's well past time we recognize and accept the threats to our way of life. We must accept the challenge to push back against the forces that would destroy the liberty we enjoy through the shed blood of the Messiah. That means we must push back where we can, when we can, and how we can. This book gives us the practical tools needed to do just that."

—Daniel J. Pilla, Tax Litigator and Author of *Salt and Light: The Secret to Restoring America's Culture*

"The Holy Scriptures are a grand narrative of God's people heeding the call to do great things for the Kingdom in the darkest moments of history. In *Fight Like Heaven*, Drenda Keesee delivers an inspiring and practical message to this generation to not grow weary in doing good and to be strong and courageous, no matter how dark things may seem. There is no doubt Christians face evil and challenges unseen in our lifetime, but *Fight Like Heaven* reminds us that Christ's victory was and never will be in question. The only question is, "Will we engage in the battle alongside Him?"

—Aaron Baer, President, Center for Christian Values (CCV.org)

"God's 'timing is everything.' *Fight Like Heaven* could not have been released at a better time than the time America finds herself in. The author does not back down from discussing the pressing issues of our time, while giving the reader biblical solutions to the issues. From the first page to the last, you will not be able to put the book down. You can feel the anointing of the Lord on the pages of this book."

—Tonda Moore, Attorney

CONTENTS

FOREWORD

Dear Drenda Keesee, woman of God, woman of faith, woman of truth, friend of the body of Christ, and spiritual mother in the Family of God. You have exceeded my expectations with this new book, *Fight Like Heaven!* You have ascended from the mountain slope, of being an encourager and a faith-builder in the body of Christ, to the mountain peak of a prophetess declaring the Word of the Lord. Your voice will surely resound like thunder in the halls of at-ease Christendom.

Like a modern, ordained, and anointed scribe, you have taken a huge mass of information, condensed it for easier inculcation, packed it full of revelation, organized it under inspiration, and sent it forth for impartation—in order to bring forth transformation in the lives of those who receive your much-needed, God-breathed insights. I see this book like a fuel-saturated, fire-starter log that will erupt in flames upon opening and immediately begin consuming the combustible hearts of those who love the truth.

I have deeply desired to write a book on some of the same subject matter myself, but you have done it so masterfully, weaving together all these different, yet highly related parts, that now—I don't have to do it. I will just share your book with others—and that I intend to do, vigorously—that they might be "established," not just in historical truth, but in "present truth," just as the apostle Peter urged (2 Peter 1:12).

This is time-sensitive material. We have a small window of opportunity. The globalist, Satanic agenda can be thwarted, but only by an awakened and impassioned church. Yet more than that, it must be a mobilized church, empowered with knowledge that cannot be duped by the deception of the hour. Even God complained, "My people are destroyed for lack of knowledge." (Hosea 4:6). You are part of the cure for this dilemma, and I must say, a major headache to those who want the masses to remain asleep in their ignorance. And much more than just a headache—even as Jael put a tent peg to the temple of sleeping Sisera, and courageously drove it through with a hammer, thus ending the life of an enemy of God, so you have put a nail through modern-day enemies of truth who needed to be exposed. I applaud your tenacity in producing this book and your courage in publishing it.

—Mike Shreve, B.Th., D.D., Evangelist and Revivalist, Founder of "The True Light Project" and Author of 15 books, including three #1 best sellers, *65 Promises from God for Your Child, Powerful Prayers for Supernatural Results,* and *25 Powerful Promises from God.* www.shreveministries.org / www.thetruelight.net

"AND THE LIGHT SHINED IN
DARKNESS, BUT THE DARKNESS
SIMPLY DIDN'T HAVE THE
ABILITY TO OVERCOME IT,
TAKE IT DOWN, SUBDUE IT, OR
DOMINATE IT."
(JOHN 1:5)

PREFACE

Don't be unaware...

After ministering 30 plus years to individuals all over the world, I have seen the power of God's Word change lives in miraculous and incredible ways. The greatest frustration I have experienced is recognizing that many of their problems, pains, and even ailments were propagated by traps laid through sinister schemes to addict, make sick, or break people. We would be wrong to dismiss the impact of schemes that have landed people in the snares and traps of Satan.

Second Corinthians 2:11 (NIV) says, "...in order that Satan might not outwit us. For we are not unaware of his schemes."

If we do not want Satan to outwit us, we must be aware of how earthly systems have been set up in all spheres of impact and influence to rob people of the abundant life Jesus came to give them. From medicine, finances, government, entertainment, media, and even religion, the enemy has laid traps through his cohorts to hurt people, destroy families, and take their peace, provision, and healing.

In this cultural guide, I expose the schemes that ensnare people. Sadly, these are mostly purposeful and cause great sorrow, whether they entice families into debt or cause chronic disease. Traditions and wrong beliefs, whether truth or lie, when believed have just as much impact if a person believes them to be true. I'm not saying that all persons who work in these areas or vocations have ill motives; they do not. But someone above them in higher places does.

I met a doctor once who said to me, "I know how many people have to walk through my door to make a living and how many surgeries I have to perform to make a great life." It's a business. We are naive to think that everyone has our best interests at heart. We can neither live in naivety, because Satan "roams around looking for someone to devour," nor in fear thinking everyone is out to get us. We must not be unaware of the schemes and must think, pray, research, and get answers. That's what this book will do to help uncover schemes in the culture and answers in God's plans for the people He lovingly created.

While we know that Jesus has already won the battle, 1 Corinthians 16:13a (NIV) commands us to "*Be on your guard; stand firm in the faith.*"

ACKNOWLEDGMENTS

There will be no limit to his authority and no end to the peace he brings. He will rule on David's throne and over his kingdom, to establish it and to uphold it with justice and righteousness from now on, into eternity. The zeal of the Lord of Armies will accomplish this.

—Isaiah 9:7 (EHV)

I wish to express my deepest heartfelt thanks to the many friends, family, and associates who brought this work to fruition. The army of the Lord, under His promptings, has done exceedingly abundantly above all I could ask, think, or imagine! His power is working in you! You have continually labored to awaken the people of God to this hour of warfare and on how to have victory in Him. You know who you are, and I appreciate and love you more than words can express!

And a special thanks to my Lord and Savior, Jesus Christ and my husband, Gary, for his encouragement to say, "Yes!"

—Drenda Keesee

INTRODUCTION
CLIMB THE MOUNTAIN

Drenda, what were you thinking?!!

I winced as I pulled a stick from my flesh. I was exhausted, soaking wet, and I was bleeding from a small branch-sized puncture in my right leg. This was not going the way I had planned at all. I looked back at my mud-covered husband, who had waited to see which path was safest to cross. Smart man. I had two options. Wet rocks or a large log were all that served as a bridge for crossing a rushing stream that stood between us and the peak of the mountain—a mountain I was determined to climb.

I made the wrong choice!

Mountains have spiritual context throughout Scripture and life. They represent consistency, inspiration, spiritual awakening, and overcoming obstacles.

Depending on the weather, mountains and oceans are my favorite retreats. Oceans in the winter. Mountains in the summer—majestic, rugged, wild, and untamed, especially in tumultuous weather. We had great weather when we started this journey. That was why I pushed for us to continue—something I began to regret.

In the summer, to drive to the mountains and ascend above the heat of the day into the crisp thin air, walk the trails, and gaze at wildflowers and tundra refreshes my soul. Mountains have always drawn me in and amazed me. I've driven through the most beautiful mountain scenery and climbed amazing mountain trails, whether the rugged Rockies or in island jungles.

This time, it was different. We had taken on more than we could handle. Gary knew it. I knew it. But all we could do was press on. After all, we had been in tough spots before.

It seems most of the time I've climbed a mountain, I was unprepared to do so, with the wrong attire and provisions. It was too often unplanned, impromptu. Clothed in a summer sports dress and Michael Kors tennis shoe slides, I looked more suited for a day at the country club than a rugged climb.

I picked myself up and continued across the wet rocks that had deceived my footing just earlier.

Almost there!

In my exhaustion, my mind ran to previous climbs. At Camelback Mountain, I chided Gary to enter the initial climb. "Let's just go far enough to see a view!" Before long, I was saying, "Let's just go a little further." The next thing I knew, we were so close to the summit, I couldn't justify stopping. We made it to the top, and it was worth it! This would be worth it too.

Life is like that. Just keep going!

Here we were once again, history repeating itself. Kalalau trail at the Na Pali Coast in Kauai was a hard trail to be sure. We were warned by a park ranger, "Do not go any farther on this hike. You are not prepared, and you will not make it." I appreciated his warning, but, honestly, I took it as more of a suggestion. I mean, he didn't know what I was capable of. Voted most likely to succeed in my class and the unofficial mascot for a "sure you can!" attitude, I wasn't going to back down. It only challenged me. I know, there are dangers in not obeying authorities, and as I looked at my leg, they were all too real. There's just something about a mountain begging to be scaled or an adventure that awaits. When we reached the river, we were met with warning signs about danger and death. This river laid between us and reaching the top, so we weren't going to stop. This was the place it all fell apart, the place I fell.

Drenda, what were you thinking?!

After I gathered myself, we made it across the violently rushing waters, to the amazement of the mostly Hawaiian young men swimming in the lovely pool and falls at the top of the mountain. We made it! We were much older hikers than anyone would ever expect to interrupt their dip. We didn't stay long, but I can still remember the feeling of reaching the top. The waterfalls were glorious to behold. The shocked looks on the faces of the young men said it all; we had accomplished a tough feat. We had conquered the mountain! The wind in our hair and the view of the world below was a reward worth the climb. We had gained perspective from the peak. It changed us.

When we finally made it back to the parking lot and guzzled the water from two coconuts while suffering from near exhaustion,

I realized the significance of the mountains and my need to climb them. There's something about a mountain that begs to be climbed, because we are made to climb them.

What if I told you that there are mountains that are so important for us to climb that our lives literally depend on it?

What if I told you that there is a plan to dominate each area of influence to move us toward an agenda you wouldn't believe?

There are seven mountains of influence that control the world around us. Whoever stands atop these mountains directs the fate of our world. I'll prove it to you.

The cultural mountains of influence: government/politics, economy/business, health/medicine, education, media/entertainment, religion, and family have their challenges to climb and possess. They are not without danger, and much of the church world has shied away, even feeling intimidated to enter these adventurous, but sometimes treacherous, fields of impact. In shrinking back from taking the journey, another influence has dominated them. And unfortunately, some who have risked the climb were caught unprepared and swept away by the current or by heatstroke or thirst. There are only two kingdoms—the Kingdom of God and the kingdom of Satan. If God's people fail to risk the trek, we hand it over to our adversary by default.

While researching for this book to discover more about the seven mountains of influence in our culture, I discovered shocking information that made me have a greater awareness of the time we are living in...

Where are we in the time line of history, and is it the end?

What is your purpose for being here in this time, and what can you do?

The mountains of influence are converging for the end of times, and you are needed to influence them for eternity.

Our adversary has set snares in these areas to trip people up and make them stumble and fall into ruin, chaos, and disorder, ultimately taking their futures and destinies from them. We need to know what our assignments are and know how to take the journey from those who have seen the dangers and know the terrain. We need to engage.

> **THE MOUNTAINS OF INFLUENCE ARE CONVERGING FOR THE END OF TIMES, AND YOU ARE NEEDED TO INFLUENCE THEM FOR ETERNITY.**

Mountains are perilous in certain conditions, but if we know the path to trek, and how to make the journey, the satisfaction of making the trip is worth it all. The view, the trip, the people you meet, and the mountains you take are completely worth it!

Jesus spoke of mountains metaphorically as obstacles to tackle. If anyone says to this mountain, "Be removed and cast into the sea" and doesn't doubt in his heart, it shall be done for him (or her). There are obstacles on the path, but the other option is not an option at all—to stay comfortably in the parking lot while seeing or doing nothing to stop the adversary from placing his flag in the territory that God says belongs to you.

A culture cannot fall into ruin unless God's people refuse to engage it, refuse to develop a strategy to capture the attention of those climbing. The parking lot has a dismal view. It's time to get out of the car and take the journey. If you choose, you will have success in the mountain God has given you to possess, and you will capture the attention of others. God will make your way prosperous and let you become the example others are looking for. Let me be your trail guide. Many will walk this pathway, and you can give their feet a steady rhythm and the right answers in life to navigate the tough spots, the hard places that make people want to quit on their marriages, their families, their health, their faith, or their businesses. There are mountains, and this book will prepare you to take the journey and your mountain!

It's time to fight to take the mountains of influence!

THE WAR IS ON!

While out for a fun evening at "Medieval Times," an entertaining quasi-reenactment with knights jousting in a feudal battle of kingdom against kingdom, I was reminded that throughout history, there has always been a war of jousting for control, for power to rule. Who or what will rule? From defeat in World War I, in a more "civilized" world, the disastrous seeds of World War II were sown into a young man named Adolph Hitler. Were it not for a miracle and the intense resistance of people who valued freedom more than personal sacrifice, Hitler's maniacal plan of world domination would have destroyed Europe if not the world.

Today we are witnessing the seeds from World War II coming into fruition like birth pains. In 1971, a man named Klaus Schwab, from Germany, founded what is now known as the World Economic Forum (WEF). The WEF began as a nonprofit organization called the European Management Forum (EMF), which invited business leaders to an annual conference to strategize how European leaders could emulate business practices in the United States. Expanding to include business and political leaders internationally in 1976, the

EMF provided membership for "the 1,000 leading companies of the world." In fact, it became "the first non-governmental institution to initiate a partnership with China's economic development commissions." The EMF changed its name to the "World Economic Forum" in 1987. In 2015, the Forum was formally recognized as an international organization.[1]

The WEF's nebulous mission is "to demonstrate entrepreneurship in the global public interest ... founded on the stakeholder theory, which asserts that an organization is accountable to all parts of society."[2] Its philosophies can be found in "the Davos Manifesto 2020," which called for a "better kind of capitalism."[3]

According to the WEF manifesto, "[a] company is more than an economic unit generating wealth. It fulfills human and societal aspirations as part of the broader social system. Performance must be measured not only on the return to shareholders but also on how it achieves its environmental, social, and good governance objectives." WEF's strategic partners are comprised of "the leading companies from around the world, each selected for their commitment to improving the state of the world" and include Amazon, BlackRock, Dell Technologies, Google, GE, Intel, Meta, Microsoft, Johnson & Johnson, Pfizer, PayPal, UBS, and Visa, to name a few.[4]

Through the COVID-19 pandemic, the WEF, through Schwab, inserted itself into global affairs, stating, "To achieve a better outcome, the world must act jointly and swiftly to revamp all aspects of our societies and economies, from education to social contracts and working conditions. Every country, from the United States to China, must participate, and every industry, from oil and gas to tech, must be transformed. In short, we need a 'Great Reset' of capitalism." Schwab further contended that "incremental measures and ad hoc fixes will not suffice to prevent this scenario," adding, "We must build entirely new foundations for our economic and social systems."[5] Klaus sums up the Great Reset succinctly when he stated that "the pandemic represents a rare but narrow window of opportunity to reflect, reimagine, and reset our world."[6] "You'll own nothing, and you'll be happy.[7] [8]

Schwab has even written a book entitled *The Fourth Industrial Revolution*, in which he states the need to advance "a range of new technologies that are fusing the physical, digital, and biological worlds, impacting all disciplines, economies, and industries, and even challenging ideas about what it means to be human."[9] When interviewed, Klaus has repeatedly stated that "the difference of this fourth industrial revolution is it doesn't change what you are doing; it changes you. If you take genetic editing, just as an example, it's you who are changed, and of course it has a big impact on your identity."[10]

Klaus' position is corroborated by the WEF's stated position that "In the Fourth Industrial Revolution, new gene editing tools are likely to overtake biological evolution."[11]

The WEF's twisted plan for the Great Reset, which includes transhumanism, is perhaps articulated best through Schwab's right-hand man and WEF advisor, Yuval Noah Harari. This is the person who Schwab, Mark Zuckerberg, Bill Gates, Harvard, Stanford, and *The New York Times* have revered and even described as a "prophet."[12] [13]

Harari speaks at the WEF, Stanford, TED and TimesTalks. At one time, his books simultaneously topped two slots on *The New York Times'* nonfiction best-seller list.[14]

I could never come close to painting the picture of the world Harari describes, so I will let his words speak for themselves. On the COVID-19 pandemic, Harari has stated as follows:

- "What's happening now? It's [the COVID crisis] really a watershed in the history of surveillance. First of all, we see mass surveillance systems entering and being adopted in democratic countries, which previously resisted them. Secondly, we see the nature of surveillance changing from over the skin surveillance to under the skin surveillance. Over the skin surveillance is, say, the government or corporation watching, monitoring where you go, what you buy, what you watch on television. Under the skin surveillance starts with monitoring your body temperature and blood pressure, but ultimately, it's about hacking your body and brain and knowing what you're feeling each and every moment, not just pain or coughing but, you know, our emotions."[15]

- "Maybe in a couple of decades when people look back, the thing that they will remember from the COVID crisis is that it was the moment that everything went digital and when everything became monitored, that we agreed to be surveyed all the time, not just in authoritarian regimes but even in democracies. And maybe most importantly of all is this is the moment when surveillance started going under the skin."[16]

- "Now, it took just two weeks to identify the correct virus sequence, its entire genome, and develop reliable tests. So, we are really in a better position than any time before. Uh, we have the scientific knowledge. What we don't necessarily have is the political wisdom to make use of our immense power. Maybe the biggest problem of all is the lack of international cooperation and of global solidarity. I'm not so afraid of the virus. I'm much more afraid of the inner demons of humanity."[17]

On the person of God, Harari has proclaimed:

- "We're giving up on gods but will turn ourselves into new kinds of gods."[18]

- "Jesus Christ rising from the dead, being the son of God, this is all fake news."[19]

- "Science is replacing evolution by natural selection with evolution by intelligent design. Not the intelligent design of some God above the clouds but our intelligent design and the intelligent design of our clouds. The IBM cloud, the Microsoft cloud, these are the new driving forces of evolution."[20]

Consider how Harari feels about humans:

- "Humans are now hackable animals."[21][22]

- "You know, the whole idea that humans have, you know

this, they--they [sic] have this soul or spirit and they have free will and nobody knows what's happening inside me. So, whatever I choose, whether it's in the election or whether in the supermarket, this is my free will, that's over.[23]

- "Today we have the technology to hack human beings on a massive scale. Everything is being digitalized; everything is being monitored."[24]

- "In the 21st century, we may see the emergence of a new massive class of useless people; people who have absolutely no economic value."[25]

- "You have a small elite that pushes things in its own interests even if it doesn't benefit the vast majority of the population; ... one of the biggest dangers to the planet today is this technological utopia because probably for the elite it will work, [but]... when the flood comes, the scientists will build the Noah's ark for the elite leaving the rest to drown, the rest of the people and the rest of the ecosystem." [26]

- "Data might enable human elites to do something even more radical than just build digital dictatorships. By hacking organisms, elites may gain the power to re-engineer the future of life itself. Because once you can hack something, you can usually also engineer it."[27]

- "If indeed we succeed in hacking and engineering life, this will be not just the greatest revolution in the history of humanity. This will be the greatest revolution in biology since the very beginning of life four billion years ago."[28]

- "Does data about my DNA, my brain, my body, my life-- Does it belong to me or to some corporation or to the government, or perhaps to the human collective?"[29]

- "You don't have any answer in the Bible on what to do when humans are no longer useful in the economy. You need completely new ideologies, completely new religions, and they are likely to emerge from Silicon Valley [ ] and not from the Middle East. And they'll [ ] give people visions based on technology, everything that the old religions promised— happiness, justice and even eternal life—— but here on earth with the help of technology and not after death with the help of some supernatural being."[30]

Harari shares his following views on immortality:

- "We don't need to wait for Jesus Christ to come back to Earth in order to overcome death. A couple of geeks in a laboratory can do it."[31]

- "Even Lenin and Marx with all of their ambitions never went as far as promising people immortality … yes, paradise on Earth, but eventually, even in the socialist paradigm, you die. And they kept their mouth shut about what's happening to you after you die. But the new religions we see emerging in the Silicon Valley and similar places across the world, they even promise immortality here on Earth with the help of technology. For example, Google has established 2-3 years ago a sub company called Calico, whose stated mission is to solve the problem of death."[32]

Unfortunately, Harari is not alone in his views or allegiance to the WEF. After having established the WEF, Schwab later recruited, indoctrinated, and trained a band of leaders across the world through his group, "Young Global Leaders," (birthed in 1993 as "Global Leaders for Tomorrow"). These leaders were groomed to move into position and wield the power of their sword, the sword of "their" lord.

YGL leaders' and their WEF predecessors' and counterparts' names are very familiar on the world stage today: Vladimir Putin (Russia); Bill Gates (Microsoft); Justin Trudeau (Canada); Angela Merkel (Germany); President Emmanuel Macron (France); Governor Gavin Newsom (California, with the fifth largest world economy); Tony Blair (England); Prime Minister Jacinda Ardern (New Zealand); and an array of government officials and politicians leading most of the nations and policies around the world.

Add to these social media moguls, celebrities, scientists, business leaders, and news media personalities like: George Stephanopoulos (television journalist); Leonardo DiCaprio (actor/environmental activist); Mark Zuckerberg (Facebook/Instagram/Meta); Sheryl Sandberg (Facebook COO); Marissa Mayer (Yahoo); Sergey Brin and Larry Page (Google cofounders); Peter Thiel (PayPal's cofounder); Pierre Omidyar (eBay cofounder); Jimmy Wales (Wikipedia cofounder); Eric Schmidt (Former Google CEO and chair of the National Security Commission on Artificial Intelligence); Jeff Bezos (Amazon); Jack Ma (Alibaba); Alexander Soros (son of George Soros, who has donated over $32 billion to Open Borders in support of liberal and progressive causes); David de Rothschild; and, of course, many others.[33 34 35 36 37 38 39]

YGL's vision and mission are this: "The Forum of Young Global Leaders accelerates the impact of a diverse community of responsible leaders across borders and sectors to shape a more inclusive and sustainable future." The organization continues by stating, "We foster collaboration in the global public interest. Our growing membership of more than 1,400 members and alumni of 120 nationalities includes civic and business innovators, entrepreneurs, technology pioneers, educators, activists, artists, journalists, and more. Aligned with the World Economic Forum's mission, we seek to drive public-private cooperation in the global public interest."[40] [41] [42]

In the last two decades, we have seen their alliance tread into every area of life to dominate the world stage in a huge power grab. They have stepped into all seven spheres of influence—the seven mountains of family, government, church, education, media, arts, health—and are now breaking and making rules that seem to have greater authority than nations, constitutions, and governments. Citizens and believers sit back and watch in dismay as they take freedom of speech, personal expression, exercise of religion, bodily autonomy, health decisions, and children's education from the people and wield their sword of fury toward a Fourth Industrial Revolution and Great Reset—the New World Order.

Human genes are being edited. Inflation has hit a 40-year all-time high. Children are being indoctrinated in schools to accept the "genderbread" model of determining their sexuality among dozens of "new options." Family and marriage have been redefined and almost completely discarded. Christianity and what have been the norms of life have become the enemy, as well as persons of Anglo-American descent.

Anyone who gets in their way is snuffed out by misinformation campaigns or censorship of social accounts. They are labeled bigots, racists, misogynists, and other condemning words crafted by the elite's brilliant marketing in a take-over campaign. Many opposing this dogma rightly feel the global strategist's plans are taken directly from a Marxist playbook. Anyone who dares to disagree with their agenda for a new world order, perhaps made in their own image, is an enemy of their "free society of open borders."

So-called progressives in education and higher learning have used their influence to: sow seeds of discord, replacing democratic principles and national loyalty with a one-world ideology; create division among ethnicities and sexes; and stir up economic and heightened social class warfare. Their goal is to magnify differences and invent "new and improved" sexual identities as a basis for identity politics and a fight for individuality. It's enough strife and division to keep everybody fighting one another as they swiftly drive their agenda, unnoticed by most.

Destruction of the traditional family was the number one place of assault, removing the protecting force of parents guarding children in the home. The nuclear family is the strength or downfall of any society and nation. As the family goes, so goes the nation. The family has been weakened and likewise democratic governments. Education has been seized by anti-God, anti-family ideologies and used to indoctrinate children and higher learners. Entertainment and the arts reflect the moral depravity with which they spin sin as freedom and self-centered pursuits of "exploring your identity" as gratification. And social media lords censor any message that doesn't fit their narrative and drive their agenda, brainwashing generations, just in case any escaped their educational systems' propaganda.

Many churches have left the teachings of Jesus and principles of the Kingdom of God for psychology and worldly acceptance. Others have shut their doors for fear of COVID or the next pathogen or bio-lab created disease as pharmaceutical companies and government agencies restrict freedom and sell their wares in a forced fashion of "Do this or die" and "Do this or you can't make a living for your family."

As the seven mountains of influence are being conquered, a frail world is teetering on collapse and replacement by a New World Order, a Great Reset to control economics or whatever name is used to replace freedom, democracy, and autonomy before God, our Creator. Government desires to become God, like "the one (Satan)" influencing their controlled chaos to create a New World Order. This is the Tower of Babel all over again, and they are blatant in their attempt to become like God and rise above His Word of power.

How you are fallen from heaven, O Lucifer, son of the morning! How you are cut down to the ground, you who weakened the nations! For you have said in your heart: "I will ascend into heaven, I will exalt my throne above the stars of God; I will also sit on the mount of the congregation. On the farthest sides of the north; I will ascend above the heights of the clouds, I will be like the Most High."

Yet you shall be brought down to Sheol, to the lowest depths of the Pit. Those who see you will gaze at you, and consider you, saying: "Is this the one who made the earth tremble, who shook

> *kingdoms, who made the world as a wilderness and destroyed its cities…?"*
>
> —Isaiah 9:14-17 (NKJV)

We can see this wilderness wandering as we have turned from God's values. Across the nation, cities are laden with crime, drug-infested cesspools of humanity. We have witnessed our cities burning on the evening news and autonomous zones of lawlessness declared by emboldened youth who are funded partly by global world deconstructionists. They have a plan to collapse what has existed, the foundations and pillars of society, in order to position their new plans for life. You will not like these plans if you know their endgame!

The Antichrist spirit has invaded the "seven mountains" of life and culture, and we can see the breakdown and consequential pain of disobedience to His Kingdom commands and way of living. It can be disheartening to watch, but we must stay focused on the answers and victories that lay ahead based on God's Word.

We must learn to fight like heaven and kick hell out of our way of life, our government, our children's education, and our churches.

How are we to handle the warfare in this eleventh hour and know the right decisions to make for our families, our freedoms, our nation, and the Gospel? Is it possible to stand up and fight this "war on God" as a believer and find peace and provision above this world's chaotic systems? I say a resounding, "Yes!" How do we engage this battle in the realms of heaven while having an impact in the seven spheres (mountains) on Earth?

We are in a war with cultural, spiritual, and personal battlefronts. And although the stakes are high for the people of this age, the victory has already been determined. It is up to every individual to decide which side they will fight for and stand with—God or Gog?

WE ARE IN A WAR WITH CULTURAL, SPIRITUAL, AND PERSONAL BATTLEFRONTS. AND ALTHOUGH THE STAKES ARE HIGH FOR THE PEOPLE OF THIS AGE, THE VICTORY HAS ALREADY BEEN DETERMINED. IT IS UP TO EVERY INDIVIDUAL TO DECIDE WHICH SIDE THEY WILL FIGHT FOR AND STAND WITH—GOD OR GOG?

Are we living in the last days? Every sign screams, "Yes!" "But haven't we heard these stories for years?" some may say or even mock. Funny that we can see this very question in Scripture. This is nothing new. In the Old Testament in Jeremiah 17:15, the people mocked Jeremiah, and he said to God, "Listen to what they are saying to me. They are saying, 'Where are the things the Lord threatens with? Let's see them happen.'" And they did happen just as Jeremiah had warned they would. Those who heeded were prepared and cared for by God. Those who didn't met destruction. The world—and more importantly, its people—hang in the balance. Only heaven has the answer. And unless we learn to fight like heaven, we will never kick hell out. There are only two sides. Will you fight? Like it or not, you have already joined the battle.

AND UNLESS WE LEARN TO FIGHT LIKE HEAVEN, WE WILL NEVER KICK HELL OUT. THERE ARE ONLY TWO SIDES. WILL YOU FIGHT? LIKE IT OR NOT, YOU HAVE ALREADY JOINED THE BATTLE.

RELIGIOUS LIES ARE THE WORST!

It was a crisp Sunday morning in our small church of 40. We were young and full of zeal and vision for God. After all, we had seen Him do incredible things in our personal lives. My husband, Gary, was just beginning a teaching on the Kingdom of God when, all of a sudden, it happened.

I looked to my left as I heard a commotion that was unearthly. To my surprise, it was a woman visiting our church. She was trying to lift her dress up; and by the look in her eyes, I knew she wasn't doing this of her own volition. My spirit leapt into action to confront the demonic presence that was manifesting as she slithered to the floor. As my hand reached out to her, the first words out of my mouth were, "I bind you, in Jesus's name!" The demonic presence writhed in pain as it was confronted by the power of the Living God. The spirit's voice spoke through hers as it tried to reclaim dominance over her life.

"She is mine!"

Gary was at my side then, both of us laying hands on her and binding the demonic spirit. Her body stiffened like steel, and it felt as though she was pushing herself off the ground, almost levitating. It was completely unnatural. The Spirit of God stirred even stronger in me as I spoke again to the opposing spirit that was tormenting her.

"She is not yours. She's free, in Jesus's name!"

She coughed several times, stirred, and her body went limp, relaxed. As she opened her eyes, I saw a sweet countenance return to her face, as she was always meant to have. She was free.

It was not a normal service that Sunday, but in many ways, this conflict was nothing new in God's Kingdom. Satan has always been after people, ever since the beginning. After all, Jesus cast out many demonic spirits in His time on Earth. He said we should do the same.

Recently, I was researching the organized church of our opposition when I came across a troubling revelation: Satan has a plan. The crackle of a 1990s VHS recording made the voice of the stoic representative of the Church of Satan all the more ominous as he sat opposite evangelist Bob Larson in an interview. His voice was chilling, but more importantly, what he said grabbed my attention. When asked if Hitler was wrong for killing millions of innocent people, he simply replied "No, there is no wrong or right." Bob Larson prodded him deeper with a second question about the church of Satan's stance on the mentally ill or crippled. His response was scathing. "The Church of Satan is not for the weak masses. It is for the elite, the world leaders ... The church can have the weak."

Righteous anger rose in me as I heard his voice. This man, missing an ear and wearing all black, was being used by Satan, and though I wanted to stand up and yell at the screen, I was also moved with compassion. Here sat a man who had no true understanding of light or love. His life, like many others used by Satan, would end in destruction without repentance. I tell you these things to open your eyes and your heart to the real battle that is raging for the hearts and minds of people every single day. Since the Garden of Eden, Satan has been hard at work to stop what God has set into motion. God uses people, and so does our opposition.

Throughout history, we can see the fall of mankind demonstrated in the fall of Noah's generation and in every empire since history began. It wasn't long after the flood that people were conspiring to build the Tower of Babel. In the Greco-Roman world of the apostle Paul, temples were dedicated to Isis and Serapis (a Greek conflation of the Egyptian gods Osiris and Apis with the Greek god Zeus and others).

The best way to perpetrate a lie is to mix it with an element of truth. Religion and secret societies throughout history have done just that. Religion is man's attempt to create his own way to get to God and can best be seen at the Tower of Babel. The Tower of Babel in the Bible was a structure built in the land of Shinar (Babylonia) sometime after the Deluge. The story of its construction, given in Genesis 11:1-9, explains the existence of diverse human languages."[43] In Hebrew, the word is Sin'ar. The Hebrew שנער Šin'ar is equivalent to the Egyptian *Sngr* and Hittite Šanḫar(a), all referring to southern Mesopotamia.[44] [45]

In the Book of Genesis, the beginning of Nimrod's kingdom is said to have been "Babel [Babylon], and Erech [Uruk], and Akkad, and Calneh, in the land of Shinar." Genesis 11:2 states that Shinar enclosed the plain that became the site of the Tower of Babel after the Great Flood. After the Flood, the sons of Shem, Ham, and Japheth stayed first in the highlands of Armenia and then migrated to Shinar.[46] The Book of Jubilees 9:3 allots Shinar to Ashur, son of Shem. Jubilees 10:20 states that the Tower of Babel was built with bitumen (asphalt) from the sea of Shinar. David Rohl theorized that the tower was actually located in Eridu, which was once located on the coast of the Persian Gulf, where there are ruins of a massive, ancient ziggurat worked from bitumen (asphalt).[47]

Genesis 11 shares this story:

> *Now the whole world had one language and a common speech. As people moved eastward, they found a plain in Shinar and settled there.*
>
> *They said to each other, "Come, let's make bricks and bake them thoroughly." They used brick instead of stone, and tar for mortar. Then they said, "Come, let us build ourselves a city, with a tower that reaches to the heavens, so that we may make a name for ourselves; otherwise, we will be scattered over the face of the whole earth."*
>
> *But the Lord came down to see the city and the tower the people were building. The Lord said, "If as one people speaking the same language they have begun to do this, then nothing they plan to do will be impossible for them. Come, let us go down and confuse their language so they will not understand each other."*

So the Lord scattered them from there over all the earth, and they stopped building the city. That is why it was called Babel— because there the Lord confused the language of the whole world. From there the Lord scattered them over the face of the whole earth.

—Genesis 11:1-9 (NIV)

"Come, let us make a name for ourselves." Their intention was to come together as one and challenge God Himself by building a tower of defiance. Whether metaphorically or not, this tower represented their desire to dominate, to be like the Most High, just as Lucifer said, "I will make myself like the Most High." The building of the United Nations in Manhattan, which will be discussed further in Chapter 3, is a representative figure of the will of man to control the world's events, like the Tower of Babel, removing faith in God and His Holy Word, the Bible, from the mountains of life. The building or tower is only the structure that represents the ideology that they would conspire against the Lord and any who would acknowledge Him.

The Egyptians worshiped thousands of gods, though only about 1,500 are known by name. The Hebrew forefathers of the children of Israel, on the other hand, knew only one God. Because of this contrast, during the prelude to the Exodus, their enslaved descendants in Egypt witnessed the power of the one true God over any other.

The defining of Egypt's gods and goddesses as idols meant that Israel would stand out against all other nations in respect to whom they would worship. Eventually, once they reached Mount Sinai on their journey from Egypt to the Land of

Promise, they would receive the Ten Commandments in codified form, two of which relate to other gods. The First Commandment speaks to the exclusive relationship between God and His people: "You shall have no other gods before Me" (Exodus 20:3). This prohibits a relationship with any other (foreign) god. The Second Commandment rules against creating or worshiping representations of such 'gods,' whether their origin is earth, sea, or sky (verses 4-5). The Israelites were not to fashion nor to prostrate themselves before such images or idols.[48]

Wherever God has given people instruction to live and to follow His ways, there are people who want to return to Egypt, return to man's ways of worship. This is exactly what the Hebrews did after God had delivered them from slavery under Egypt. They left Egypt, but that didn't take Egypt out of them. They carried their false trust system and idolatry with them.

"While the idea of idolatry was to be alien to them, by the time of the Exodus, they had lived for centuries within Egyptian society, surrounded by multiple deities. Is this why so soon after leaving Egypt under God's hand, they easily induced even Aaron to build them a metal idol? In Moses's absence for about six weeks as he received the Ten Commandments, we are told the people *corrupted themselves ... They have made for themselves a golden calf and have worshiped it....*' (Exodus 32:7-8, ESV)."[49]

Throughout history, God has had men and women He would use to orchestrate a showdown with Satanic occult powers. Elijah confronted Jezebel and the prophets of Baal and their death cult of sexual immorality and offering children in death rituals. Moses was raised as a deliverer to confront Egypt as God heard their cries and said, "Let My people go." Through plagues that made a mockery of the Egyptian gods, it was clear that Moses's God was the true and living God.

In our own country's past and European history, secret societies incorporating pieces of Christianity mixed with Egyptian idolatry and occultism have attempted to create

THROUGHOUT HISTORY, GOD HAS HAD MEN AND WOMEN HE WOULD USE TO ORCHESTRATE A SHOWDOWN WITH SATANIC OCCULT POWERS.

religious practice. Egyptians worshiped Isis and Osiris and many false gods.[50] Freemasons adopted symbolism and occultist rituals in their levels of involvement with curses and bizarre initiations.[51] The Skull and Bones Organization formed at Yale University picks its 15 highly secret members from 15 juniors with a special consideration to alumni children.[52] There is an initiation in a tomb with artifacts and physical beatings. Initiates are then awarded a new name, and secrets are divulged.[53] George H.W. Bush; John Kerry; Earl Graves, Jr.; CIA and Supreme Court Justices; and many in the media have been involved in Skull and Bones.[54]

A man by the name of Adam Weishaupt from Bavaria, Germany on May 1, 1776, founded the Enlightened Ones, later developed to become the Illuminous and Illuminati, loosely based on the Freemason's rank and file classes and orders. He would closely oversee member's training, and in time would reveal to them special occult knowledge as they advanced through the ranks of the Illuminati. His first recruits were law students adopting an alias. The group grew slowly until the recruitment of master Mason occultist Adolph Freiherr von Knigge, who recruited royalty and powerful politicians into the group, including Duke Ferdinand of Brunswick, a towering figure in European Freemasonry, and the writer Johann Wolfgang von Goethe. Membership swelled to more than 3,000 believers with lodges in Germany, Switzerland, Austria, Italy, and other locations.

Some of our own Founders involved in these extra-curricular societies, although outspoken Christians, synergized Scripture with man-made rituals from Freemasonry and European societies. After much controversy and fallout in Germany and other areas over the Illuminati, in August of 1798, George Washington, then a private citizen and once Master Mason, received a letter and copy of John Robison's "Proofs of a Conspiracy Against All Religions and Governments of Europe, Carried on in the Secret meetings of Freemasons, Illuminati, and Reading Societies" from G.W. Snyder of Fredericktown, Maryland. Snyder expressed concern that some of the Masonic lodges in America might have caught the infection of the Illuminati's plan to overturn all Government and all Religion, even natural.

In his response Washington claimed, "I have heard much of the nefarious, and dangerous plan and doctrines of the Illuminati." By the late 1780s Thomas Jefferson was accused of belonging to the mysterious secret society. John Quincy Adams, a Mason who later became the sixth President of the United States in 1825, accused Jefferson in writings of using Masonic lodges for subversive Illuminati purposes.[55]

Whatever the role Freemasonry, the occult, and the Illuminati have played in our history, their secret rituals and symbolism are alive today. The Baphomet, a pagan hermaphroditic winged human figure with the head and feet of a goat, is seen in music videos, concerts, and performances of the likes of Lady Gaga, Justin Bieber, Jay Z, Beyoncé, and such a multitude of performers we could not exhaust the list here. The all-seeing eye afloat on the pyramid as seen on our Great Seal of the United States and the back of the U.S. dollar bill are evidence that the Illuminati's influence infiltrated the ranks of the Founding Fathers and future government decision-makers. The eternal flame represents the Illuminati's immortality, and, according to some, the fire represents Lucifer, the bringer of life. The symbol appears on Standard Oil and Columbia pictures. The distorted cross, the inverted cross, or the double cross allegedly represents the Illuminati's slandering of the Cross of Christ and God Himself.

Albert Pike, the U.S. Leader of Illuminous and head of Scottish Rite Free Masonry reportedly penned a letter to Italian revolutionary leader Guisseppeo Mazzini on August 15, 1871 that said Judeo-Christianity must be defeated to usher in a New World Order:

> We shall unleash the nihilists and the atheists, and we shall provoke a great social cataclysm which in all its horror will show clearly to all nations the effect of absolute atheism; the origins of savagery and of most bloody turmoil. Then everywhere, the people will be forced to defend themselves against the world revolutionaries and will exterminate those destroyers of civilization and the multitudes disillusioned with Christianity whose spirits will be from that moment without direction and leadership and anxious for an ideal,

but without knowledge where to send its adoration, will receive the true light through the universal manifestation of the pure doctrine of Lucifer brought finally out into public view.[56]

Pike's remarks, the precise source of which is controversial, are consistent with his Satanic and occultist theology. Consider how he described Satan: "LUCIFER, the *Light-bearer*! Strange and mysterious name to give the Spirit of Darkness! Lucifer, the Son of the Morning! Is it *he* who bears the *Light*, and with its splendors intolerable, blinds feeble, sensual, or selfish Souls? Doubt it not!"[57]

From these early perversions and distortions of pure Judaism or Christianity came other apostate religions and secret societies of the world. Mormonism was started April 6, 1830 by Joseph Smith in Kirtland, Ohio moving westward. It incorporated teachings of the Bible but added the Book of Mormon and other heretical teachings that were either extra-biblical and/or anti-biblical, including sacrifices for deceased relatives and many elements of Free Masonry. Joseph Smith himself was a freemason. "Mormons do not realize that their temple Endowment ceremony was copied directly from occult rites in freemasonry."[58]

The Mormon temple ceremony has no basis in Christianity. "The all-seeing eye of freemasonry is a prominent feature on the Salt Lake City temple in Utah. There is an inverted pentagram on the temple building as well." It's important to say that many of the well-meaning Christians who joined these groups started with some knowledge or faith in God or Jesus Christ but were deluded into deception over a period of time. "A little leaven (or falsehood) leavens the lump."

Taking bits and pieces of various world religions "in the last 45 years, we have seen the explosive growth of new-age (or occult) religious cults with their roots in classic Hindu thought. Today, there are literally hundreds of large and small cults in America with Eastern ideas and practices.... The different Hindu sects, while practically appearing as different religions, in reality, regard themselves as different sects and divisions of the One Eternal Religion of India."[59]

Hollywood latched on to these Hindu sects and New Age.[60] Gurus like Rajneesh, whose teachings were rejected at home, came to the U.S. and have had an impact on Western New Age thought. His followers were involved in criminal activity, poisonings, threats to government, and he was deported to India, dying at age 58. Today, his meditation centers are still operating, in their words, "liberating the minds of future generations from the shackles of religiosity and conformism." Many Hollywood and Bollywood personalities now follow his teachings.[61]

The top religions of the world, according to the Pew Research Center, are: 1) Christianity (2.3 billion), 2) Islam (1.8 Billion), 3) Unaffiliated (1.2 billion), 4) Hinduism (1.1 billion), 5) Buddhism (500 million), 6) Folk religions (400 million), 7) Other religions (100 million), and 8) Judaism (10 million).[62] The three that worship one god instead of several are Christianity, Islam, and Judaism. These groups trace their origin back to Abraham, the father of many nations. Judaism and Christianity are tied to Abraham through Isaac, the son of promise. Islam's roots are tied to Abraham's first son, Ishmael, born of a servant woman. Other religious groups either sprang from one of these monotheistic faiths or worship many gods as a synergy of various beliefs, societies, and even occult practices originating from Satan.

Judaism and Christianity both believe in the Messiah (Savior) as prophesied in Old Testament Scripture. "It may be possible for someone to fake one or two of the Messianic prophecies, but it would be impossible for any one person to arrange and fulfill all of these prophecies. Jews await a Messiah that Christians believe has already come in Yeshua, Jesus Christ, whose life and ancestry perfectly align with every Old Testament prophecy, a 10^{50} chance (a figure with 50 zeros) from just considering 48 Messianic prophecies.[63] There are 456 prophecies about Messiah! Yeshua (Jesus) fulfills all 456 pre-written in the Old Testament before His birth, including His birth in Bethlehem![64] One rabbi jokingly said, "At His coming, Jews will say, 'What took you so long?' and Christians will say, 'Welcome back.'"

What was the spiritual climate when Jesus carried out His ministry? "The age which saw the advent of Jesus Christ was an age rich in religion stretching from the crass animism and sex worship of the great majority of the world to the Roman pantheon gods and the Greek mystery religions. The Romans had a multiplicity of gods and goddesses, philosophy, and enlightened attitudes."[65] Babylon and Egypt's polytheistic influence in Rome was undeniable. This was the culture of Jesus's day and ministry, a mirror of things to come in our times.

Jesus told us in Matthew 7:15-23 to beware of false prophets that would come to us in sheep's clothing, but inwardly they are ravenous wolves. "You will know them by their fruits," He reminded. "Every good tree bears good fruit; but a corrupt tree brings forth evil fruit... and every tree that does not bring forth good fruit is hewn down and cast into the fire... Not everyone that says to me, 'Lord, Lord' shall enter the Kingdom of heaven; but he that does the will of my Father which is in heaven. Many will say to me on that day, 'Lord, didn't we prophesy in your Name? Didn't we cast out devils? And in your name done many things?' And then I will profess to them, I never knew you. Depart from me you that work iniquity."

I have personally visited the ruins of Pompeii, near Naples, Italy, destroyed in 79 AD by the eruption of Mount Vesuvius. Just as Lot's wife was turned into a pillar of salt, fleeing Sodom and Gomorrah, due to Pompeii's quick burial, the people were literally frozen in daily activity, preserved in suspended animation. The town's ruins reveal the hedonistic sex shops and phallic street markings. It is rumored that disciples came to preach Christ and warn the city to repent, and they did not. Sex cults of the day and paganism brought a fire of judgment, unexpectedly burying everything under nine feet of ash.

The 1970s in America saw an outward, incredible rise of Satanism accompanied with LSD and psychotropic drug usage. Michael Aquino, U.S. Army Officer, did a tour of Vietnam and in 1968 was a specialist in psychological warfare. He would return from the war practicing Satanism under the direction of Church of Satan Founder Anton LaVey. Dissatisfied with their association, he would break away and start his own, Temple of Set. "In 1975, he sought a new mandate to operate by invoking the devil; Satan responded by appearing as Set, the ancient Egyptian deity."[66] He and his wife also ran a daycare center. Accused of child molestation, he and other occult members infiltrating government ranks seemed to walk away from any form of accountability. Occult activity reached a heightened level of glorification in the media in the 70s.

But the pendulum swings, and conservative Ronald Reagan would become President in 1980. The born-again experience became mainstream, but it didn't completely accompany national repentance. Underneath the surface, Marxist occult ideology continued unchecked while the Berlin Wall came down. We have seen—as Scripture describes, "like birth pangs"—the coming forth of an evil plot toward one world, an attempt that Satan has tried from Babel onward. Babylonian, Egyptian, and cultic worship is back stronger and more blatant than ever. One need not look far to see Hollywood stars and entertainment boast of pyramids, Illuminati symbolism, blood, and sex rituals dating back to ancient Egyptian pyramids.

In Egypt, God's people were subjected to hard slavery making bricks for Pharaoh. Today, Satan attempts to persecute God's people as never before for his days are short. Christians have been subjected to torturous treatment in our own generation. "More Christians have died for their faith in the last 100 years than in all the other centuries combined."[67] The persecution of Jews is also on a tremendous rise, with world leaders attacking Judaism, especially from the UN and its mandates. Jesus said, "They will kill you and think they have done God a favor" (John 16:2).

We witness nations realigning against God and His people. Prophetic predictions are unfolding before us. Once Israel became a nation again and her people were gathered back from dispersion, as prophesied in Scripture, we have steadily seen a fast-speeding train toward the one world order where no man can buy or sell without the mark—the mark of the Antichrist, 666.

How is the religious world paving the way for the New World Order? Pope Francis, the first Jesuit priest to occupy the position of Pope in history has raised more than eyebrows. Catholic priests of the Jesuit order incorporated the practice of charity and educational work with a military hierarchical organization that Marquis de LaFayette, who trained the American Continental Army under Washington, would remark, "It is my opinion that if the liberties of this country (the United States of America) are destroyed, it will be by the subtlety of the Roman Catholic Jesuit priests, for they are the most crafty, dangerous enemies to civil and religious liberty. They have instigated most of the wars of Europe." With the guise of charitable and educational work, the Jesuit priests were able to move into operations that were predominantly political. Abolished by Pope Clement XIV, he stated he had sealed his death warrant, and he was dead months later.

The Jesuits' Order was expelled from over 83 nations between 1555 and 1931 for engaging in political and subversive plots as revealed by Jesuit priest Thomas J. Campbell's writings. The Jesuits created a military hierarchy and used it against the Protestants of Europe. When expelled or caught in political subversion, they learned to change tactics and reenter through charity and education. Hitler said, "I learned much from the Jesuits ... until now, there has never been anything more grandiose, on Earth, than the hierarchical organization of the Catholic Church. I transferred much of this organization into my own party. I am going to let you in on a secret... I am founding an order... In my 'burgs' of the Order, we will raise up youth which will make the world tremble."[68] [69] Hitler's acting diplomat was Franz von Papen, a sinister Nazi helping him come to power. "The Fuhrer had come to power thanks to the votes of Catholic Zentrum (centrists) overseen by Jesuit Ludwig Kaas."[70] Additionally, it was the synergy of the Jesuits' hierarchy and the Ordo

Novi Templi, a theosophical occult group believing in Eugenics and a superior race, that influenced Hitler's ideology and mythology.

Today's Jesuit priesthood operates universities and colleges like Georgetown University, Boston College, College of the Holy Cross, University of San Francisco, Loyola, and many others, focusing on business, economics, psychology, and ideologies that are leftist for the Catholic Church.

"Liberal Jesuit Catholic Priest Father James Martin has come under fire for appearing to defend puberty blockers in children who identify as transgender. Martin, who also serves as an editor-at-large for the Jesuit publication *America Magazine*... took criticism... when he appeared to challenge Texas Attorney Ken Paxton's assertions that sex change operations and puberty blockers prescribed to kids is child abuse."[71]

Pope Francis has been sharply criticized by many, including Archbishop Vigano, for statements that seem more one world government than the Kingdom of God. "Vigano levels his most pointed condemnation at 'prelates who betray their mandate' as ministers of Christ by working as agents of the New World Order." "Prelates who betray their mandate, who are almost always just as corrupt in doctrine as they are in morals, have occupied the Church of Christ in order to transform Her into a state church, a zealous servant of the New World Order and apostate in its faith." He continues to call out Catholic educational facilities and the churches by saying, "The stance of inoculating oneself with an experimental vaccine as an act of love and duty denies the evidence of facts but also the existence of a global plan that has deliberately caused this psycho-pandemic in order to bring about a ruthless reduction of the world population, especially the elderly, and impose forms of control and restriction of the natural rights of citizens."

"Far from pulling any punches, Vigano writes that 'it is not surprising that the deep church is totally subservient to the deep state, that Bergoglio (Pope Francis) wants to put himself forward as a candidate for the Presidency of the Religion of Humanity that the New World Order intends to establish.' He goes on to make note of 'those who have disguised themselves as saviors of humanity while in fact seeking to subjugate the peoples of the world and exterminate citizens or make them chronically ill.'"[72] Just as the humble yet bold Archbishop called out Pope Francis for his complicity in covering up pedophilia and homosexual abuse of children, Vigano is a voice crying out for truth and a return to Christ.

A NEW KINGDOM IS COMING, BUT IT WILL NOT END THE WAY THE GLOBALISTS HAVE PLANNED, AND I'M SURE WILL NOT DISAPPOINT THE FAITHFUL WHO STAND UP IN THIS HOUR FOR TRUTH AND RIGHTEOUSNESS.

A new Kingdom is coming, but it will not end the way the globalists have planned, and I'm sure will not disappoint the faithful who stand up in this hour for truth and righteousness. Jesus set up a Kingdom that was different than what the disciples expected. The Roman government was cruel and oppressive, especially to God's people. The followers of Jesus expected this "Kingdom" He spoke of to be established as a government on the earth and to overthrow the Romans. He tried to explain to them His Kingdom was not of this world. Daniel says,

...The God of heaven will set up a kingdom that shall never be destroyed, nor shall the kingdom be left to another people. It shall break in pieces all these kingdoms and bring them to an end, and it shall stand forever, just as you saw that a stone was cut from a mountain by no human hand....

—Daniel 2:44-45 (ESV)

Jesus's Kingdom represents the stone that crushes the previous kingdoms with their false religions. This happened when Jesus came the first time, establishing His Kingdom spiritually. He came as an infant and died as a man, becoming our Savior. But when He returns, He will come as our King of kings and Lord of lords, conquer the kingdoms of the earth, grind them into a fine powder, and set up His earthly Kingdom. The disciples hoped that Jesus would overthrow the cruel oppression of the Roman government and set up an earthly Kingdom. But He did something far better! In His first coming, He established a spiritual Kingdom, redeeming all of mankind who would receive Him. In the second coming, He will establish both a spiritual and natural Kingdom on Earth. This is what the disciples longed for.

THE MOUNTAIN OF THE LORD WILL BE BEAUTIFUL AND WILL RISE ABOVE ALL MOUNTAINS. WE ARE GOING TO HEAVEN NOT BY OUR WORK BUT BY THE WORK THAT JESUS DID, BUT "TAKING THE MOUNTAIN" BRINGS REWARD.

We are witnessing the preparation for that day. Knowing this, as believers, we possess the Kingdom now spiritually by faith and use our voices to snatch people from darkness and bring them into the light before His return.

The mountain of the Lord will be beautiful and will rise above all mountains. We are going to heaven not by our work but by the work that Jesus did, but "taking the mountain" brings reward.

I played a little basketball and coached, so I like to think of this time in terms of the fourth quarter of the game. Time is running out on the clock. We must play a strong defense and offense at the same time. We are in a full court press with everything we've got!

We are in the most suspenseful part of the movie. It looks frightening, the pace and intensity immense. God loves a climactic ending, and He promises not to disappoint! Those who perpetrate crimes on God's men, women, and children will not get away with it! When the armies of the world wage war upon Israel, Jesus (Christ, the Anointed One), with an incredible army, will descend into the battle and strike down His enemies. The blood will run deep and will vindicate the saints of God. No evil deed will go unpunished.

Jesus will set up His reign of 1,000 years on Earth at His coming. Where are we in the timeline? The Scripture tells us a day is as a thousand years in the Lord. There were seven days of creation, six days to work, and one day of God's rest. There were 2,000 years between Adam and Abraham, another 2,000 from Abraham to Jesus, and close to 2,000 years since Jesus's death to today. Calculations place that 2,000 years to culminate around 2030. At His return, He will set up His Kingdom here on the earth, and the earth will live in peace for 1,000 years. These days add up to 7,000 years, seven days of creation. Is this a revelatory answer? Many believe so. We don't know the day or hour, but Scripture is clear: We will know the season.

When Jesus returns, He will set up His earthly Kingdom. The reign of Christ as King on Earth will be the day of rest in the physical realm as it was placed in the spiritual realm at His first coming. This is an exciting time to live and take the mountains to influence others for Christ through your life. Your life and time were determined by God, and He chose you for this time!

Instead of only seeing the evil about us, we must see the purpose for our destiny coinciding with this day. Scripture compares the relationship of Jesus to the church. The wedding feast is prepared. The Galilean wedding and the Marriage Supper of the Lamb are being prepared for the day the Father will tap His Son on the shoulder to go and get His bride, His church.

> WHEN JESUS RETURNS, HE WILL SET UP HIS EARTHLY KINGDOM. THE REIGN OF CHRIST AS KING ON EARTH WILL BE THE DAY OF REST IN THE PHYSICAL REALM AS IT WAS PLACED IN THE SPIRITUAL REALM AT HIS FIRST COMING. THIS IS AN EXCITING TIME TO LIVE AND TAKE THE MOUNTAINS TO INFLUENCE OTHERS FOR CHRIST THROUGH YOUR LIFE. YOUR LIFE AND TIME WERE DETERMINED BY GOD, AND HE CHOSE YOU FOR THIS TIME!

In Revelation's seven churches, some lost their love, and their lives became tarnished, lukewarm in faith, and even apostate in allowing sinful actions. But two churches were promised to escape the terrible day, the faithful church and the persecuted church. Jesus called the other five to repent or their lights would be removed. In the final judgment, He will separate the sheep from the goats and say to the goats, "Depart from me, you workers of iniquity. I never knew you."

My desire is to hear, "Well done, good and faithful servant. Enter into all I have prepared for you since the foundations of the earth." It is God's pleasure to give you His Kingdom. He has instructed us to ask Him, and He will give us the nations for our inheritance. Take mountains at home, in nations, in every corner of the earth. For this Gospel of the Kingdom will be preached throughout the earth, and the end will surely come.

TWO KINGDOMS
IN CONFLICT

There are forces and people driving the agenda for a New World Order. Prior to the exploitation of the COVID pandemic, globalist proponents devised the novel tactic of the threat of "environmental Armageddon" by way of "climate change" in the 1970s.[73] One of the strongest advocates of the global governance movement, the Club of Rome said, "The common enemy of humanity is man. In searching for a new enemy to unite us, we came up with the idea that pollution, the threat of global warming, water shortages, famine, and the like would fit the bill. All of these dangers are caused by human intervention, and it is only through changed attitudes and behavior that they can be overcome. The real enemy then is humanity itself."[74]

Seizing upon the idea, former Soviet leader and Communist Mikhail Gorbachev quickly positioned himself to promote this New World Order. He explained at the State of the World Forum, "The emerging 'environmentalization' of our civilization and the need for vigorous action in the interest of the entire global community will inevitably have multiple political consequences. Perhaps the most important of them will be a gradual change in the status of the United Nations. Inevitably, it must assume some aspects of world government."[75]

The UN began to sponsor a series of international meetings, specifically featuring the environment and how to "save planet Earth."[76] In 1992, more than 50,000 NGOs, diplomats, and 179 world leaders, including U.S. President George H.W. Bush, met in an "Earth Summit," in Rio de Janeiro, Brazil. Here, four governing documents and treaties emerged outlining how the UN would spearhead saving the planet, the most important of which was named Agenda 21.[77] Its supporters promoted it as a "Comprehensive blueprint for the reorganization of human society."[78] All 179 world leaders signed and adopted the document, including President Bush, agreeing to put its goals into national policy "in every area in which human impacts on the environment."[79] Agenda 21 was supplemented by the UN's 2030 Agenda, signed by Obama, which gives more detail on how that is to be done and states in its preamble that "all countries and all stakeholders, acting in collaborative partnership, *will implement* this plan."[80]

At its core, Agenda 21 is about impoverishing huge portions of populations and bringing down developed nations by imposing restrictions on land use, air, energy, industry, water, agriculture, and every other area "impacted by humans." The end goals are to eradicate small business, competition, borders, laws, private property, and concentrate wealth into a global government at the behest of major corporations, i.e., to facilitate the creation of a One World Government.

Why through the environment? According to the UN's Biodiversity treaty presented at the 1990 UN Earth Summit, "Nature has an integral set of different values (cultural, spiritual, and material) where humans are one strand in nature's web and all living creatures are considered equal. Therefore, the natural way is the right way, and human activities should be molded along nature's rhythms."[81] The environment does not follow national boundaries, rivers don't head borders, the air in one country becomes the air in another, and oceans are not subject to man's control. Thus, if the UN and other globalists can control nature, they can control people.

However, even if those behind the environmental movement were not as sinister as I just described (how I wish it were true), and are simply well-meaning people in their pursuit of environmental causes, their understanding of world events places the planet and the creation of more importance than the humans God created in His image to live on it. Their view of life, purpose, and the order of humanity has been skewed by a worldview that places themselves and saving the planet as the priority and heightens their role of self-importance. Whether they view themselves as atheists or have recreated God in their own image, as in some sects of Christianity and the world's religions, their actual allegiance is to a kingdom, but it is not God's Kingdom. Jesus made this very clear when He said, *"Whoever is not with me is against me, and whoever does not gather with me scatters"* (Matthew 12:30, ESV).

These thought leaders did not invent a "one world" idea on their own, no matter how brilliant they would represent themselves to be. They have simply joined the wrong side of the original battle of the ages. There are two kingdoms in conflict, and the lives of men, women, and children have been targeted by the enemy of heaven, Satan. He was cast from heaven after leading a rebellion that included one-third of heaven's angels in a prideful display of arrogance. Satan is a great deceiver. He conspired against God in heaven. He conspired against God to get the allegiance of the first family, Adam and Eve. He conspired against God in Noah's age, resulting in a watery judgment on Earth, and he conspired against God at the Tower of Babel. He conspired against the Son of God, Jesus, to crucify Him, but that backfired beyond his wildest schemes!

Defiance against God is Satan's modus operandi, and his endgame is to destroy the object of God's love and devotion, you. Yes, beyond any "thing" created on Earth, God saw you and me as the reason for the creation. A father builds a house for his family. A mother may plan a vacation for her children. God, in His goodness, gave men and women dominion (authority) to rule over the earth He created for them, with His guidance. They chose to listen to another voice and give their gift away, but God had a plan to rescue them back through His Son. Satan's fate is sealed, and if he can take God's beloved with him, all the better in his game of vengeance to kill, steal, and destroy.

The conflict is escalating, and we observe the impact of the spiritual world manifesting in the natural world daily in headlines, wars, rumors of wars, famines, pestilence, and evil beyond our comprehension. To understand what is happening in our time, we need to realize that not only are there two kingdoms, but also every person is part of one or the other. Depending on where we have chosen to align ourselves, we are in allegiance to God or Satan. Are we gathering with God or scattering and contributing to

> **DEPENDING ON WHERE WE HAVE CHOSEN TO ALIGN OURSELVES, WE ARE IN ALLEGIANCE TO GOD OR SATAN.**

demonically inspired chaos? There are no other options, according to Jesus's words that state we are either for Him or against Him. First John 4:6 describes the two kingdoms in different terms: the Spirit of truth and the spirit of falsehood, or deception.

How do we recognize the Spirit of truth so that we are not deceived?

> *But the person without the Spirit does not receive what comes from God's Spirit, because it is foolishness to him; he is not able to understand it for it is evaluated spiritually.*
> —1 Corinthians 2:14-16 (CEB)

God's Word is the truth, yet those who do not receive His Spirit through the born-again experience will not discern what God calls good versus what God calls evil. Jesus said, *"Unless one is born again he cannot see the kingdom of God"* (John 3:3b, ESV).

From a biblical worldview, God created the earth for man and woman, and He set in place commandments and principles to govern life under His divine leadership, but in the globalists' view, the earth is to be elevated, perhaps even worshiped, over the beings created in God's image that inhabit it. *"They have traded God's truth for a lie and worshiped and served the creation instead of the creator who is blessed forever"* (Romans 1:25, CEB). These mindsets are belief systems that originate apart from God and drive everything from morality, politics, social constructs, abortion, gender fluidity, and radical environmentalism to socialism and communism.

The further we stray from a biblical worldview or the Kingdom of God, the more we are deceived; and the more deception, the more opportunity Satan has to influence and destroy the objects of God's love, people. Those who want to engineer life and determine its outcomes "play God" and determine what is valued and what is not, who or what fits into their plans for the future, and who is expendable. The result? Take abortion, for instance: 63 million children in the United States have been murdered in the womb since abortion was legalized in 1973.[82] "Abortion was the leading cause of death globally in 2021 with nearly 43 million unborn babies killed in the womb, according to data provided by Worldometer."[83]

I hope that number causes you to gasp, as was my response! But instead of a gasp, these global leaders clap in approval because depopulation helps further their social and environmental goals. How did we get here? The basis of this deception becomes clearer as we observe the family backgrounds of current world leaders driving these decisions.

"The father of Bill Gates, Bill H. Gates, Sr., was on the board of Planned Parenthood. The Bill & Melinda Gates Foundation brags on its own website that it gives $1.7M to Planned Parenthood. In fact, the Gates Foundation and Warren Buffet (as trustee of the Gates Foundation and founder of the Susan Thompson Buffett Foundation) are among the biggest donors to Planned Parenthood. Of course, George Soros, through his organization, Open Society Institute, is also listed as a major financial supporter of Planned Parenthood.[84] Planned Parenthood commits over 30 percent of America's abortions—887 abortions a day, 1 abortion every 97 seconds, and over 320,000 abortions last year alone."[85] Delving into the backgrounds of many world leaders, it's not hard to see the influences driving much of their ideologies started with their parents' influence.

The deception that the earth is more important than its people gives these influencers the moral outcry to destroy human life to "save the planet." This view of genocide—and that is what it is, make no mistake—is justified by their anti-biblical worldview that the greater good is worth the destruction of human life. They have been educated with a globalist view; they must control the planet, its people, and resources because they have a higher understanding than you and I do.

> *"Professing themselves to be wise, they became fools and changed the glory of the incorruptible God into an image made like the corruptible man..."*
>
> —Romans 1:22-23 (AKJV)

We are warned in Scripture that in the last days, gross darkness will cover the earth. People will be lovers of money, boastful, arrogant, proud, lovers of self rather than lovers of God. They will be haters of good, disobedient to parents... (2 Timothy 3:1-5). Jesus said to those who would choose to reject God:

> *"You are of your father the devil, and your will is to do your father's desires. He was a murderer from the beginning, and does not stand in the truth, because there is no truth in him. When he lies, he speaks out of his own character, for he is a liar and the father of lies."*
>
> —John 8:44 (ESV)

There are only two kingdoms, and when people reject God and His Word as truth, they choose to listen to another voice and live from the kingdom of darkness. It manifests as the origin of their thoughts and decisions, then produces lies, and, eventually, murder.

The seven mountains of cultural influence dominated by man's arrogance are converging often in partnership against the Lord, but we have this hope-filled promise in Isaiah 2.

> *Now it will come about in the last days, the mountain of the House of the Lord will be established as the chief of the mountains, and will be raised above the hills, and the nations will stream to it. And many peoples will come and say, "Come, let's go up to the mountain of the Lord."*
>
> —Isaiah 2:2-3a (NASB)

Regardless of the evil we observe, God's mountain will rise above every tower man has made and man's every ill-concocted idea. God will establish those who build their lives on His Kingdom.

This is a day like no other, a day of deception, but a day of great opportunity too. We do not have to be deceived in these times. The conflict is great, but God is greater in you than he that is in this world. We need to discern the days we are living in and recognize their significance. We cannot determine what is right or wrong without God's Word as our moral compass. The only basis for truth comes from an unshakable standard, viewing life through God's eyes and His Word. This is not the first attempt of humankind to create a one world rule where the top lead and decide what is right or wrong apart from God, but it always ends badly. The Kingdom of God and His way of living will produce life and truth and invoke His blessing. Apart from Him, we can do nothing that has a lasting positive effect.

God's Kingdom is a Kingdom of true love and light for God is love, and His Word and ways are the light. Jesus stated that *"I am the light of the world"* (John 8:12, NIV) and Matthew 4:16 (NIV) says, *"The people living in darkness have seen a great light."* The kingdom of darkness counterfeits the real source of love and light with false imagery that sparkles but ends with turmoil and destruction.

Sometimes, it is hard to see through the facades! We need heavenly help to avoid being deceived by their glitter.

Second Corinthians 4:4a (NLT) says "*Satan, who is the god of this world, has blinded the minds of those who don't believe. They are unable to see the glorious light of the Good News.*" The world's system is temporal, and just like those who sought to build the Tower of Babel, it will not succeed long term. Sadly, those who foster it create great misery and destruction for people while they experiment with their lives. We are reminded in Scripture that we see the wicked and then

THE KINGDOM OF DARKNESS COUNTERFEITS THE REAL SOURCE OF LOVE AND LIGHT WITH FALSE IMAGERY THAT SPARKLES BUT ENDS WITH TURMOIL AND DESTRUCTION. SOMETIMES, IT IS HARD TO SEE THROUGH THE FACADES! WE NEED HEAVENLY HELP TO AVOID BEING DECEIVED BY THEIR GLITTER.

they are no more. Though they possibly have great accolades on Earth, their lives end morally bankrupt. Satan merely uses people as his minions to destroy.

Jesus said, "*My Kingdom is not of this world*" (John 18:36, ESV). We know that Jesus exemplified the will of the Father and His goodness. When Moses asked for God to show him His glory, God said, "I will show you my glory in my goodness." God is a loving Father, and He controls eternity. Satan is an evil tyrant who is the "*god of this world*" (2 Corinthians 4:4, ESV) with limited time to deceive the world's systems. The result of living in God's unlimited light and following His way is it produces wholeness. His faithful followers are given the authority to rule and reign with Christ throughout eternity. This is in contrast to Satan's limited kingdom of darkness, which results in those who follow him being ruled over by a tyrant, Satan, and incurring his same eternal judgment in the end. These are choices people make, and the outcomes of their decisions can be clearly seen in this life.

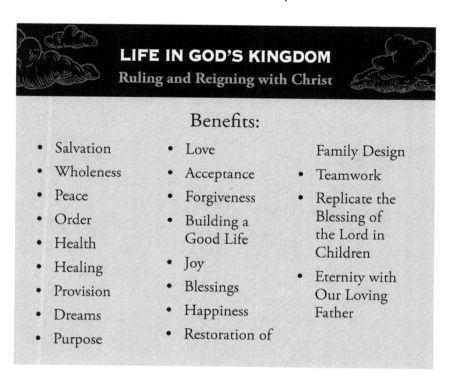

LIFE IN GOD'S KINGDOM
Ruling and Reigning with Christ

Benefits:

- Salvation
- Wholeness
- Peace
- Order
- Health
- Healing
- Provision
- Dreams
- Purpose

- Love
- Acceptance
- Forgiveness
- Building a Good Life
- Joy
- Blessings
- Happiness
- Restoration of

Family Design
- Teamwork
- Replicate the Blessing of the Lord in Children
- Eternity with Our Loving Father

LIFE WITHOUT GOD/ SATAN'S LIMITED KINGDOM
Being Ruled Over by Satan

Curses:

- Broken Lives
- Fear
- Anxiety
- Dread
- Torment
- Control
- Anarchy
- Sickness
- Disease
- Pain
- Broken Homes
- Children Indoctrinated and Used for his Agendas

- Infidelity
- Lust
- Strife
- Anger
- Resentment
- Fits of Rage
- Unforgiveness
- Condemnation
- Guilt
- Bitterness
- Addictions
- Bondages
- Strongholds

- Enslavement to Debt
- Poverty
- Worship Things and Lust for More
- Infidelity
- Death
- Destruction
- Rat Race
- Never Satisfied
- Never Enough

As a young college student at Oral Roberts University, I was required to watch the series "How Should We Then Live?" by Francis Schaeffer. Dr. Schaeffer shared how a civilization's spiritual knowledge of God and His values are reflected in the areas of its culture. He demonstrated how throughout history, a society's religion and acceptance or rejection of God is reflected in its arts/entertainment, government/politics, media, education, health, family, and religion. As a society becomes more immoral, its arts and entertainment demonstrate the fallen state of its people. The laws become unjust, and the people suffer from poor leadership. Poverty and resulting sickness abound as people are treated poorly by those who have absolute tyranny over their lives.

Satan is the first tyrant, and all those who are godless will follow their leader. They produce after their kind, just like a seed does. They have been seeded with the fallacy that man is his own god. Schaeffer said, "God has ordained the state as a delegated authority; it is not autonomous. The state is to be an agent of justice, to restrain evil by punishing the wrongdoer, and to protect the good in society. When it does the reverse, it has no proper authority. It is then a usurped authority, and as such it becomes lawless and is tyranny." We are witnessing this tyranny today, and without God, men will assume headship as gods just as Satan attempted a usurped authority.

> **SATAN IS THE FIRST TYRANT, AND ALL THOSE WHO ARE GODLESS WILL FOLLOW THEIR LEADER.**

In light of Scripture and every prophetic sign of Jesus's coming, it appears we are living in the end of the age. We must ask, as Ezekiel 33:10 (KJ21) says, "How should we then live?" Further, we must ask: "Do I have the personal commitment to God and His "equipment" to enter my personal battle and win?" "Am I walking in accordance with God's Word? and "How will I fulfill my destiny for myself and those counting on me in my family, my community, nation, and the world?"

There is a way to escape the corruption of this world and live in His divine nature. It is dual in that we have a spiritual escape, but we also have promises that give us the answers to life, its meaning, and, more importantly, how to live. And we have a calling to not only escape the corruption of the world but also to share with others how to do so.

My husband, Gary, has a gift of revelation concerning the Kingdom of God and its operations like no one else I have heard. I marvel and walk humbly by his side even as his wife. For the most part, Gary is a simple person, low-maintenance, and likes things pretty basic. Yet, when he begins to teach on the Kingdom of God, jaws drop, mine included. I am sharing a very basic yet profound understanding I received from Gary concerning 2 Peter 1:3-4:

> His divine <u>power</u> has given ME everything I need for life and godliness through MY knowledge of Him who called ME by His own <u>glory</u> and <u>goodness</u>, so that through them, I may <u>participate</u> in the divine nature and escape the corruption in the world caused by evil desires.

God has given us everything we need for life and godliness, and in a world of chaos, that is very comforting to hear. Otherwise, self-preservation and fear could take over our lives. How does this "everything I need" come? Through my knowledge of Him, according to this Scripture. Our knowledge of what? Our knowledge of Him, the One who called us. And how did He call us to be His? By His own glory and goodness. God's glory is His demonstrated power and goodness. In other words, He has the power to do what He promised to do. We must believe He has the power, and we must also believe in His goodness. In other words, His will toward you is good. This is His goodness. If we believe He has the glory (ability), and we believe He has good intentions, then we must choose to participate in the promise. This principle determines whether we receive the promises, or we could say "experiences," described and promised in the Word of God.

Years back, our youngest daughter wanted me to skydive on a break in our ministry trip to Australia. I wasn't too certain about skydiving, but I was willing to go there for my daughter, whom I love very much, and the idea excited me a bit too! I asked the instructor who was going to be tandem jumping with me two questions. "How many jumps have you completed?" I was determining if he had the ability, or the power, to do this. He said, "2,500!" I was satisfied. My second question was, "Do you want to die today?" He chuckled and said, "No!" I was trying to evaluate if his will toward me was good. Did he want to complete the jump successfully (his goodness toward me, and perhaps to himself)? Once I knew he had the glory (ability) and the goodness (good desire), then I had to choose to participate. I had to say, "Yes," and I also had to sign up by placing my agreement, my signature on the legal paperwork, accepting my responsibility.

God has a part to play, and so do we. Will we, as individuals who love Jesus, sign up, agree with God, and take our responsibility to escape the corruption of the world, a world He has given us to occupy until He comes? He has given us His promises, the equipment, the weapons, and the power to do mighty exploits for such a time as this if we choose to believe and engage His Kingdom.

1 Believe God has the power. **(GLORY)**

2 Believe His will toward you is good. **(GOODNESS)**

3 Choose to participate in the promise. **(AGREEMENT/FAITH)**

We will approach God and His Word differently if we accept that His will (His Word) is good toward us and that He has the power and authority to perform what He promised.

It is the supernatural presence and power of God that gives us hope and courage in a world gone mad. We are partakers of that divine knowledge, and it changes everything. We personally have thousands of stories of this divine intervention that answers every need in life and causes those who believe God's Word to escape the corruption of this world. "He has given us everything we need for life and godliness," and we can escape the corrupted world. These are your commissioning words to start to turn the world upside down (really right side up) for Christ. By choosing to live in the Kingdom of God, you can get your life back the way God intended and then share the truth with others.

> **IT IS THE SUPERNATURAL PRESENCE AND POWER OF GOD THAT GIVES US HOPE AND COURAGE IN A WORLD GONE MAD.**

Thus says the Lord: "Let not the wise man boast in his wisdom, let not the mighty man boast in his might, let not the rich man boast in his riches, but let him who boasts boast in this, that he understands and knows me, that I am the Lord who practices steadfast love, justice, and righteousness in the earth. For in these things I delight, declares the Lord."

—Jeremiah 9:23-24 (ESV)

THE SEVEN MOUNTAINS OF INFLUENCE

Mike and Nora moved to the United States from Uzbekistan with no friends, unable to speak English, and with only $2,000 to their name. Mike found a low-paying job that barely covered their bills, where he worked for nine years. They lived in a small two-bedroom apartment with their four children. Nora hoped that one day they might be able to afford a three-bedroom apartment for their family, but she told herself that's all they could ever afford. They attended an underground church in their country before coming to America. It was dangerous even to attend. They found churches in the U.S. disappointing as many did not seem committed to the Bible or living their faith. Mike said, "Mostly, they just offered milk and no meat," but he wanted their faith challenged.

They visited our church and were inspired as they heard the Kingdom of God taught and saw stories of life transformation others had experienced. They learned who they were in Christ, Kingdom principles, and their potential as children of God. Mike decided that he would ask God to give him a better job. He quit his job after years of promised increase that never came, not knowing where he would go. He found a job driving a truck, which paid him more money than he had ever earned. Mike and Nora began to dream of someday building a home of their own. Together, they believed God could bring the money, and they saved. They were so thrilled when they finally built their own home with over 5,000 square feet of space. This was living a dream! Although their lives were changing, Mike was on the road all the time. With little time for family, again they prayed and decided to start their own business. Eventually, he began to hire drivers and built his own trucking company.

In just four years from the hardships of a small apartment and limited future, Mike has employees that help him carry the load and contracts with large corporations. His English may be a bit broken, but he is not! He is able to enjoy time with his children and wife as they run their business from home. Their transformation has encouraged and inspired others to discover God's Kingdom. They have impacted many other people because of their story of God's Kingdom transforming their finances, family, and life. Their life story is a ministry that preaches without a pulpit. We have thousands of stories like this in every area of need. The early church exploded with growth because of transformation and miracles just like Mike and Nora's.

People's stories preach the best sermons! When people experience God for themselves, others are drawn in. It is often assumed that ministry is carried out by clergy members or church pastors. There has been a sense that only uber-serious Christians go into ministry, and the rest of Christendom sits on the sidelines, second-class spiritually, filling "secular" roles, especially business leaders. Pastors have been paid to handle "the ministry." This couldn't be further from the example of the early church that turned the world upside down. Jesus called His disciples from fishermen, tax collectors, and new converts. The apostle Paul funded his ministry through tent-making. It was through his business that he made a lifelong relationship with Priscilla and Aquila. He went so far as to state that he came at no expense to minister but rather funded his ministry by the work of his own hands.

I remember clearly in our own situation when my husband decided to enter financial services after attending college at Oral Roberts University, he was warned by well-meaning family members that he was going to be in trouble for "missing the call of God." Gary had an experience with God on his nineteenth birthday that would change the trajectory of his life. He had a vision and heard a voice say, "You're called to preach My Word" while seeing himself teaching people who were sitting in folding chairs. At graduation, He asked God to show him what to do and where to fulfill that vision. A position in financial services was offered to him, and he felt strongly to pursue that leading. It was new territory and a bit frightening, but an interesting thing happened. He found the call of God in his financial services business!

The financial disparity we experienced ourselves "doing finances" the normal way, according to the standard of the world's system, landed us in deep debt. We questioned the "debt system" that we were raised to place our trust in. That caused us to search Scripture for answers and discover that there are actually two kingdoms, they operate completely differently, and the results are different too. Although we were believers, we had trusted financial guidance that didn't match the counsel of the Word of God. We decided to "switch kingdoms" not just spiritually but in our financial dealings too. We aligned our trust in God's principles to receive provision His way. The biblical principles were opposite from what we had learned in our training in school, home, and through the media. We began to see there was a serious breakdown and disparity between God's instructions versus what we were conditioned to believe in every area of life.

Those teachings became the bedrock of our life's work and ministry. To this day while pastoring a large church, we operate a company we launched over 30 years ago. Our company helps families get out of debt and invest safely. The business has helped families understand the Kingdom of God's biblical provision and develops free plans showing them "how" to get out of debt. This is a viable ministry, and yet it comes in the package of business. People open up to us in business and share their problems and family situations, because finances touch every person in some form. They share information that few people are willing to share with their pastors. What an incredible opportunity to share God's Kingdom as we help them navigate their finances.

Climbing the mountain of business, we became the number one office out of 5,000 offices with our vendor. We became marketplace ministers first, and eventually, this would lead to other areas of ministry. Spiritual impact doesn't have to look like a cookie-cutter ministry. God uses all of us in various ways to touch someone. Your common ground with others or business services you offer can become your mission field. God calls people to spheres of influence and to carry the Kingdom with them! Your personal example speaks loudly, and you can interject God's life principles as you model a different way to live.

The same type of epiphany happened with marriage. As we helped people with finances, their marriage issues consistently surfaced as well. Just like finances, God has a completely different standard and approach toward marriage and family than those driven by celebrity culture. Ideologies contrary to the Bible permeate media, psychology, and education. Sexual intimacy has no sacredness, and acceptance of premarital sex, one-night stands, and the exploration of every imaginable form of sexual immorality is normalized. In the last 40 years, relationships between men and women shifted from a biblical worldview of marriage to any and every type of modern family arrangement imaginable. This ultimately doesn't work out well, and people are hurting. Where there's hurt, there's need and a desire for hope and help. That's an opportunity!

I have written and spoken on these topics in marriage conferences, sharing God's design for family. As we lived those principles in our family, and shared them with others, just like the success we experienced in finances, we saw incredible transformation in marriages too. We realized that the churches' lack of effectiveness was in part because of compromise. Doing life just like the rest of the culture robs believers of a life that mirrors God's principles instead of the world's. People are looking for answers and want results, but somehow, the messages weren't resonating and didn't help people tackle life with real answers and results. It became religious but not transformational.

In some ways, the church abandoned the six other mountains for religion alone. Business, government, family, media, arts/entertainment, education, *and* religion influence our society. What influences society is a missed opportunity if we are not engaging people there. I believe this is what Jesus referred to when He said, "Occupy until I come." This is a military reference to "take territory, invade, and take over." That sounds like world impact to me! Wrong perceptions that ministry is only for clergy keep believers from "occupying" and also from "modeling" for others the results of following Jesus.

What are we to occupy? Everything, every area of life, all seven mountains! Each of us is drawn to various interests, whether it's vocationally or recreationally or artistically. God created you with unique abilities and interests, but guess what? There are others like you. These are areas you can occupy and can bring your faith with you to impact people for Kingdom purposes. And there must be joy in our endeavors! If you're not enjoying your faith, why would anyone else want it?

Church became religious and not applicable. Waning commitment increasingly pushed faith out of mainstream influence, shrinking church attendance over the last 25 years. I am certainly not saying to make church worldly, but it must be appealing! Satan has a better marketing campaign for a faulty product. Wrong attitudes toward faith and perhaps lack of teaching permeated pulpits and separated ministry from everyday life where people live, work, rest, play, lead, learn, and take care of their health or finances. Although there is not a scriptural reference for the seven mountains of influence, we are charged to, "Go into all the world and preach the Gospel." We need to view this as "go into every person's world" and be a representative, "an ambassador of Christ" in that arena.

Unfortunately, when we vacate these opportunities or allow an increasingly hostile culture to minimize our involvement, what fills the void of what was once a vibrant life-producing faith is religion but of another kind—false or dead religion. Both are empty. If we compromise the teachings of God's Kingdom to "reach" people, when we get an audience with them, there are no life-changing messages or results of doing things God's way. It is a balancing act to maintain the commitment to truth and a relevant application to life and culture.

There must be purpose attached to our faith, and every believer must be on a Kingdom assignment in some area of impact. Leaders need to teach people that it is their mission to share the Kingdom by example and in their unique assignments, whether it's running a business, running for office, teaching classes, gaming, or hosting small groups. When there is life transformation,

> **THERE MUST BE PURPOSE ATTACHED TO OUR FAITH, AND EVERY BELIEVER MUST BE ON A KINGDOM ASSIGNMENT IN SOME AREA OF IMPACT.**

we want to share it with someone! We must ask, "How can I intentionally use what I enjoy or do for a living to take territory?

Apathy, compromise, and cultural resistance to Christianity have weakened our voices, but it's not too late to get back our megaphones. As we have allowed the attacks of sinister forces to silence and hush us, we have lost tremendous territory, making Christianity counterculture. But that's an opportunity in itself! Corporations and educational institutions have adopted policies to forbid and limit people of faith from sharing their views and beliefs, whether from wearing apparel reflecting faith or by educators being restricted from displaying a simple Bible on their desk or any references to their faith in classroom examples. Loud voices have drowned out the choir. For the most part, these attitudes toward religious expression have not been equally applied to other beliefs.

Particularly, Christian faith has been singled out, ridiculing students for their faith and censoring freedom of expression, and especially "Christian" expression. It's not unusual to open slick, beautifully designed magazine spreads for home, health, or fashion filled with chic imagery of people in meditation poses or rooms decorated with Buddha and other gods, including occult figures and symbolism, all associated with living the good life. Christian symbols and expressions are rarely seen and deemed offensive when portrayed. Across the nation, daily meditation groups and classes meet to practice yoga and forms of martial arts that may invoke spiritism, emptying oneself and receiving from other spiritual forces. These have become ways of everyday life in the culture, including for many Christians. Health food stores, exercise, fashion, entertainment, media, and arts openly display gods of world religions and occult "worship," and no one complains.

Music and all forms of artistry incorporate occult imagery and symbolism with very little blinks of the eye, but not so with Christian imagery. It is censored as offensive. In brainwashing fashion, the media consistently remarks how narrow-minded and intolerant Christian views are and are shaming many into silence. Our views aren't intolerant. They're just different than the world's. Our world celebrates difference but not in our faith expressions.

One article went so far as to sing the praises of the Muslim faith and advocate for its "right" to control lawmaking because, unlike

Christianity, it is both a religious faith and a system of law that should be allowed into our governing systems. What about Moses's Levitical law and the formation of our American Republic and legal system originally based in the faith of the Bible, its moral code, and the Ten Commandments? Judeo-Christianity is being shoved out of the public square and halls of education. There is a purposeful effort to remove Christian teaching, principles, and faith from all seven spheres.

It is said, "Money makes the world go round." The desire to control and rule has spread into every sphere of society, impacting all of culture. Historically, the arts and entertainment industries' primary funding and patronage originate from the wealthy; and at the bequest of philanthropists, they determine what is commissioned and gains popularity. Politics are driven by powerful elite forces with banking connections and funding to engage candidates and the power to make or break them in media, again funded by ad campaigns from large conglomerates. Socialist corporatism is swallowing small businesses and economies. Healthcare is controlled by these same large corporate forces. Government leaders can easily become puppets to a group of global leaders and social engineers building the world they command.

And the church's impact? Most Christian publishing and music companies have been bought out by secular companies, and the messages carefully crafted to be "inclusive" no longer reflect the exclusive commands of our God concerning faith, sexuality, family, economics, and morality. Some churches have closed their doors, and other religious organizations have abandoned the faith, joining together with powerful world alliances to help further agendas of equity and wield political power. These organizations help emerging leadership to solidify global agendas in the guise of religion but are void of truth.

Jesus warned against a form of godliness but without His power. Religion is simply the skeleton of what used to be alive. When God is no longer the center of it, man and his plans take over and produce an apostate church. Jesus said, "Because you are neither hot nor cold, I will spew you out of my mouth." Archbishop Vigano has accused his own church, the Catholic church of taking up such globalist causes without scriptural integrity.[86] His works and words bear much truth and are worth hearing. He has been censored like the prophet Jeremiah, who was thrown into a cistern because of his truth telling. Thankfully, there are those who are willing to risk the consequences for freedom and a heavenly cause. Our strength remains in the power of truth. Let's utilize a strategy and work together to proclaim it!

There is great opportunity in spite of all the pressure. Maybe we took too much for granted and became comfortable with our faith as a whole. Unlike Nora and Mike, who had to meet underground to worship, we have never felt that level of pressure and persecution. I see an awakening happening across the nations. Parents are realizing that their children's education has been taken from them and replaced with indoctrination into social agendas. Government approval ratings are at all-time lows. People want change,

> **PEOPLE WANT CHANGE, AND WE KNOW THE CHANGE THEY NEED THAT CAN TRANSFORM THE CULTURE JUST LIKE IT HAS THROUGHOUT HISTORY, A VIBRANT, RED-HOT FAITH THAT CHANGES LIVES AND HOMES.**

and we know the change they need that can transform the culture just like it has throughout history, a vibrant, red-hot faith that changes lives and homes.

If we will pray fervently over these areas, ask God for His strategies to have greater influence, and then add to our prayers commitment, action, and involvement, we can contend for the faith and reach into our personal spheres of influence to make a difference. You have been called into the Kingdom of God for such a time as this. We can infiltrate the seven mountains again with the right mindset and reclaim lost or missed opportunities. We are experiencing exciting results from using media to tell transformational stories that demonstrate God's Kingdom and the life change happening for people just like Mike and Nora. We must engage people where they are, in the place of their felt needs, and bring answers that work, with both spiritual and practical applications. Take every mountain!

HOW DO I FIT IN THIS BATTLE?

God had servants, the angels, but He wanted a family. You are the dream, design, and creation of a loving Father. You are one of a kind, irreplaceable in the heart of your Father. It's hard for us to comprehend the battle we are in without truly understanding what the battle is over. It is over you! Imagine you have a child that you envisioned before its birth. You hold that child in your heart and finally in your arms. Your love for that child is overwhelming. You

GOD HAD SERVANTS, THE ANGELS, BUT HE WANTED A FAMILY.

have other children, but no two are alike. Each one has the dearest place in your heart. Unique in every way, you deeply love them and long to be with them. But one day, a past enemy with the most evil intentions breaks into your home while you are away and lures your beloved child into their car, promising them a gift they want badly. That kidnapped child is lost and out of your reach. You cannot free them without offering your life as a ransom for theirs. What do you risk for their life?

Jesus risked it all and did this for the family that God created, you, the apple of His eye. God is about family. Religion can misconstrue God's love for us by making us feel that God is only about what we can do for Him, painting the picture of us as servants or slaves instead of sons and daughters. God created you with a choice to follow your destiny or to reject His love and follow your own. He created you with purpose in His mind. "I knew you before you were in your mother's womb." You were not created to be a slave. You were created in His likeness and His image and possess His characteristics and DNA. Sons and daughters share an inheritance with their father, and the inheritance comes from being part of a family, not from performing as a slave. God chose us, but it is up to us to choose Him.

The angels ask, in Psalm 8:

> *"When I see and consider Your heavens, the work of Your fingers, the moon and the stars, which You have established, what is man that You are mindful of him, and the son of [earthborn] man that You care for him?*
>
> *Yet You have made him a little lower than God, and You have crowned him with glory and honor. You made him to have dominion over the works of Your hands; You have put all things under his feet."*
>
> —Psalm 8:3-6 (AMP)

The devil hates you so much because God created you higher than the angels, and made you, as the Scripture says, "a little lower than Elohim (the word for God)." Children are made in the likeness and image of their father, and you are made in His image and likeness. Angels are a separate creation apart from man and are not sons.

Satan despised God's creation of mankind and tried to exalt himself above the Most High. When he led the rebellion in heaven against God and was banished to Earth, he became an archenemy of the Kingdom of God through treason. He led Adam and Eve in this same treason against God as well. He had no authority over them in the earth until they gave it to him. His only strength against them was to lie and deceive them into handing their leadership over the earth to him. That is why Scripture calls him the god of this world. The same cunning, crafty, and maniacal lies he used to deceive them into treason was how he operated in heaven against God.

The host of angels that rebelled against God along with Satan are now dark spirits operating to deceive people into the same treason of their lives. The whole world is under the sway or influence of this darkness. People blaspheme God and try to remove His influence out of the world and every area of life. There are pervasive lies set up to craftily lure people into bondage and pain and then blame God for the wars, death, sickness, and destruction. He creates terror under the guise that God is the one to blame.

James 1:17 states that every good and perfect gift is from above, coming down from the Father of heavenly lights in whom there is no shadow, no turning, no darkness. This is not the picture of someone who does evil. Why does God give you good gifts? Because He loves you! God has given His children everything that pertains to life and to godliness just as a good and loving parent gives their children the necessities of life, but even more.

"If you being evil (corrupted by sin) know how to give good gifts to your children, how much more will God give good gifts to those that love him." And even beyond that, "He delights in the prosperity of those who serve Him." And beyond that, "I will give you the desires of your heart." This is the heart of our Father who loves you and wraps you in His love. Our worship is not mandated; it is our response to His love.

Satan and a horde of demonic forces are aligned against humankind and targeted at those who come to Christ and choose to be translated into the Kingdom of God. We become new creations in Christ when we accept Jesus, the rescuer Savior, and God's Spirit comes inside us and breathes new life and power into us that we were originally created to carry. Just as God breathed the breath of life into Adam and Eve when He created them, His life force comes into ours, and we are "born-again" with that new breath of His Spirit, the Holy Spirit.

With our new recreated spirits alive to God, we can learn who we are in Him, our inheritance, and destiny. Until then, we are just Satan's pawns operating in his kingdom of darkness and a limited life of searching. We must learn our weaponry and how to use it to fight spiritually in heavenly realms we cannot see with our natural eyes but that are revealed to us by His Spirit. It is in using those weapons that we apprehend the victory already purchased for us as an heir of God and a benefactor of royalty in His Kingdom. There are principalities, might, and dominant forces in the heavenly atmosphere that are these fallen demonic spirits that try to war against people and the Kingdom. We must submit our hearts and weaknesses to God, then He gives us the power to resist them in His strength that comes through the Holy Spirit. These weapons don't look like the ones we use in natural conflict, but they are spiritually discerned and mighty.

They pull down any strong force against us and destroy the lies that hold us captive. Scripture says we are seated with Him in heavenly places, positioned with His authority, but we must learn how to exercise that authority with faith and decisive power.

God loves you so much more than any attack against you. With our new lives, we have dominion and authority over Satan and his angels. You have been given power over all the power of the devil, and nothing shall by any means harm you. Satan hates that you are over him in Christ!

It is important that you know how great God's love is for you. Otherwise, you can faint in the midst of the battle when obstacles align against you and become tempted to give way to fear. We don't live in fear because God's love, when perfected in us, casts out fear. Greater is His love in you and for you! Greater is He that is in you than he that is in the world. God is love, and you cannot imagine just how deep that love is for you, but He reveals it to you by His Spirit. God's love in you is greater than all the warfare around you.

Satan wants to pervert God's character, to make you believe that God is the bad guy, that He is mad at you, and He's the one who does bad things to people to teach them. These are doctrines of devils. The enemy steals and then gets people to believe God did it. Our mission is to expose the lies of the enemy in every area of life and influence people toward freedom in the Kingdom of God.

When you have a right relationship with God, peace, and joy in the Holy Spirit, you exude God's goodness. This is the most important foundation to influence others. We must have a vibrant relationship.

God wants to give good things to those who follow His ways. When you are well-provided for and in health as your soul prospers, God is exalted. The glory of children are their fathers. The reflection of a father's care is seen in how well his children are provided for, so why would this not also be a reflection of God's care to others who observe our lives? It's all right not to have it all together, but people do observe our lives and the outcomes. Jesus declared, "You will know them by their fruit." When we go through trouble, then go through to the other side, God is glorified. Attacks and issues happen in everyone's life, but how we handle those skirmishes, and the outcome of our lives, speaks to others and has great influence. We cannot give someone something we do not possess ourselves.

Being a Christian doesn't mean you won't have any trouble; it means you have victory in spite of it! Satan is waging an all-out war trying to steal the hearts of people away from God. The world is influenced by the enemy.

> *We know that we are of God, and the whole world lies under the sway of the wicked one.*
> —1 John 5:19 (NKJV)

The people have been blinded by the culture.

> *Whose minds the god of this age has blinded, who do not believe, lest the light of the gospel of the glory of Christ, who is the image of God, should shine on them.*
> —2 Corinthians 4:4 (NKJV)

It's our calling—each and every one of us—to represent the truth to them and to model the Kingdom of God in our faith, families, and callings to work with our hands so that we may have something to give and that others may see our Father's goodness.

The devil wants to rip you off! The litmus test of whether something is from God or Satan is this: Does it steal, kill, or destroy?

> *The thief does not come except to steal, and to kill, and to destroy. I have come that they may have life, and that they may have it more abundantly.*
>
> —John 10:10 (NKJV)

Another translation says, "to the fullest." God's desire is that you have life to the fullest.

The enemy knows if he can use influences in the culture to pull people into disobedience, to operate in the law of planting and harvesting (sowing and reaping) in a negative way—by sowing sin—that they will open themselves up to him! He attempts to steal from people through attacks, financially, through temptations, discouragement, division, sickness, and rebellion. Anything to get them to turn against God so they become prey to him. Remember, Satan hates you because you have been given the position, inheritance, and authority that he covets!

Sin is Satan's trap to rob you of dominion in Christ. He tries to bring adversity to you to oppose you and keep you from God's good life and plan for you. That's why Scripture says, "Be sober minded; your enemy is looking for someone he may devour. Resist him steadfast in the faith." We must stay steadfast in God's love knowing that we are loved. When you are tempted to get under the weight of life's problems, remember to be patient in affliction, unmoved, and refuse to compromise. You are secure in the love of a Father and His Son, Jesus, who risked it all.

WARFARE BASICS

If we are in a war, and we surely are based on every sign, then it is imperative that we not only know our enemy and how he operates, but we also need to understand the basics of how to operate our weaponry and how our Leader in the Kingdom of God operates. This may seem obvious, but it is shocking to me how many believers have not been taught the fundamentals of warfare. Great athletes, businesspeople, and performers know that it is always the basics that must be mastered and understood to be successful in these endeavors.

The most basic foundational truths we need to grasp to reclaim the seven mountains is to understand these four basic principles:

- God is good.
- Satan is evil.
- God has power over the enemy.
- He's given you His power over Satan.

God Is Good

Throughout my 30 years of ministry, I have heard very confusing conversations about such a simple topic. In order to engage in any type of warfare, I must know who the good guys are and who the bad guys are! Every soldier knows he must have a clear understanding of whose team he is on and that the government or force he is fighting for is worthy of allegiance. How many believers confuse God's works and the enemy's? They often attribute bad things that happen as God doing this to teach them something. God does not give someone a disease or bad situations to teach His children any more than a good parent would do these things to their child. We would consider it child abuse if a parent intentionally gave their child a disease. Yet, this is often the mask that Satan wears to misrepresent God, just as he did in the Garden when tempting Eve to doubt God's character.

> **THROUGHOUT MY 30 YEARS OF MINISTRY, I HAVE HEARD VERY CONFUSING CONVERSATIONS ABOUT SUCH A SIMPLE TOPIC. IN ORDER TO ENGAGE IN ANY TYPE OF WARFARE, I MUST KNOW WHO THE GOOD GUYS ARE AND WHO THE BAD GUYS ARE!**

If we are not sure that God is good and always good, we will attribute evil and wrongdoing to God, and we certainly can't find the answers we are looking for or help in time of need from the one we assume to have perpetrated the evil upon us. And if we believe God is the source of the wrongdoing, then why would we resist what came from God in the first place? This is the confusion created by religion and those who do not have answers. They somehow find it more comforting to blame God for things that go wrong than to examine the real culprit or admit that perhaps they failed to carry out their part in the battle plan (God's Word). Maybe they were not battle ready or knowledgeable on how to use their sword, but either way, we cannot credit our King or Captain of the armies for life's problems, attacks, or failures in battle.

James 1:17 (CEB) says:

> *Every good and perfect gift is from above, coming down from the Father of the heavenly lights, who does not change like shifting shadows.*

God only gives good gifts, and we can trust Him in battle. We can be certain that God is consistently good, all the time. He is the same yesterday, today, and forever. Regardless of what may happen in the world, our Father is faithful, and His Word is true. Any contrary thought is a lie, a deception to get us to doubt His character.

Satan Is Evil

This leads to the most basic of secondary truths. Satan is evil. Satan comes to steal, kill, and destroy (John 10:10). The Scripture calls Satan the Father of lies from the very beginning (John 8:44); the accuser of God's people (Revelation 12:10); the destroyer; and the author of confusion, poverty, and sickness. Jesus went about doing good and healing all that were *oppressed by the enemy* for God was with Him (Acts 10:38). Clearly, it is the enemy who oppresses with sickness, and Jesus came to set straight or heal that which was from the enemy.

In John 8:44, Jesus addressed those who were of a religious spirit and were confusing people concerning God's character and using religion as a form of godliness yet with no power.

> *You are of your father the devil, and you want to do the desires of your Father. He was a murderer from the beginning, and does not stand in the truth because there is no truth in him. When he lies, he speaks from his own nature, for he is a liar and the father of lies.*
>
> —John 8:44 (MEV)

God Has Power Over the Enemy

And third, God has power over the enemy. Too often, we are made to believe that God and the enemy are co-equal in this warfare, and we are led to believe that the enemy possesses the capability of God or is a match for Him. Stories that glorify the enemy create a mental picture that God and Satan are in a dueling match, boxing for the victory. This couldn't be further from the truth. This is absurd and is obviously a lie that has been perpetrated by the enemy himself, but, sadly, too many churches have helped propagate the attitude that exalts Satan as one to fear in the minds of many and elevates his position, when in fact Jesus has made an open spectacle of him and his hierarchy.

TOO OFTEN, WE ARE MADE TO BELIEVE THAT GOD AND THE ENEMY ARE CO-EQUAL IN THIS WARFARE, AND WE ARE LED TO BELIEVE THAT THE ENEMY POSSESSES THE CAPABILITY OF GOD OR IS A MATCH FOR HIM.

The enemy has been defeated by Jesus. It was no great feat for God to cast the prideful archangel Lucifer (Satan's previous identity) from heaven. Satan's lies and treachery led one-third of the angels to join him in rebellion against Almighty God. And once the enemy deceived the newly crowned recipients of the earth into giving it to him, God's plan was already in place to rescue Adam and Eve and all future people from the sorrow and pain that they brought upon themselves through disobedience. Jesus took the keys of death and hell and rendered him (Satan) powerless.

Yes, Satan is the prince of the power of the air and he has limited authority in this earthly realm because the first man and woman gave it to him... but Jesus, the second Adam, born of God has conquered this foe, and Satan is defeated by the Blood of Christ.

God Has Power Over the Enemy, and You Have Been Given the Same Power

If a church or believer grasps the first three principles of warfare, the fourth one is often the breaking point. That is simply stated: He's given you His power over the enemy.

- I have given you power over ALL the power of the enemy ... and NOTHING shall by any means harm you. (Luke 10:19)
- These works and greater works shall you do because I go to my Father. (John 14:12)
- As He [Jesus] is, so are we in this world! (1 John 4:17)

You are authorized to exercise that same power of "law enforcement" as Jesus did, who went about doing good and destroying the works of the enemy. We have a dear friend who works with us in our Kingdom Advance. He is a law enforcement agent. He has an area of the city he works, a jurisdiction, enforcing the law and keeping lawbreakers from hindering the daily operations of the local businesses and citizens in their daily pursuits. He is deputized to carry out the laws written on the books. He is operating under the same authority as those who commissioned him represent authority, and he is backed up by the government itself. Although he does not have the power in himself as one man to stop a tractor-trailer, the driver of the truck stops not because he fears him, being only one man, but he stops because of the government that his badge represents. It is this delegated authority that authorizes him to say, "Stop in the name of the law."

YOU ARE AUTHORIZED TO EXERCISE THAT SAME POWER OF "LAW ENFORCEMENT" AS JESUS DID, WHO WENT ABOUT DOING GOOD AND DESTROYING THE WORKS OF THE ENEMY.

At least that is how law and order worked until lawlessness was perpetrated from high places in our government. These attempts to violate the law and stop its enforcement, by people in high places, is exactly how the enemy tries to intercept your position and place himself in position to misconstrue the law and steal the authority of the church (you). If he can get away with robbery and theft, he will continue in his charade. "Satan masquerades as an angel of light" and "he roams about seeking whom he may devour." We are instructed to resist him steadfastly in faith.

Jesus has given you His same position, by delegated authority, as a citizen in His Kingdom. He has deputized you as an agent of His

Kingdom. We are not just children of God relationally. We are coheirs and rule on behalf of the government of God in an authoritative position. Scripture says that you are seated with Christ in heavenly places far above all principality, might, and dominion (Ephesians 2:6, Ephesians 1:20-21). These evil principalities are a hierarchy of demonic forces that try to oppose mankind and break the law. These lawbreakers wreak havoc on unsuspecting Christians who do not understand their authority in Christ or the laws of His Kingdom. They beg and plead for God to help them when Jesus has already defeated the enemy and given them the keys of His Kingdom.

If our friend on the police force went to work every day and begged his sergeant to give him authority to be an officer—and he sat in the office drinking coffee, begging to be in the field even though his boss had already given him an assignment and authority—at some point, he would lose his position. Perhaps the bad guys in his jurisdiction would take advantage of him and steal his role of authority. Instead of order and peace, they would perpetrate crimes against the people. Yet the officer already had the authority to use his delegated power to stop evil all along. That's the church, you and me! We have the keys from Jesus to enforce His Kingdom, open doors, and prohibit evil:

Jesus said,

> *"I will give you the keys of the kingdom of heaven; whatever you bind on earth will be bound in heaven, and whatever you loose [release] on earth will be loosed [released] in heaven."*
> —Matthew 16:19 (NIV)

"I have given you authority to trample on snakes and scorpions and to overcome all the power of the enemy."

—Luke 10:19 (NIV)

We have our own personal stories of how God brought us out of bondage to debt, delivered my husband from fear, healed our daughter from a debilitating sickness, and built a good life for our family according to His promises. Was there warfare? Yes. But have we prevailed? Absolutely! And we have thousands of stories from others who have learned the basics of warfare and have obtained the victory that already rightfully belonged to them. We must see the truth of who we are and what we have in Christ, and then we can annihilate the spiritual enemies of our lives.

WE MUST SEE THE TRUTH OF WHO WE ARE AND WHAT WE HAVE IN CHRIST, AND THEN WE CAN ANNIHILATE THE SPIRITUAL ENEMIES OF OUR LIVES.

If we have been given this power over the enemy, why are so many people living below their potential, suffering under the curse of poverty and sickness? Why do bad things happen in people's lives? As we examine the patterns of this world, we begin to understand the reason Scripture instructs us, *"No longer be conformed to the pattern of this world, but be transformed by renewing of your mind"* (Romans 2:2, NIV). The areas that most influence life have been invaded to set up mirages, misinformation, and deceptive practices to mislead people into traps. This gives Satan and a horde of demonic spirits access to our families, finances, health, and peace.

The limited knowledge of economics and the system we learned to trust in were rooted in debt; it looked simple enough to "build credit" and to make purchases, but afterwards, the 23 percent interest rate delivered the consequence of our ignorance. Eventually, these money schemes steal destinies, time, and relationships with family as we sell ourselves into financial slavery.

People perish for the lack of knowledge (Hosea 4:6) of how God designed life to be lived and fall into the adversary's tricks. We are warned, "Don't be ignorant of Satan's schemes" (2 Corinthians 2:11). The dangerous deception of our day is that it seems there are no consequences for wrongdoing, but there are grave consequences that can result in death.

> *We know that whoever is born of God does not keep on sinning. But whoever has been born of God guards himself, and the wicked one cannot touch him.*
>
> —1 John 5:18 (MEV)

How do we keep ourselves? We stop living lives of wrongdoing and sin, which opens our lives to destruction. Sin or wrongdoing gives Satan legal jurisdiction into our lives, just as it did with Adam and Eve. And it doesn't matter if we are ignorant of God's ways: we get the same outcome as the person who knew about wrongdoing and yet violated God's law. The results are the same.

The lies and traps presented in the world's systems primarily appeal to the pride of life, the lust of the eyes, and the lust of fleshly appetites. We want something so badly that we violate God's principles and sound judgment to get it. We can better understand the enemy's plan to harm us if we uncover how he operates in areas of influence in life. God wants us to live in His free zone, under His loving authority, ruling and reigning as sons and daughters with Christ where there is peace, joy, and provision.

Throughout each chapter, I will expose the schemes and deeds of darkness and then counter those pitfalls with God's promises, truth-filled principles, and practical applications to win and live the lives that God planned for us to live in Christ Jesus. Let's get started!

Warfare Declarations:

God has made me alive together with Christ, raised me up with Him, and made me sit with Him in the heavenly places in Christ Jesus that in the ages to come He might show the exceeding riches of His grace in His kindness toward me in Christ Jesus. (Ephesians 2:6-7)

I am seated with Christ, who is seated at the right hand of God in the heavenly places far above all principality, power, might, and dominion, and His name is above every name that is named not only in this age but in the one that is to come. And God has put all things under His feet and gave Him to be head over all things in the church. (Ephesians 1:20-22)

Since Christ is seated above all evil forces and I am seated with Him, all the forces that are under His feet are under my feet in Christ Jesus.

THE SEVEN MOUNTAINS CORRUPTED BY DARKNESS

As we navigate these years of COVID-19 lockdowns and attempt to regain life and economic stability, more disruptions are happening and brewing, wars and rumors of wars, famine, disease, government IDs, digital currencies, and more and more government control. What does the future hold? Everyone wants to know, and only one book has the answer, the Bible. Although we see dimly and many interpret details differently, the overarching future is laid out in the books of Revelation, Daniel, Ezekiel 37-39, and Matthew 24. These books paint a picture of the last days and a final battle in which the nations of the earth form an alliance under beastly powers that seek to defy God. Aligned with Satan, a political figure, the Antichrist, a False Prophet, a religious figure use their power to carry out Satan's final attempt to destroy people through deception, treachery, and a final war. The seven mountains of culture are manipulated by the beast; the false prophet and the Antichrist government influence people as they lean to, visit, and are influenced by these areas that form our culture.

The mountains themselves are not evil, but because they are areas of influence corrupted by sin, they have been penetrated and honed to influence people, sadly, in a wrong direction. We have seen the collaboration and alignment of these areas of influence. It's as if there is one agenda and all roads lead to the same destination. We are not to fear but to be aware and beware of the path that leads to the wrong destination.

The systems of the world, regardless of the names associated with them, have a primary influencer. It should be the church, but unfortunately at this time, it is not. But she is awaking and rising to her destiny. Both are influencing the decisions of men and women across the world. How is this alignment fulfilling biblical prophecy in our lifetime?

Economic disruption, inflation, and scarcity are certainly signs of our times and those foretold in the Scripture. Financial forecasts, stock markets, and savings are overshadowed with plans for a financial reset and digital currency. It appears that all seven mountains of influence have been corrupted and aligned for the end of times. Corrupted by Satan, the arts, the media, the economy, government, education, medicine, and even religious powers across the globe are aligned for blasphemy against God. Is this the pages of Revelation discussed in biblical prophecy?

The Four Horsemen of Revelation

There are four horsemen presented in Revelation 6:2-7. They represent forces and messengers at work in the world. The white horse represents a false system or the world's system of allegiance to power/government. The red horse represents civil war and strife, removing peace. The black horse is a symbol of economic disruption. And the final, fourth horse is one of death from famine, war, and starvation.

The end-time book of the Revelation of Jesus Christ, in chapter 6:1-6, says:

> Come and see. And I looked and behold a white horse. He who sat on it had a bow; and a crown was given to him, and he went out conquering and to conquer... and another horse, fiery red, went out, and he who sat on it was to take peace from the earth, that people should kill one another... So, I looked, and behold, a black horse, and he who sat on it had a pair of scales in his hand. And I heard a voice in the midst of the four living creatures, saying, "A quart of wheat for a denarius, and three quarts of barley for a denarius."

This passage reveals severe inflation, as one would remark that the price of food or gas is high today. In some parts of the world, the scarcity is so great as to be a famine. Scripture says, "A loaf of bread for a bag of gold." Food and commodities become the priority.

After the black horse, just before the fourth pale, dappled horse of death by famine, disease, and war, there is the admonition, "*Do not harm the oil and the wine.*" Some have interpreted "oil and wine" to mean luxuries and to indicate that the scarcity will not be worldwide. But biblically, oil is used to consecrate, as an anointing oil. Oil signifies anointing, restoration, joy, healing, and completeness. This is the Holy Spirit's work, the oil and seal of our redemption. The wine represents the blood of the New Covenant, of Jesus Christ, the Messiah, the One who has purchased our atonement. Do not harm the oil and the wine. Are the oil and the wine the anointed ones purchased by Jesus and sealed with the Holy Spirit? I believe so. Do not harm what belongs to Him.[87]

There is a strong connection between these horses or messengers, and each of us have witnessed the impact of these forces of power, war, economics, and death at work together in the world, some more than others. They are interconnected. Great power, or those who would try to control and wield that power percolate wars, resulting in economic disruptions and death, whether by famine, disease, or war. One of the cards can be laid first to yield the results of the other, but after the first one is laid, the others will show their hand. The world's system deceives, and if we adapt to receive it as our source, it results in missing God and His plans.

> **THE WORLD'S SYSTEM DECEIVES, AND IF WE ADAPT TO RECEIVE IT AS OUR SOURCE, IT RESULTS IN MISSING GOD AND HIS PLANS.**

> *What causes fights among you? Don't they come from your desires that battle within you? You desire but do not have, so you kill. You covet but you cannot get what you want, so you quarrel and fight. You do not have because you do not ask God ... don't you know that friendship with the world means enmity against God? Therefore, anyone who chooses to be a friend of the world becomes an enemy of God.*
>
> —James 4:1-4 (NIV)

We want to be friends and to be accepted, but friendship with the world means we miss God's plan for us. The temptation is to accept the activity happening in the world's system, embrace it as "that's just the way it is," and to compromise our values and biblical mandates of right and wrong to find acceptance, promotion, finances, and success. This is the very heart of control that makes the alignment of systems into a one world system so plausible to those who do not see the endgame. There's a way that seems right but ends in destruction.

It's important to understand the history of how the enemy maneuvers to use people, families, and debt to control areas of influence. Demonic influence can pervert and align for negative purposes. When did these world alliances begin to form, and how are they coming together?

"In an increasingly interconnected and interdependent world, some issues are too big for countries to handle on their own. Countries need to work together, and they do so partly by international organizations that encourage cooperation and diplomatic resolutions to global problems."[88]

This certainly sounds reasonable, but when these organizations begin to work in sync toward goals that most citizens in America and free democracies would find abhorrent, we have a problem. These organizations are worth investigating so as to be aware of how their cooperation impacts all seven areas of influence.

The United Nations and the New World Order

These organizations formed after wars and prominent events, "fears" to protect the world from domination by the "Hitlers" of the world, and have gained such astounding control that arguably it could seem to be the antithesis of their original stated missions. These organizations, like the UN (United Nations, 1945), the WCC (World Council of Churches, 1948), WHO (World Health Organization, 1948), NATO (North Atlantic Treaty Organization, 1949), the WEF (World Economic Forum, 1971), EU (European Union, 1993), WTO (World Trade Organization, 1995), G-20 (Group of 20, 1999), Interpol (International Criminal Police Organization, 1938 then revamped 2001), and ICC (International Criminal court, 2002), have continued to move toward global goals and international mandates moving more power from democratic countries to world powers.

Of these organizations, "The United Nations is the world's most important international organization in the world with 193 member states and a total budget of 5.81 billion dollars." The United Nations encompasses all the nations and territories of the world except Palestine and the Vatican City. The United States is the third largest country ... with a population of 328 million people and a GDP of 21.43 trillion dollars, the U.S. is one of the most influential countries in the world."

New York is the seat of the UN, and Manhattan is the home of the 505-foot tall skyscraper, the centerpiece of the headquarters of the United Nations. This is the crossroads of the earth. It is also the headquarters of the New World Order and prophetically represents the world. The lot on which the skyscraper sits in the Turtle Bay area is considered the United Nations' territory, although it remains part of the United States. The UN has three other subsidiary regional headquarters in Geneva, Switzerland (opened 1946), Vienna, Austria (opened 1980), and Nairobi, Kenya (opened 1996). The UN has a treaty agreement with the United States, and the buildings are under the sole administration of the UN. The UN's specialized agencies, like UNICEF, are also headquartered there.

A large portion of the UN's budget is donated by the US. The UN has a total of 37,000 staff worldwide. The aim of the United Nations is to be a forum between nations where dialogue can be held and global peace achieved. This means that the UN aims for collective decision-making, multi-lateral agreements, and compromise. This limits the power the UN has as it means it must act in the interests of a collective group of nations.

In contrast, the United States is a single, independent nation. Its only objective is to act in the best interest of its citizens. "Essentially, the United States has a simpler objective than the UN—achieve prosperity and security for the population of the United States. The only way the United Nations affects the United States is in terms of laws and treaties the US has signed-up to, or if a UN resolution is passed against the US ... Although the United States is an independent country, it is subject to international law."[89]

How did the UN get there, and more importantly, how does it fit into the prophetic times we are living? John D. Rockefeller gave the land to establish the United Nations as a headquarters that would never allow another world war. That was the selling point at least. However, the United Nations is a club of which nations voluntarily join and pay dues.[90] From its inception, some envisioned a much larger role for the UN. "They envisioned the end of independent sovereign nations in which they charged were the root of war, strife, and poverty. They claimed that for true freedom to exist, everything must be equal, including food, possessions, and opportunity. To achieve that, individual nations must surrender their sovereignty to the greater good—global governance overseen by the United Nations."[91]

Many want to dismiss the idea of a New World Order as a conspiracy theory; however, President George W. Bush shared a vision for the New World Order multiple times, including in his speech on September 11, 1990 amid the Persian Gulf Crisis:[92]

> A new partnership of nations has begun, and we stand today at a unique and extraordinary moment. The crisis in the Persian Gulf, as grave as it is, also offers a rare opportunity to move toward an historic period of cooperation. Out of these troubled times, our fifth objective—a *new world order*—can emerge: A new era—freer from the threat of terror, stronger in the pursuit of justice and more secure in the quest for peace. An era in which the nations of the world, east and west, north and south, can prosper and live in harmony.
>
> A hundred generations have searched for this elusive path to peace, while a thousand wars raged across the span of human endeavor, and today that *new world* is struggling to be born. A world quite different from the one we've known. A world where the rule of law supplants the rule of the jungle. A world in which nations recognize the shared responsibility for freedom and justice. A world where the strong respect the rights of the weak.

This is the vision that I shared with President Gorbachev in Helsinki. He and the other leaders from Europe, the gulf and around the world understand that how we manage this crisis today could shape the future for generations to come. 'The Test We Face Is Great.'

This is the first assault on the *new world* that we seek, the first test of our mettle. Had we not responded to this first provocation with clarity of purpose; if we do not continue to demonstrate our determination, it would be a signal to actual and potential despots around the world.

At the time of this conflict, Iraq controlled 10 percent of the world's oil and Kuwait twice that. Iraq threatening to control Kuwait would affect oil across the world. These same concerns loom today.

More recently, Joe Biden said on March 21, 2022 there would be "a new world order" established and led by the United States while speaking at a roundtable to discuss Russia's war on Ukraine and the economy. "You know, we are at an inflection point, I believe, in the world economy—not just the world economy, in the world. Occurs every three or four generations," Biden said. "As one of the top military people said to me in a security meeting the other day, 60 million people died between 1900 and 1946, and since then, we've established *a liberal world order,* and that hadn't happened in a long while." He continued, "A lot of people died but nowhere near the chaos, and now is the time when things are shifting. There's going to be a *new world order* out there. We've got to lead it, and we've got to unite the rest of the free world in doing it."[93]

Across the street from the United Nations is a taller tower than the UN building called the Trump Tower, and like him or not, Donald Trump has sounded an alarm about the New World Order, or maybe better known as the deep state. In his one short term as President fighting the "deep state," America became energy independent, but in less than a year, the Biden administration completely reversed this course, again placing American dependence upon world oil. Why? Also, ISIS was defeated and the economy and dollar soared during the Trump Administration. Many feel this was a prophetic sign to show Americans that freedom towers over the one world Tower of Babel. Clearly, his term unmasked the lies and deception that we could not have energy independence or avoid the constant regional wars and conflicts we have participated in since WWII. We had peace and prosperity, and Jerusalem was recognized as the capital of Israel; prophecy fulfilled.

Biblical Prophecy of Kingdoms to Come

In chapter 13 of Revelation, the apostle John describes a beast that rose up from the sea. This creature had the body of a leopard, the feet of a bear, and a mouth like a lion (Revelation 13:2). John described it as having *"ten horns and seven heads, with ten crowns on its horns, and on each head a blasphemous name"* (Revelation 13:1, NIV). John's vision was nearly identical to that of Daniel, who saw four creatures approximately 600 years prior—a lion, a bear, a four-headed leopard, and a fourth terrible sea creature with ten horns (Revelation 13:2, Daniel 7:1-7, NIV).[94] As for the dragon, which is the source of power for this beast, Revelation 12:9 (NIV) tells us *"The great dragon... [is] that ancient serpent, called the devil, or Satan, who leads the whole world astray."*

In Revelation 17:9-10 (NKJV), the seven heads of the beast are identified as "*seven mountains*" or "*seven kings*." According to Daniel 7:24 and Revelation 17:12, horns symbolize kings or kingdoms.

Biblical prophecy predicts the rise and fall of kingdoms. Jeremiah says concerning the Medes destroying Babylon:

> *"Make the bright arrows; gather the shields: the Lord hath raised up the spirit of the kings of the Medes: for his device is against Babylon, to destroy it; because it is the vengeance of the Lord, the vengeance of his temple."*
>
> —Jeremiah 51:11 (KJV)

These seven heads have come, and some have gone. The four largest empires that were part of Daniel's dream in Daniel chapters 2 and 7, which precede the end-time, are the: Babylonian Empire, Medo-Persian Empire, the Greek Empire, and some argue the Roman Empire (Daniel 8:3-4; Daniel 8:20).[95]

According to most biblical scholars, the Babylonian Empire is the gold head of Daniel's vision. A lesser kingdom took it, the Medes (the bear); and then joining them, the Persian Empire became great as the leopard with four wings, representing the four kings of Persia. The belly and hips represent Greece, and the legs of iron point to Rome.[96] [97]

Bible prophecy reveals that what follows, a great political, military, and economic superpower will arise—the Antichrist—and set up a system of one world government.[98]

John writes in Revelation,

> *And I heard another voice from heaven saying, "Come out of her, my people, lest you share in her sins, and lest you receive of her plagues. For her sins have reached to heaven, and God has remembered her iniquities."*
>
> —Revelation 18:4-5 (NKJV)

This final one world government will not be supported by Jesus Christ but by a counterfeit power led by the "dragon," Satan. The good news is that, as revealed by Nebuchadnezzar's dream, the statue that represented world-ruling power was destroyed. As Daniel explained to King Nebuchadnezzar:

> *"You watched while a stone was cut out without hands, which struck the image on its feet of iron and clay, and broke them in pieces. Then the iron, the clay, the bronze, the silver, and the gold were crushed together, and became like chaff from the summer threshing floors; the wind carried them away so that no trace of them was found. And the stone that struck the image became a great mountain and filled the whole earth."*
>
> —Daniel 2:34-35 (NKJV)

The stone that demolished the carnal empires represented the coming Kingdom of God. As Daniel proclaimed,

> *"And in the days of these kings the God of heaven will set up a kingdom which shall never be destroyed; and the kingdom shall not be left to other people; it shall break in pieces and consume all these kingdoms, and it shall stand forever."*
>
> —Daniel 2:44 (NKJV)

The most important takeaway is that we know Jesus comes to set up His Kingdom, the stone that crushes them all, and makes the kingdoms of the world the kingdoms of our God. He did so in His first coming and will finalize it at the battle of Armageddon at His second coming.

The Hebrew people, Israel, are represented throughout the Old Testament as God's people because He chose them. But the coming of our Savior Jesus would create a new government, a new Kingdom that would be preached to the world, to all people, every tribe and nation, before the end of time. Jesus's disciples thought He was going to overthrow the Roman Empire, but instead, He overthrew all the kingdoms of the world spiritually and established the body of Christ. When He returns, He will do this on the earth physically too. We can actually say that through media, the Gospel is now preached in every part of the world, another end-time prophecy fulfilled, although everyone has not heard. And we must continue fervently at warp speed.

> **THE MOST IMPORTANT TAKEAWAY IS THAT WE KNOW JESUS COMES TO SET UP HIS KINGDOM, THE STONE THAT CRUSHES THEM ALL, AND MAKES THE KINGDOMS OF THE WORLD THE KINGDOMS OF OUR GOD. HE DID SO IN HIS FIRST COMING AND WILL FINALIZE IT AT THE BATTLE OF ARMAGEDDON AT HIS SECOND COMING.**

EGYPT (ca. 2100 B.C. to ca. 1400 B.C.)

A son of Ham was the first king of Egypt. When Joseph went to Egypt, foreign "Shepherd kings" may have been in control. The Hamites were back in power at the time of the Exodus.

ASSYRIA (ca. 1100 B.C. to 606 B.C.)

The ancient city of Nineveh finally rose to power over her rival, Babylon. The Assyrians ruled the world with force and fear and demanded great sums of tribute.

BABYLON (606 B.C. to 538 B.C.)

Babylon was even older than Nineveh. Daniel lived in the great, impregnable city and saw it fall to the Medes and Persians. (Daniel 2:37-38, 7:4, 5:1-31)

MEDO-PERSIA (538 B.C. to 333 B.C.)

Cyrus the Great freed the Jews to return and rebuild the Temple in 538 B.C. About 445 B.C., Artaxerxes allowed them to rebuild Jerusalem. (Daniel 9:25)

GREECE (333 B.C. to 146 B.C.)

Alexander the Great conquered the world in only 10 years! The Greek culture and language later greatly helped to spread the Gospel. (Daniel 2:39, 7:6, 8:5-8)

ROME (44 B.C. to 455 A.D.)

By the time Jesus was born, Augustus Caesar ruled the Mediterranean world with almost complete control. This period of world peace allowed the Gospel message to spread more easily.

TODAY, the feet of iron & clay

symbolize two modern superpowers (EU? and Russia?) whose governments are a mixture of Militarism and Big Business. (Daniel 2:41-43)

World's Last Empire
In the final days of this present age, the False Prophet and Antichrist with his ten toes (nations that form from his empire) will preside over the most terrible time in the history of the creation, but it will also see the greatest finish with the return of Jesus Christ to rule the earth with His saints for the next thousand years. (Daniel 2:44-45)

SEVEN WORLD EMPIRES

REVELATION 13 AND 17
1. Egypt
2. Assyria
3. Babylon
4. Medo-Persia
5. Greece
6. Rome
7. Antichrist

HEAD OF GOLD: BABYLON — Lion with eagle's wings

BREAST & ARMS OF SILVER: MEDO-PERSIA

Bear raised up on one side. Ribs: three conquered kingdoms

Ram with two horns (the Persian and Mede kingdoms)

BELLY & HIPS OF BRONZE: GREECE

Great horn: Alexander the Great

Little horn: Antichrist

Four horns: Alexander's successors (Egypt, Assyria, Turkey, Greece)

Leopard with 4 heads (Egypt, Assyria, Turkey, Greece), Wings: Speedy conquest

LEGS OF IRON: ROME (DIVIDED INTO EAST & WEST)

ANTICHRIST BEAST
10 horns/nations, 3 broken by the Antichrist "little horn" The world shall worship him. Mouth speaks blasphemies. World's worst warmonger (Daniel 7:7-8, 19-25; Rev. 13:1-10)

FEET OF IRON & CLAY

THE END!

ROCK Christ's Kingdom overthrows all the world's governments!

FALSE PROPHET BEAST
2 horns like a lamb Speaks like a dragon Master of deception Controls world's economy (Revelation 13:11-18)

(Adapted from a TFI publication.)

History of Satan's Influence in the Western World

From the preaching of the Gospel, a group who sought religious freedom would dedicate the newly formed nation of America to God, choosing to place His Word as their foundation. God chose Israel, but America chose God. However, there were always workings of compromise and warfare against that choice that would challenge the young nation to succumb to a trap of bondage. It involved money, power, and Satanic influence. It's a story we don't often hear as it is revealing how Satan has always jockeyed to rule nations and the world from ancient history to today.

America fought for independence, and France did so as well almost simultaneously, but their fights were for different causes. America's Revolutionary War was a fight for independence from the tyranny of Britain. "One of their chief complaints was the right not to be taxed without representation, the right to not be taxed without the consent of elected representatives." When this became impossible to achieve within the British Empire, Americans declared their independence and then won it on the battlefield. That is, Americans fought for tangible goals; they fought to preserve their rights rather than to overturn an established social order. Ours was a revolution more about home rule than about who should rule at home."[99] America sought to establish freedom from Britain and to create a sovereign state, a republic. The difference between a republic and a democracy is that the constitution sets the rules in a republic while the rules in a democracy are decided and set by the general public, a majority rule.

"The French on the other hand, defied Reason above not only

experience, but also above religion and divine revelation. Indeed, they transformed Notre Dame into a Temple of Reason and held pseudo-religious festivals in honor of this new deity. Reason unrestrained and unguided by history and experience proved unable to establish stable government or to secure liberty to France. Instead, it led them to descend into the Terror, the reign of Napoleon, and ultimately to the restoration of the monarchy."[100]

France's fight was funded and fueled by those who wanted to destroy the monarchy utilizing rabble-rousers and troublemakers for other reasons, namely financial. Interestingly enough, it was financial leaders in Britain who placed bets on stocks concerning the French war and became forces to control banking from the early days.

One of the primary names was the Rothschild family, who owned and operated the East India Trading Company. The company was used to expand Britain's imperialism, conquering and controlling territories across the world. Slavery and horrific treatment of people in Asian, Indian, and African territories, owned and exploited, brought disgrace over time.

From the battle of Waterloo against Napoleon in 1600, the British Empire arose out of the abyss. This empire arose again at the Battle of Waterloo where Napoleon was defeated. It was rumored through history that a man named Mayer Rothschild was given information about the war's outcome before others, and he appeared to sell his British stock holdings, but it was a ruse to purchase other traders' stock. As others followed his lead to sell, he was secretly buying up their stocks through a proxy. He became handsomely rich and would become the Master of Finances and banking across Europe from his windfall. The Duke of Wellington became prime minister of Britain, and the alleged seat of power was the monarchy, but it was more in appearance, with the monarchy as a figurehead.

The Crown of Britain actually is a corporation called "The City," a square mile that houses the greatest banks and wealth under the direction of the corporation. The Rothschild family enterprises are still operating there today. Most think Britain is ruled by the monarchy, but it's the City that is the seat of power in London. The writ created in history established the City as a corporation. "Over the 950 years, the City has won powers and privileges that were unheard of... but have gone on to form the basis of the modern parliamentary representative democracy. They continue to set the City apart from other parts of the United Kingdom. The involvement of the Royal Family with the Livery Companies is by no means a modern phenomenon. Monarchs of note such as King James I, Henry VIII, and Elizabeth I have all been members of Livery Companies. Livery Companies are chartered companies of the City of London originating from the craft guilds. In modern times, the Crown retains a special relationship with the City. Indeed, the Sovereign is the only person who outranks the Lord Mayor in the City, and even so, the Lord Mayor's permission is sought before the Sovereign enters the City. Many members of the Royal Family are active in the City's Livery Companies."[101]

It is reported that the powerful banker Mayer Rothschild said, "Permit me to control the money and currency, and I care not who wears the crown." His son Nathan Rothschild received his father's propensity for business and knew the ins and outs of banking. "You will lend and not borrow." They loaned money to kings funding wars and enterprise, and their family banks became extremely rich.

Many stories have circulated about the Rothschild family throughout history, and it is difficult to determine truth from fiction. Historically, a pamphlet, considered years later by some to be anti-Semitic propaganda, was written about the family and circulated. It was later called into question, but that information was carried in the 1931 Britannica Encyclopedia, which I have viewed.

A verifiable family history on the Rothschild family's own site shares their involvement in secret societies like Freemasonry:

> Members of the Rothschild family have been involved with the Freemasons, a fraternal organization whose members are concerned with moral and spiritual values, self-improvement, and helping their communities with charitable endeavors. By 1900, different branches and generations of the family owned thousands of acres, so the Vale of Aylesbury almost became a Rothschild enclave, the most famous property being Waddesdon Manor, built by Baron Ferdinand de Rothschild (1839-1898). Ferdinand de Rothschild Lodge, No. 2420 was established in Aylesbury in 1892. It was consecrated at the Five Arrows Hotel, Waddesdon on 30th May, 1892. The founding of the lodge brought Freemasonry to the district of Waddesdon, its name being derived from Baron Ferdinand who it was intended should be the first Master.
>
> The Concordia Lodge was consecrated in 1893, and met at Red Lion Hotel, Lee Common, Wendover, Buckinghamshire. The badge for Concordia Lodge features the Rothschild

symbol of the five arrows. The name Concordia Lodge may have been inspired by the local Rothschild family, and the Rothschild family motto, Concordia, Integritas, Industria, although "Concordia," meaning harmony, has been a common name for other masonic lodges with no connection to the Rothschilds. Both the Ferdinand de Rothschild and Concordia lodges are still active.[102]

The Rothschild Archive maintains historical information about principal residences of the Rothschild family in England, France, Germany, Austria, Switzerland, and Italy. For brief information concerning over 75 Rothschild estates and properties in England, France, Germany, Austria, Switzerland, and the Netherlands… Rothschild collections of art and objects d'art are among the finest ever assembled." Regardless of any information circulating, we can verify the European banking and imperialism that brought immense wealth and the connection to Freemasonry which exists to this day.

The 1931 Britannica Encyclopedia states:

> Rothschild Family, the most famous of all European banking dynasties, which for some 200 years exerted great influence on the economic, and indirectly the political history of Europe. The house was founded by Mayer Amschel Rothschild (b February 23, 1744, in Frankfurt) and his five sons … Mayer and his sons became international bankers, establishing branches in London, Paris, Vienna, and Naples by the 1820s…. Intended for the Rabbinate, Mayer studied briefly, but his parents' early death forced him into an apprenticeship in a banking house. Soon after becoming court factor to William IX, Mayer set the pattern that his family was to

follow so successfully—to do business with reigning houses by preference....

Mayer and his sons eventually became bankers to whom the French Revolutionary and Napoleonic wars of 1792-1815 came as a piece of good fortune. Mayer and his eldest son, Amschel, supervised the growing business from Frankfurt, while Nathan established a branch in London, Jakob settled in Paris in 1811, and Salomon and Karl opened offices in Vienna and Naples, respectively, in the 1820s. The wars for the Rothschilds meant loans to warring princes and smuggling, as well as legal trading in key products such as wheat, cotton, colonial produce, and arms. Peace transformed the growing Rothschild business: the banking group continued its international business dealing but became more and more an agent in government securities... The banking group continued to expand after the 1850s and, in particular, achieved an important position in the world trade of oil and nonferrous metals... Successive generations of the Rothschild family have been similarly active in international finance and politics.

The Rothschilds were much honored. Mayer's five sons were made barons of the Austrian Empire, a Rothschild was the first Jew to enter the British Parliament, and another was first to British peerage. The head of the British branch of the family has always been considered the unofficial head of British Jewry. Members of the British and French families, the only ones still engaged in banking after the seizure by the Nazis of the Austrian house distinguished themselves as scientists and often as philanthropists. In 2003-2008, the British and French houses were merged, marking the reunification of the Rothschild family business for the first time in nearly two centuries.[103]

The British maritime museum contains what little records remain available and the history of the Rothschild's East India Company.[104] [105] British imperialism flourished under the East India Company until their attack of China and "the end justifies the means, whatever it takes to start a world order" attitude caused their reputation to tarnish.[106] Amidst public outcry over their violent and cruel behavior, the East India Company dissolved, and the Rothschilds moved more investment into oil and other endeavors. [107]

Their goal of world dominance was thwarted through this blow, but the protégé trained in their group of associations that produced the likes of Karl Marx, father of Communism, was Nathan's cousin and was hired into their business.[108] Karl Marx developed ideologies that the state would rule absolutely in all the affairs of men in a totalitarian state eliminating the middle class.[109] According to Marx, "Religion is the opium of the people. It is the sigh of the oppressed creature, the heart of a heartless world, and the soul of our soulless conditions."[110]

Charles Darwin was also a member of the East India House.[111] Darwin's contribution to the creation of a new world order was his hypothesis for a scientific explanation for the origin of all life. He articulated his theory of evolution in his 1859 book, *On the Origin of Species*. This theory removed God from man's creation and destiny. Darwin's teachings helped people rationalize eugenics developed by Thomas Malthus, another Rothschild protégé.[112] [113] Marx was "exceedingly enthusiastic over Darwin's book *On the Origin of Species*. Karl Marx wrote a letter to [Friedrich] Engels in December of 1860 declaring that *On the Origin of Species* was 'the book which contains the basis in natural history for our views.'"[114]

His views on eugenics inspired Margaret Sanger (Planned Parenthood), who championed Malthus's beliefs.[115] [116] She drove an agenda of birth control and abortion, especially on the Black population.[117] Her racist belief system was acceptable to Darwinian beliefs since human life was no longer viewed as sacred from God. All of these were rooted in humanistic views of man and that without God, man could create his own race and the Tower of Babel, one world orchestrated by man apart from God.

Adolf Hitler also was influenced by these teachings of eugenics and sought the perfect race by the systematic murdering of the Jews, the Jewish bankers he hated from war grievances impacting Germany.[118] [119]

A man by the name of John Ruskin advanced Christian socialism and legislated socialism in Christian circles by teaching a form of social justice that included socialist and communistic dogma.[120] [121] Cecil Rhodes became an outspoken proponent of Ruskin.[122] Rothschild funded Rhodes's diamond mines in Rhodesia, named for him, as well as the Rhodes scholarship to fund and raise up leaders toward a one world initiative.[123] Today, this group has morphed and is called the Chatham House.[124] [125] Global leaders mentored in the wargames of banking, financing war, eugenics, or population control, and debt to enslave countries and citizens continue today.

How did this affect the United States of America? From America's inception, there were forces trying to stop the newly free country from standing apart from Britain. Three primary occurrences have had a lasting impact on America and our banking system.

If the borrower becomes a slave to the lender, as Proverbs 22:7 states, then to get America into debt would be the most plausible way to end freedom and autonomy, and then to steal her spiritual heritage. Jesus said, "You can't serve two masters. You'll love the one and hate the other."

A famous traitor buried at St. Mary's church in London, named Benedict Arnold, was a British spy against America. His comrade, Aaron Burr, who was also a spy, became Vice President of the United States and was supposed to be influenced by British banking lords. Burr was a British plant and wanted a British bank to control America. Alexander Hamilton vehemently opposed any banking connection to Britain; he wanted a central bank in the US. In disagreement, Burr shot Hamilton.

The East India Company utilized Albert Gallatin, originally Swiss born but became an American. He created the Ways and Means Committee and made certain American forces were weakened by refusing to build up the Navy, which many felt paved the way for the War of 1812. It was only divine intervention that caused America to prevail and survive. Eventually, the Civil War was also boosted by elite bankers. Their goal was to divide the people and conquer them from within. Once again, the strong principles and faith of Abraham Lincoln refused their loans to fund the war.

A group called the Knights of the Golden Circle funded both the north and the south during the Civil War, so either way they profited, whichever side won. Lincoln refused to borrow their money or take debt, and they eliminated him through one of their members, John Wilkes Booth. The contention was not just slavery but rather debt, banking, money, and the states' rights, which affected slavery. These internationalists were behind the killing of Abraham Lincoln. The East India Company and coalition of elites would operate like the Wizard of Oz from behind the curtain, and the world would fall deeper into the control of their debt.

In the 1890s, the banking houses contracted credit and created economic conditions that were dismal, eventually giving way to the Depression of 1907 and igniting economic conditions to create a central bank. In Jekyll Island, Georgia, The Federal Reserve Act was created, and Congress passed it on Christmas Eve with low attendance. President Woodrow Wilson, a professor, had been run by the bankers and positioned to not veto The Federal Reserve Act. The Federal Reserve Act became law in 1913. This propelled the indebtedness of America to outside forces.

World War I ensued, the first of its kind, with the assassination of the Archduke of Austria. The red horse of Revelation brandished its sword of war and took peace from the earth through war. This British Empire began to diminish, and

World War I was underway. Woodrow Wilson ran again on the campaign promise that we would stay out of war, but weeks after elected, he entered the US, borrowing great sums from the Federal Reserve Central Bank. After World War I, a super government was desired to keep peace across the world. The allies and war delegates met in Versailles to divide the spoils of battle and create 14 points for a League of Nations, some say a New World Order. The League of Nations was developed in Europe, but Woodrow Wilson failed to get Congress to pass it as Republican senators rejected the idea.

THE LONG-AWAITED COMING OF CHRIST IS AT HAND. PROPHETIC EVENTS ARE ALL IN PLACE. JESUS CAME IN HUMILITY AND DIED, BUT HIS NEXT COMING WILL BE A TRIUMPHANT ENTRY OF THE KING OF KINGS, WHERE HE WILL APPEAR AS A CONQUEROR AT THE HELM OF HEAVEN'S ARMIES.

Their next plan would involve a man named Adolf Hitler with a Marxist view of socialism. He was perceived admirably by Wall Street bankers, and the plan was once again to reignite a war in Europe and re-establish the one world plan. They used him as a tool but didn't know he was a megalomaniac and would recruit Japan and Italy into the war. Ultimately, he attempted to exterminate the Jewish bankers and all Jews. He attacked Poland in 1939. Japan attacked Pearl Harbor. Churchill resisted the tyranny, and through America's intervention on D-Day, the plan was foiled.[126]

Why is this history important? These tactics to draw nations into wars and finance them have continued and been manipulated to put individuals and nations into debt and control their destinies and ideology.

After 80 million deaths from WWII, there was no resistance to setting up the United Nations in America. Britain had almost ceased but rose out of the ashes of defeat with their allies' help. Is this possibly the eighth head of empires that rose out of the seven in Revelation 17? Revelation 17:11 (NLT) says, "*The scarlet beast that was, but is no longer, is the eighth king. He is like the other seven, and he, too, is headed for destruction.*"

The United Nations was positioned in none other than New York's Manhattan. These events are projected and foretold in the book of Revelation. A false prophet arises to lead this New World Order. Daily, we witness events aligning to form a Great Reset with the discussion of a New World Order.

Is this the beast that swallows the world and deceives its people, beckoning the Scripture, "When He returns, will He find faith in the earth?" The merging of the seven mountains of influence and the eighth empire of prophecy are happening in our lifetime before our eyes. "He who has ears to hear," Jesus said, "Hear!"

The long-awaited coming of Christ is at hand. Prophetic events are all in place. Jesus came in humility and died, but His next coming will be a triumphant entry of the King of kings, where He will appear as a Conqueror at the helm of heaven's armies.

Then the seventh angel blew his trumpet, and there were loud voices in heaven, saying, "*The kingdom of the world has become the kingdom of our Lord and of his Christ, and he shall reign forever and ever*" (Revelation 11:15, NLT).

FINANCIAL SCHEMES

There's a saying, "There's nothing new under the sun." From the earliest times, people have struggled under an earth curse system of financial bondage, trying to make ends meet, while those who are smarter, or perhaps more devious, figure out ways to enslave people to high interest rates and taxation. The rich rule over the poor, and the borrower becomes a slave to the lender. America is up to her eyeball (the one on the back of our Federal Reserve bills atop a pyramid) in over $30 trillion in debt with a present borrowing cap of $31.4 trillion![127] The power of compounding interest and the wiles of a banking industry

DEVIOUS POWERS ARE PLAYING AMERICA FOR A COLLAPSE FINANCIALLY AND A GREAT RESET. BUT GOD.

threaten our existence as we know it. Devious powers are playing America for a collapse financially and a Great Reset. But God. Three watershed events in the 20th Century have put America in her most vulnerable state since the Civil War. They are: (1) the creation of the Federal Reserve System, (2) the abandonment of the gold and silver standards, and (3) the ratification of the 16th Amendment (the income tax). While I will not go into detail on the 16th Amendment here, it is undeniable that the income tax is part of the unholy trinity, an essential part of the Marxist plot to destroy the wealth of the middle class.

America abandoned the gold standard in 1933, and the silver standard in 1968. This left the government free to print money indiscriminately with no intrinsic value. This caused soaring prices. By 1980, inflation reached 12.3% and was threatening to destroy the economy.[128] In 1971, President Nixon reneged on the U.S.'s pledge to redeem with gold U.S. dollars held by foreign governments. In retaliation, OPEC nations refused to sell oil to America, causing gas prices to nearly double between 1972 and 1975. I remember as a child seeing the long gas lines. My dad would be gone for hours just to get gas.

In 1972, Nixon became the first sitting U.S. President to visit China.[129] He went to negotiate a trade deal. China was granted Most Favored Nation Trade status in 1980 (reviewed annually), and given permanent MFN status in 2000.[130] Between 1980 and 2004, trade between the U.S. and China rose from $5 billion to $231 billion annually.[131] In 2006, China surpassed Mexico as our second largest trading partner. [132]

Unfortunately, we exported a massive number of jobs and manufacturing facilities to China in the process. It is estimated that America lost 5.8 million jobs along with 67,000 manufacturing facilities as a result of the U.S. China trade deficit.[133]

Today, everything we need, from medications to oil, is dependent on foreign nations, especially nations like China that now have power to control us for goods. We are at a tipping point as a nation. Not only is the nation in an inconceivable amount of debt, but also over 66 percent of Americans live paycheck to paycheck, and 40 percent do not have $400 in the bank to cover an unexpected bill.[134] What security or peace is there in living under that kind of stress? None! The following story pretty much illustrates the state of the American family.

Gary was asked to visit a woman who said she wanted his help in putting a plan in place to eliminate her debt. We arrived at her home, and we were invited to sit down at her kitchen table where she began to tell us her story. She admitted that she had over 30 credit cards, all maxed out, and her last one had just stopped working, which prompted her to call him. In tears, she said that she could not continue to live like this and had to get out of debt. He told her that if she really wanted to get out of debt, she would have to stop using credit cards and live on her current income. When he said that, it was as if someone slapped her across the face. She suddenly cried out, "How am I to buy shoes?" And then she burst into uncontrollable sobbing. We were shocked by her statement. Buying shoes? That was her concern? Trust me, she had all the shoes she needed. In fact, he could tell from the credit card statements that she probably had a closet stuffed full of them.

Or take the client that called him in tears asking him to come over because they just had to get out of debt. The wife just could not stand leaving her baby at the day care any longer and wanted to go part time. When he sat down with them, in tears, they said they had learned their lesson. Debt had a stranglehold on their life, and they were done with it. He asked them his normal questions regarding their financial issues, taking notes, which he then took back to the office to examine and put together a plan. He was excited to see they could be out of debt, including their home mortgage, in about five years. We knew they would be so excited to see that!

As he returned a week later to go over the plan, he noticed a brand-new, top-of-the-line Cadillac in the driveway with temporary tags. He did not think much of it, thinking it was probably a friend visiting. But as he sat down, they admitted that the new Cadillac in the driveway was theirs. He just could not believe it! The payment was over $600 a month. He asked them why they would go into so much debt and burden their family with another debt payment after they, in tears, had begged him to help them get out of debt. They told him that they knew when he came back, he would tell them to stop using debt. So, before they made that commitment, they wanted to buy one more thing! Are you kidding? He just could not believe it.

As crazy as both cases are, they are not that abnormal. We have personally counseled tens of thousands of families in over 30 years helping people with their finances, and just let me say it this way: Debt has become a way of life in America! Or let me state it this way: Slavery has become a way of life in America!

Our family once lived in that financial slavery until we figured out what was happening and finally got off the merry-go-round. Here is our story, and, in many ways, it is the typical story of middle-class Americans trying to figure out how to survive financially, falling into money schemes out of desperation, and losing their dreams along the way. We made many regrettable mistakes, and it is miraculous that our marriage and family survived. And we probably wouldn't have if we had not allowed God to teach us how life was supposed to work and learned how to handle money God's way. We eventually learned and applied God's principles, and we have thrived beyond anything we had ever imagined. Our story is a raw, real, and ugly story, but we share it to help others avoid the traps and to have the courage to admit their own messes and to get help.

My husband, Gary, tells our story the best:

> Drenda and I started out with no money when we were married. Well, actually, we borrowed $500 from a friend to get married, so we really started out in debt. We lived on commissions working with an insurance company which I really believed in; however, I was extremely shy and dreaded talking to people, which you can imagine did not go well with my insurance business. Nevertheless, I plodded through my fears, made my calls, and became pretty good at selling insurance. I was making decent money, and Drenda and I had some free time since I set my own appointments and most of those were in the evenings.
>
> It wasn't too long, however, before I found out that it takes money, and a lot of money, to have things, do things, and be able to function in life. My commissions were just not enough to keep up. Without knowing better, we began to use credit cards to buy what we needed, then when that was not enough, we used finance company loans to consolidate those cards. When money got tight again, we would get new credit cards. We had two car loans also, and then, of course, we bought a house which we could not afford and did not really qualify to purchase. Drenda's parents loaned us the down

payment, and my boss wrote a letter which exaggerated our income to the bank. They approved the loan, but we did not have the first payment when it was due!

We scraped by. When things broke, we used more debt. We did not have money for taxes, so I did not file, thinking that I would get around to it when the money was there. Well, it did not show up, we eventually had to file, and we owed thousands of dollars that led to tax liens and extreme stress. The bottom line is that after just six years of marriage, we had accumulated 10 maxed out and canceled credit cards, two car loans on old run-down and broken cars, three finance company loans at 28 percent interest, judgments filed against us, and thousands of dollars in tax liens. On top of that, we owed our parents tens of thousands of dollars which we had borrowed just to survive.

Life was horribly stressful, and I ended up having panic attacks and was put on antidepressants to cope. Stress caused me to deal with hypoglycemia as well, and doctors said I would end up being a diabetic. I woke one day, found my body paralyzed, and fear gripped me. I became so stressed that I was afraid to leave my house. My wife began to plan how she and the kids would survive, thinking that she may have to go back home to Georgia. Let me just say that it was hell on Earth. It was not life.

The media has fed you a lie. Even your parents may have trained you to trust in debt. They may have offered to cosign for your first car. But debt is not an accident. It is a well-thought-out plot to steal every ounce of vision and strength you have. I can remember the time that I was expecting a check in the mail for about $2,000 from a case I had written. I needed that $2,000; that was big money to me back then, really big money. Knowing the pay cycle of the insurance company and knowing that the insurance policy had been issued, I knew that the check would be in the mail and arrive in about five days. So, I wrote out about $2,000 worth of bills and mailed them off, thinking that I had timed things perfectly. But Friday came and no check, and I knew that most of those checks I had written would hit the bank that night. I did not know what to do, so I had a brilliant idea. I would open a new checking account at a nearby bank and write a $2,000 check on the new, empty checking account and deposit it into the account that the checks were going to hit that night.

Monday morning, I checked my account, and the plan worked perfectly. All the checks cleared that night as paid. Confident that the real check would be there, I went to the post office, but to my horror, there was no check there. I figured the same strategy would work in reverse, so I wrote a check this time from my real bank account and deposited it into the new checking account I had only opened to perpetrate my plan. Like magic, it worked again. Well, for some reason, that check did not show up for two weeks. Meanwhile, other bills came in, and of course, there were groceries to buy. So, the $2,000 check now became about $2,600 each day going back and forth between the banks.

This all went well until one morning I received a call from one of the banks. I recognized the voice on the phone immediately. It was the teller I always talked to when I made my deposits, the branch manager. I had been sharing with her how knowing Jesus could change her life. I even had one of those Christian images printed on my checks. She opened the conversation with no introduction but simply said, "I know what you are doing! I have closed your account, and you are to bring into the bank the full balance you owe us or we will press charges. And by the way, you can never have an account in our bank again."

I cannot tell you how embarrassed I was, how humiliated. Luckily, the check finally showed up that day and I was able to pay the bank all I owed. Shame was the only way to explain how I felt walking back into that bank and meeting with her. I told her that this was all my doing and that God had nothing to do with it. It was my own stupidity, and I told her I was sorry. My life was full of these types of events, full of shame and financial despair.

I hated being in debt, and I dreamed of what it would feel like to be free of debt. I could not imagine how that would feel. As time went on, things got worse. No groceries, pawning the few things I had just to buy food, IRS liens, bill collector phone calls on a daily basis, no food in the house, no heating oil in the winter, and much more. I wish I could say that this was all just a blimp in the road, an anomaly. But it was our life for nine years!

Finally, an attorney called us and said they had waited long enough for payment and were filing a lawsuit on behalf of their client. When I got that call, I realized I was done. There were no more debt options left, no relative who would give me one penny more. I simply had no options.

In fear and hopelessness, I climbed the stairs to our little bedroom in the broken-down farmhouse, laid across the bed, and cried out to God. Surprisingly, He answered very quickly. Up out of my spirit I heard Him say, "I had nothing to do with this mess. The reason you are in this mess is because you have not taken the time to learn how My Kingdom operates." There was more He said that day to me, but I got the message. My mistake was trying to prosper the world's way, by using debt, and that would not work. God wanted to teach me how He pays for things. Of course, I had no clue what He was talking about, meaning I did not understand what He meant by learning how His Kingdom operates, but I was ready to learn. I went and grabbed Drenda's hand and repented to her, and we prayed and asked God to teach us how His Kingdom operates as we obviously did not have a clue.

The attorney who had called that day said to avoid the lawsuit, I would have to have about $1,500 to him in three days. At the time, we had no money and no business in the pipeline that would be paying out that much money in time, so I did not have an answer regarding how that money could show up. The next day, I had an insurance sales call with a family in the evening. I drove our old van to the appointment. It barely ran and spewed huge billows of white smoke as I drove it. Because of that, I would usually try to park the van several blocks away from a client's house so they would not see the state of their financial advisor's transportation. This time was no different except as I left, my client followed me to my van. I dreaded starting it with him there, knowing that it would fill the air with dense, white smoke, which it did. My client quickly asked me to turn off the van and pop the hood. He poked around a bit and then came to my window and said, "You have a broken head gasket. Drive it home and get it fixed as soon as possible." I did not need anyone to tell me the engine had a problem, of course; that was obvious. What also was obvious was that I did not have a dime to cover any repair.

On the way home, I prayed and talked to the Lord about this Kingdom thing and my van. I said out loud, "Lord, I do not have the money to fix this van. It would be better if it just burned up and I could get rid of it." Of course, I did not expect it to burn up; I was just venting my frustration. But as I said those words, I noticed a bubble on the hood that I did not remember being there. In fact, as I drove, the bubble was slowly getting bigger. I realized after a while that in fact the engine was on fire. As I pulled into my office and brought the van to a stop, the flames burst out of the engine compartment and rose six feet off the hood. I was in shock as I ran into the building and called the fire department. To make a long story short, the van was totaled. The insurance company gave me a settlement that, after paying off the loan, left me with about $2,500, more than enough to overnight the attorney the $1,500, which I did. We had money left to buy some groceries and pay a few other essential bills.

As we sat around the dinner table that night, we were still shocked, but then we realized that we still needed a vehicle. My little, old sedan could only hold four people, and we were a family of six at the time. My father heard of our vehicle burning up and called me. He told me to come to his house in the morning, and we would go looking for a vehicle. My hopes soared. My dad was wealthy and could easily write out a check for our new van. That morning, we went to a dealership, looked at all the options, and we found one that we loved. The price was about $19,000. My dad pulled me aside and told me that if I liked the van, he would give me $5,000 toward its purchase. I did not know what to do at that point. My dad had no idea of our horrible financial condition. I knew I did not have the credit to get a loan on the remaining balance for the van. So, I had to tell my dad the truth. He quickly said that he would cosign for the van.

Knowing that I did not want to use debt after what the Lord told me, yet feeling I had no choice, I went ahead and filled out a credit application. They said they would let us know in the morning. That night, Drenda and I could not sleep. We knew we could not go through with that purchase, but we needed a vehicle. By morning, we knew we could not do it and called the dealership and told them we would not be picking up the van. We then called my dad and told him the same. Now what? We did not know.

During this time in our lives, Drenda would often stop at garage sales, looking for things that we could buy and resell to make some cash. Her parents ran a monthly household auction in Georgia and would often make trips to Ohio to buy items and then resell them there. So, Drenda was always looking for things to sell.

A few days after the van burned up, she received a call from a man that she had met months before. He had remembered her and somehow had kept her number. He worked at a nursing home and said that he had two rooms full of stuff that needed to be sold and cleared out. Would she have an interest? Drenda said, "Yes," called her parents about it, and they wired us the money to buy the entire lot. They came with a truck and took all of it back to Georgia and sold it at their auction. They did so well with the auction that they said they were going to give Drenda a commission on it. The commission was a very clean used station wagon. We were thrilled! We then had a paid for vehicle for the first time in our lives.

We had eliminated the van debt and had learned a lesson in how God's Kingdom operates. We found out freedom is a great feeling. God was training us that His ways were good and free. From there, we began to apply what God was teaching us in every area of our lives. We became completely debt free in two and half years. We began paying cash for new cars, built and paid for our dream home, and began prospering at a level where we were able to give hundreds of thousands of dollars to various ministry projects around the world. Our lives drastically changed, but our memory of those dark nine years gave us a passion to teach people about the Kingdom of God. We hate poverty and lack.

Here is the sad part of the story. We never had to go through those nine years of slavery and stress. We never had to learn how finances worked the hard way. We could have learned God's system from the very beginning and prospered. That is our prayer for you, to learn how life works without all the pain and stress. God is the Author of life, and He wrote the instruction manual, the Bible. In it, you will find the answers and the template for life. The hard way is too hard with a huge price, one that you were never intended to pay.

As far as finances are concerned, there is another system, another Kingdom with laws and principles that will free you from the slavery and hopelessness of what the world has to offer. Trust me, been there, done that, got the T-shirt.

FREEDOM IS BETTER THAN ANY "THING" YOU COULD OWN. IT OWNS YOU IF IT TAKES YOUR PEACE, FAMILY, AND DESTINY.

We violated Scripture trying to figure out life, but we have dedicated our lives to helping others find freedom and, hopefully, avoid the serious mistakes that could have destroyed our lives. Marriages have dissolved over debt, and children have become the casualties. It's not worth it! Freedom is better than any "thing" you could own. It owns you if it takes your peace, family, and destiny.

I agree, there are so many money schemes set up to steal people's destiny from them and put them in bondage to the kingdom of darkness and its money systems. No one goes into debt hoping to destroy their lives. Many times, they are just trying to survive, not realizing the game is rigged against us. Preapproved credit cards used to be mailed out to unsuspecting people like us who thought it was a blessing until we realized the real cost, 28 percent interest. No one really understood that if they just made the minimum payment, it would take upwards of 22 years to pay off that card! Banks and institutions know exactly what they are doing. They can't get that kind of return anywhere in the market!

Debt is so tempting. For some, it is the temptation to buy something luxurious like a sports car or a diamond they truly can't afford. For others, they use the card and tell themselves they will pay it off next month, but few ever do. Those with high incomes are not immune. We have been in the most beautiful mansions and found those families to be in the same scenario of debt, just at a higher level. You need to realize that there are well-thought-out traps set up to land you in the poor house. Even rental storage facilities make more by selling off the forfeited items once the person can no longer afford the monthly storage fee. When people can no longer make their debt payments, the lender comes and takes the possessions they thought belonged to them. The truth is they never were theirs. The Bible is proved true: The borrower is left to become a slave to the lender (Proverbs 22:7).

The Israelites made bricks for Egypt's Pharaoh and saw very little from their forced servitude. The media sells us on new and shiny objects we must have, banks loan us the money, and we forfeit our marriages, families, relationships, peace, and freedom for trinkets that become tomorrow's trash. Just as our nation is facing a "payday" for its indebtedness, every family will too. There are answers, but they will not be quick or easy fixes.

Scriptures for financial foundations:

> *But godliness with contentment is great gain. For we brought nothing into the world, and we can take nothing out of it. But if we have food and clothing, we will be content with that. Those who want to get rich fall into temptation and a trap and into many foolish and harmful desires that plunge people into ruin and destruction. For the love of money is a root of all kinds of evil. Some people, eager for money, have wandered from the faith and pierced themselves with many griefs. But you, man of God, flee from all this, and pursue righteousness, godliness, faith, love, endurance and gentleness.*
>
> —1 Timothy 6:6-11 (NIV)

> *For which of you, desiring to build a tower, does not first sit down and count the costs, whether he has enough to complete it?*
>
> —Luke 14:28 (ESV)

> *For the Lord your God will bless you, as he promised you, and you shall lend to many nations, but you shall not borrow, and you shall rule over many nations, but they shall not rule over you.*
>
> —Deuteronomy 15:6 (ESV)

Owe no one anything, except to love each other, for the one who loves another has fulfilled the law.

—Romans 13:8 (ESV)

Pay to all what is owed to them: taxes to whom taxes are owed, revenue to whom revenue is owed, respect to whom respect is owed, honor to whom honor is owed.

—Romans 13:7 (ESV)

The rich rules over the poor and the borrower is the slave of the lender.

—Proverbs 22:7 (ESV)

The wicked borrows but does not pay back, but the righteous is generous and gives.

—Psalm 37:21 (ESV)

FINANCIAL DREAMS

As you saw, many years ago, my husband, Gary, and I faced our own financial crisis. We had moved to Ohio to do what God had directed us would be our end-time work. We thought that because we had God's Word on the situation, and if we obeyed that Word, we would be on easy street. What we were too naive to recognize is that there is always a fight for God's Word—especially where money is concerned. We found ourselves strapped with existing debt and less income while starting all over in Ohio. The next few years would prove to be rocky with great pressures on both our finances and marriage.

One day under great distress, we talked about throwing in the towel on our business. It just wasn't working, no matter how hard we tried. After almost a year of this, we both had lost sight of why we had moved and our dreams of what it would be like to have success… and most importantly, to be an example of God to our family members.

Tearfully, we prayed and asked God what to do. Had we missed His will? Where was our promise? Was there any hope we could make it? While we were having a serious discussion, a mail delivery truck pulled up and delivered a package. We opened it, realizing it was from a ministry we had occasionally called for prayer and had sent some offerings to when we could. Enclosed was a teaching series entitled, "Don't Quit!" It couldn't have been more perfect timing!

We listened to it over the next day. Encouraged, we didn't quit, and God breathed new strength and vision into our hearts! We simply received some provision for the vision on the way to the promise God had given us. Sometimes, we expect the promise to come immediately, but we had to walk out the timing until our business started to lift off. Often, God directs His children with vision or direction, but they only know how to carry it out in the way that the earth curse system has taught them to function. We get the marching orders but not the strategy. "People perish for lack of knowledge." To take a mountain, you need a strategy.

We decided to stick with it and persevere. My husband started delivering soda pop to his father's local restaurant as a side job while he continued to build our business. It was a little cash to keep us afloat. But we didn't take our eyes off the vision while he worked part time to fund the vision.

One night not long after that, I made up my mind I would not go to bed until God spoke to me. I remember thinking, *If Jacob could wrestle with an angel to get what he wanted, I can do the same until I hear from God about our situation.* Surprisingly, I discovered that God was just as eager to spend time speaking to me as I was to hear something. I got my Bible and began to pray and search the Scriptures. I started reading in Haggai. Out of all places, God spoke to me out of that small book of the Bible.

The book of Haggai paints a picture of Israel's lack because the people had left God's work in ruins. God said to them that because His house was in ruins while they built their lives, He had not blessed their work or their lives.

I couldn't help but think about how hard we had been trying to build our business, family, and life without really seeking God first and foremost. We attended church regularly, but we had one foot in God's Kingdom and one foot in ours. We would seek God for a season, and then the circumstances would pressure us into leaning to our old ways again. Sometimes we tithed, and sometimes we didn't. Sure, we prayed and went to church, but it was more because we felt like we were supposed to rather than an all-out choice to honor and seek Him first.

I went on to read in Haggai where God says, "*Is there any seed left in the barn?*" I knew a little about planting financial seeds from my time at Oral Roberts University, but we literally didn't have any money to seed into God's house. I said, "God, I don't have anything left to give you but me. I give you my life, such as it is, and anything you want me to do to build your Kingdom, I will." God spoke back to me in my heart. "I am going to use you and Gary to help My people in their marriages and finances, and you will bring My people out of financial bondage." I pictured how God used Moses to lead the Israelites out of Egypt, but we would lead people out of debt and into their promised land.

Excited, I woke Gary up from a deep sleep. "God is going to use us to help people with their finances and marriages!" In a less-than-happy voice, he said, "I wish He'd show me first!" He was so discouraged that he struggled to see it, but I was enthused to pray and believe

God's Word again. I got the answer I was seeking. This vision of helping others would propel us through difficulties in the future and paint a picture of purpose for our fight to the finish line.

After a few weeks, God gave Gary a dream. In the dream, a caterpillar crawled out on a limb and spun a cocoon. From the cocoon came a great and beautiful butterfly. He then heard the words, "This is how your business and life will be. Follow My plan, and give your business to me."

We left the company we had been with for eight years, and God orchestrated a new focus for our business where we incorporated His Word into our business practices. We got more and more excited about sharing God's Word, and then our business didn't seem so much like a business as it did a mission! We were excited for each new day, and God began to download ideas to us both about how to build our company and help people. The Word of God became alive, and we saw things in it about money, life, and priorities that we had not previously seen. A struggling business began to take new form. It was still quite a few years before we saw it take off and fly, but it was on its way. More hurdles came that we had to persevere through, but we had learned to seek His will for our lives instead of doing our own thing and expecting Him to bless it.

A few years later, our business became the number one office out of 5,000 offices nationwide, and Gary was asked to share his success at a national convention. We had not been striving for this goal, but rather we were just following the passion of God's plan for our life. Today, that business and the seed we sowed from it has produced a harvest we could not have imagined then.

We learned that you cannot serve two masters. You will love the one and hate the other. The enemy wants to keep you serving money rather than the purpose of God. If he can press you in the area of finances, he can rob you of your time seeking God and fulfilling His destiny for your life. *Serve* is a verb, so let me ask you a question: Who or what are you serving—God or money?

We learned that as we truly placed God's mission of the Kingdom's advancement as a priority, our finances were supplied with the provision we needed to run our race. Having money or the things it can buy is not a purpose, even though that becomes the life pursuit of many. Money is to fund purpose, the purposes of God. In order to thrive financially, find your purpose in advancing God's Kingdom, and then your labors, business, and life will take on a whole new passion.

The same God who directs your steps to your purpose will give you the creative ideas and direction to fund and propel you in that purpose. God has led us to invest in businesses and areas that prospered. We have had streams of income dry up through the years, but never without God leading us to a new stream that ended up being more profitable. Don't be surprised if you pray for increase and God closes the door on a current job

THE KINGDOM OF GOD IS NOT SUBJECT TO THIS WORLD'S ECONOMY, BUT YOU DO NEED STRATEGIES FROM THE SPIRIT TO THRIVE IN DIFFICULT TIMES.

or leads you to a new business. Or He may give you a new twist for your current business. Because the Kingdom of God is within you, the direction you need to thrive in hard economic times will flow out of your spirit. The Kingdom of God is not subject to this world's economy, but you do need strategies from the Spirit to thrive in difficult times.

Our nation is far from recovering from the many years of debt-laden lifestyles, improper usage of entitlement programs, and excessive printing of the dollar. We have only begun to see the bumps in the road of financial uncertainty and the dollar's volatility in world markets. Because as a nation we have turned from the principles of God's Word, there has been a loss of individual freedoms. A day of reckoning for our gross overspending in Washington is still unfolding. However, God will protect and help His children operate in His Kingdom; and those who do will be like Elijah, fed by ravens in a famine. We do not need to fear but rather to *prepare* as Joseph did, by the Spirit of God. And we must live by faith.

I have mentioned that Gary and I started a new business after we felt led to leave our employer, but I need to let you know what that business did. I know it sounds crazy now that you know how messed up our finances were, but the business was designed to show people how to get out of debt and safeguard their investments. From personal experience, we found out just how devastating debt can be; and with the help of the Holy Spirit and a lot of research, we discovered an amazing fact. We discovered that 86% of the families in the United States can be out of debt, including their home mortgage, without changing their current income. Incredible as it sounds, it is true. When we discovered this, we realized that no one was telling the consumer that this was possible. So, we set out to develop a company that would do just that, which we did. That company is now 29 years old and still going strong.

But I asked Gary if he would share some of the things he has learned over the years that can help you overcome a well-thought-out marketing campaign to steal every dollar you make by luring you into debt:

Drenda and I have learned a lot over our 30 years of helping people get free from debt. The first thing I think you need to understand is that someone wants you in debt. For instance, I am sure your mailbox is bombarded by a continual flow of credit card offers. And I am sure that you have noticed that you get offers repeatedly from the same companies. Have you ever wondered why those companies just keep sending those offers out repeatedly when you declined to show any interest the last 10 times they sent that offer out? I think the following little financial illustration will answer the question.

Let's assume you are 20 years old, and you have $25 a month that you want to invest for your retirement, which you believe that you will probably need by age 70. So, you are going to invest $25 a month for 50 years.

Now, if you invest that $25 a month at the current five-year CD rate, which at the time of this writing is 2.25%, your money will grow to a whopping $27,692.98. But what is the bank going to do with your money? You guessed it. They are going to loan it out, and not at 2.25%, but we can assume probably at around 18%. Now, check this out. If you invested that $25 a month at 18% over those 50 years, it would grow to $12,630,390. Yes, you read that right! But what if the bank loaned your money out to someone using a retail store credit card? Those cards are not charging you 18%; instead 24 to

27% interest is the norm. At 24%, your $25 a month would grow to $1.8 billion. Now, let's think this through. The bank is going to pay you $27,692 and will loan out that money and make millions. Now, do you understand why they can afford to send out those offers repeatedly? No one is giving you a loan because they like you!

The world is full of debt traps. Ninety days same as cash and no payments for a year all sound like a deal, but 85% of the people that take those offers do not pay off their loans in the free time period. Then their loan reverts to a loan—not at 18% or 24% but as high as 36%. I will not even try to tell you how fast money grows at that rate, but be sure of this, the banker knows. No one goes out looking for a 36% loan, but a ton of people have them. The trap is thinking, *I will pay this card off next week or next month.* Stop! Ask yourself what windfall is coming in that is tempting you to think that. No, it is better to wait until you have the cash and then buy the item you are looking at. It is a fact of life that most people never do get out of debt but simply use debt as a way of life and retire broke.

So how do we get out of debt? First, stop relying on debt! Stop giving your money to others to use for their profit; you need to keep that cash and build your own future with it. You may be thinking, *I don't have extra cash.* Without being argumentative, I strongly disagree. Over the 30 years of helping people get out of debt, I found that the average family has an extra $500 to $700 a month if they know where to find it. And that is the key, so where is it? Trust me, it is there. In a very simple explanation, the money can be found in everything you are currently spending your money on.

Let me explain in a simple illustration. Let's say you are spending $300 a month on your family's cell phone plan. If you find a less expensive plan for $150 a month, you just found $150 a month. If you continue with this model through everything you are currently spending your money on, you will be amazed at what you will find. I can guarantee you that you are losing money by overpaying your taxes or by paying too much for your various insurance plans. You are overpaying for your cell phone program, your groceries, or a multitude of other things you spend money on. All this spending can be adjusted just by gaining a bit of knowledge and taking the time to compare prices to make sure you have the best rate for the best product, and if you even need that product.

In review, the scams and plans to get you and keep you in debt are endless. You will have to be determined if you want to stay free. The first key is learning how the Kingdom of God works in relation to finances and then, secondly, learning how money works here on the earth. If you are interested, our business will examine and to "print a free, personalized Get Out of Debt Plan for you at no cost. This plan will show you exactly how you can become debt free in less than seven years, including your home mortgage, without changing your income.

I know it sounds crazy, but we have been doing this for 30 years. The best part is the plan is free. Even if you are not in debt, finding extra money is always a smart and expedient thing to do. And if you have money saved and you are wondering what is safe and what is not, contact us. We focus on investing options that are safe and where you cannot lose a penny due to market swings. Secondly, we offer advice on where to invest outside the fractional banking industry with many sound investment options to consider. We also can help you purchase gold and silver. Again, our advice is free. You can call us at 1-(800)-815-0818 or go to our website at forwardwardfinancialgroup.com.

Here are some practical principles and suggestions:

1. Seek first the Kingdom of God.
2. Give tithes regularly, and give offerings by faith targeted for specific needs.
3. Get out of debt, and stay out of debt! (Get a free plan from Forward Financial Group.)
4. Seek God's way of meeting a need instead of relying on debt.
5. Sell unneeded items and create an emergency cash fund (six months' income is the goal, but start with $2,000 minimum).
6. Give God your tithe first, then pay your savings account at least 10% of your income; live off the rest.
7. Invest in gold and silver for such unstable times, as well as commodities like food and the necessities of life, since these will continue to increase in value and unnecessary items will take a downturn. Consider buying cryptocurrency to diversify.
8. Consider getting money out of national banks; consider regional or state-chartered ones or credit unions in conservative states.

9. Consider a career change if yours is not recession/inflation proof.

10. Projected business growth areas are general medical practice and related businesses, financial counsel, repair work (automotive, home, etc.), large-scale farming, skilled trades, low-ticket restaurants, and retail versus high-end.

11. For business owners, increase your customer service so your business tops competitors in client satisfaction and repeat business; make your product more affordable and appeal to larger numbers of clients.

12. Be generous and trust God to fulfill His Word on your behalf.

God has always provided for His people in times of famine, national disaster, and hardships. Build your life in His Kingdom and not the uncertainty of this world's systems that are crumbling before our eyes.

The upside to all the shaking in this world is that many will recognize their need for a Savior. Get your financial house in order so you can be ready to reach them with His love and provision. We are all called to invest our finances into the Kingdom of God, but there are those who are called with the "gift of giving" to build businesses and literally fund the assignments God wants accomplished. God promises to take care of your business as you help Him take care of His, seeking first the Kingdom of God.

> **THE UPSIDE TO ALL THE SHAKING IN THIS WORLD IS THAT MANY WILL RECOGNIZE THEIR NEED FOR A SAVIOR.**

We need to honor businesspeople and never treat them as a secondary gifting in the body of Christ. God created free enterprise. If a man doesn't work, he shouldn't eat (2 Thessalonians 3:10), but if a man or woman works and brings his or her finances to God's Kingdom work, that is a high calling indeed. Businesspersons need cheered on to take that mountain and then use that money and wisdom to take many other mountains! Everything costs money, lots of it, ministry included. We must stop penny-pinching if we want to reach a hurting world.

DRUGS, PROFITS, AND FEAR

I think it is important to understand a little history behind the mountain of health, or we could more accurately call it medication, drugs, vaccines, and surgery. If we think the economic and banking system has been manipulated by those motivated by greed and other agendas, let us not think that these same perverse spirits have not moved into the area of health and medicine. Traditionally, medicine was centered on a holistic approach and involved herbal and plant-based remedies that were passed down through several generations—but at the turn of the century, there was a concerted effort to dismiss these as "old wives' tales" and replace them with more sophisticated forms of man-made chemicals, chemicals that could be patented. Patents bring big profits; natural substances do not.

Together, the big three—The Food and Drug Administration, organized medicine, and the pharmaceutical industry—collectively engaged in a tri-fold effort to influence legislators to promote the usage of man-made drugs and restrict non-drug remedies. Abraham Flexner was engaged by John Rockefeller in 1910, who already controlled an oil monopoly in the nation. Flexner evaluated the effectiveness of therapies and procedures taught in medical schools across the country, produced a report to lambast these procedures, and concluded, "The privileges of the medical school can no longer be open to casual strollers from the highway."[135]

From this report, the American Medical Association was given the power to be a doorkeeper to policy and medical procedures in the name of public protection. They were given power to certify or decertify medical schools and approval of medical procedures and medicines. Existing medical schools declined sharply, and schools were closed that didn't comply with their orders. And you can probably guess where the orders originated. Natural or homeopathic remedies were replaced with courses in favor of pharmaceuticals. Large sums of money from pharmaceutical corporations were provided to fund medical schools, and this developed into a self-serving arrangement.

Dr. J.W. Hodge described the medical monopoly, "The medical monopoly or medical trust, euphemistically called the American Medical Association, is not merely the meanest monopoly ever organised, but the most arrogant, dangerous, and despotic organisation which ever managed a free people in this or any other age. All methods of healing the sick by means of safe, simple, and natural remedies are sure to be assailed and denounced by the arrogant leaders of the AMA doctors' trust as fakes, frauds, and humbugs."[136]

"What has become orthodox medicine utilizes poisonous substances (drugs) in non-lethal dosages in order to suppress symptoms in an affected area. This approach neither addresses the cause of the disease condition, nor is it responsible for healing the patient. Rather, the use of drugs often will temporarily mask the outer manifestations of the malady while at the same time drive the disease deeper into the body ... only to reappear at a later date as a more serious and chronic health threat."[137]

Interestingly enough, these pharmaceutical companies studied natural plant-based remedies and then sought to mimic them in chemical portrayals that could be patented and sold at much higher costs to patients. What are the consequences of injecting patients with poisonous substances over naturally derived substances? Side effects, known and unknown. This has been perpetuated over the last 70 years, and we do not see cures but rather a continuation of treatments, drugs, and vaccines with side effects we only hear spoken at 90 miles a minute at the end of commercials or completely covered up. Is this profit motivated?

Mike Gaskins, in his 2019 book *In the Name of the Pill*, uncovers the dubious history of the birth control pill. His research sheds light on scientifically documented evidence linking the pill to blood clots, breast cancer, lupus, multiple sclerosis, Crohn's disease, and 10 other effects... and yet the pill has been given a medical pass for over 50 years.

"The pill was strongly linked to the women's liberation movement in the 1960s and 1970s, and people didn't want to appear to be criticizing the movement. Secondly, the pill debuted at a time when world overpopulation was a huge issue frequently lamented on the nightly news by Walter Cronkite and the likes.... Some early feminists felt like their movement was being co-opted to promote the pill."[138]

Even more shocking is that green plasma started appearing in samples and donations taken from women who took birth control pills; doctors had never seen this before. The Red Cross published guides to identify green plasma to remove it from blood banks. Another interesting side effect was that mothers who breastfed after taking the hormonal birth control pills produced bi-lateral breast growth in their babies, both boys and girls, that eventually subsided after the mother stopped breastfeeding. It was determined that the mother's milk was altered and was in lesser quantities too. In 2009, the Yaz birth control ads were removed from the market after promising that the drug reduced PMS and treated acne. How many young women took these pills to treat acne?!

Birth control drugs shut down a woman's cycle. "The monthly bleeding isn't even a period; it's a pill withdrawal." Many doctors use it to treat polycystic ovarian disease or endometriosis as well, but it does nothing to treat the problem; it only masks it. "By shutting down the body's natural production of hormones for so long, the system essentially atrophies and leaves the woman infertile."[139]

"Bayer has paid out over $1.02 billion to settle over 10,000 blood clot related injuries from Yaz and Yasmin."[140] Are the infertility rates among so many women today related? Studies are not even on the radar as these FDA approved drugs are not brought into question.

Do we see other similar collaborative agendas between medicine and political groups? Everywhere we turn. The same type of collaborative efforts happen in gender transition medicines and surgeries, while social and political agendas proclaim equity and equality in discussions concerning gender. Many assume these rights are related to women's rights or racial equality, but underneath the facades, the drive to replace women with biological males in sports and the sterilization of youth transitioning to a plethora of sexual identities is at the core of their plan. Pharmaceutical companies profit while those who drive the political agendas and depopulation get their wish list too.

Then there's the recent handling of COVID-19 and vaccinations. Where do we even begin to unravel this? What has happened on a national level in medicine played out on an international scale with lockdowns and medical emergency orders that were not sanctioned by Congress. Against the advice of doctors across the world, vaccines were rammed down the throats, or should I say jabbed in the arms, of everyone across the planet, except those who worked for pharmaceutical companies, Congress, and corporate elites.

Doctors who wish to remain anonymous told me that to jump on board the vaccine train and advocate came with a six-figure signing agreement, and that didn't include the profits from administering vaccines. Many acclaimed doctors, scientists, and epidemiologists joined in a countermeasure by signing a document called the Great Barrington Declaration, which stated: "The most compassionate approach that balances the risks and benefits of reaching herd immunity is to allow those who are at minimal risk of death to live their lives normally to build up immunity to the virus through natural infection while better protecting those who are at a higher risk. The document was met with sharp criticism and reactions from the federal government."[141]

Weekly, we were given alternative guidelines, demands, and changing "facts." "Science doesn't flip-flop like that. Politics do. Science has become politicized. We need to decouple science from politics. It's being manipulated to serve corporate and political agendas. Anyone criticizing the science is silenced harshly."[142] This included scientists and professors like John P.A. Loannidis of Stanford University; Dr. Joseph Mercola; Dr. Vladimir Zelenko (who treated President Trump); and our friend, Dr. Avery Jackson, a respected neurosurgeon who was reprimanded for bringing protocols he discovered were saving patients that were projected to die. He said, "Since when do protocols become more important than saving human life?" A very good question!

Dr. Paul Marik, founder of Frontline Doctors and internationally acclaimed doctor for sepsis treatment, was awarded by Virginia's House of Delegates for "instead of playing it safe and going along with the so-called conventional wisdom… dared to take a truly scientific approach… and saved lives." Just days later, this same doctor received an inquiry to respond to an investigation from Norfolk-based Sentara Healthcare. "The contradiction of the simultaneous commendation and investigation of Marik demonstrates that government administrations have gone rogue to stifle doctor and patient choice and autonomy."[143] Many other doctors have faced suspension or the loss of licenses and hospital privileges because they dared to put the patient before protocols and mandates.

Since China's vaccine rollout, 84.4 million children have been vaccinated, and many parents are concerned about the lack of data available on the safety; however, not without severe consequences for some. Parents were forced to comply or their children could not attend school. "After receiving an initial dose of the COVID-19 vaccine, my four-year-old daughter developed a fever and began coughing' ... after the second shot, the father could tell something was wrong. Swelling appeared around his daughter's eyes and lingered. For weeks, she complained of pain in her legs, where bruises started to emerge seemingly out of nowhere. In January, a few weeks after the second dose, the child was diagnosed with Leukemia."[144] Children have such a minimal risk of COVID issues that this has led many to ask the questions: "Is the cure worse than the virus? Why the pressure to vaccinate children?"

"The most recent data from the CDC shows that U.S. millennials, aged 25-44, experienced a record setting 84 percent increase in excess mortality during the final four months of 2021 .... In all, excess death among those who are traditionally the healthiest Americans is up by an astonishing 84 percent. Basically, millennials experienced a Vietnam in the second half of 2021. 58,000 died in the Vietnam War, U.S. troops, so this generation just experienced a Vietnam War. It's the worst-ever excess mortality. Millennials were by far hit hardest by the wave of excess deaths, likely because taking the jab was the only way for them to stay employed. Case in point, the excess deaths were almost seven times higher than those who are 85 or older."[145]

Will we ever know the actual truth about COVID-19? Through the Freedom of Information Act, National Institute of Health (NIH) documents have been released revealing that "the agency deleted CCP virus genetic sequencing information from the Wuhan Institute of Virology at the lab's request." This gave false credence to the tale that the virus started in a wet market instead of its actual creation in a bio-lab funded inadvertently by our own NIH. Senator Roger Marshall called for an investigation into this disturbing revelation. "The American people deserve to know the truth behind the origins of COVID-19, as well as how we can best prepare for, prevent, and recover from future pandemics...." For this reason, it couldn't be more important that we get to the bottom of this deleted data.[146]

These concerns have created just as much anxiety and fear as medical problems, if not more. Mental health issues have soared, and suicide rates are at an all-time high. In addition to these disturbing numbers among millennials, deaths from overdose are now over 100,000 in a 12-month period in the United States, an increase of 28.5 percent. Deaths from opioids and synthetic opioids (Fentanyl) rose to 75,673 in a 12-month period.[147] Prescription drugs account for 12 to 15,000 of these deaths.[148]

What is even more disturbing than all the lies, financial devastation, sickness, injury, and death from the COVID vaccines is how easily most of the world was conned into serving themselves up as "hackable animals" to fulfill globalists' plans for transhumanism. As Harari said, "Never let a good crisis go to waste. A crisis is an opportunity to do what in normal times people will never agree to, but in a crisis we have no chance."[149] Through the mass administration of the COVID vaccine, even in democracies, "surveillance started going under the skin." As a result, "free will is over" according to Harari. This is the genetic editing that Schwab and the WEF promise "will change not what do, but change YOU."

In a March 29, 2022 Substack article, Joe Allen discusses "the rapid approach of transhumanism, ushered in by 'unaccountable corporations that openly force advanced tech into our bodies,' such as nanodevices to track vaccination status and compliance with medical edicts."

"Three technologies drive the plot of this horrific story," Allen writes. "mRNA gene therapy, quantum dot tattoos, and artificial intelligence. Advance machine learning, used to predict the effects of mRNA mutations in silico [via computer], allows for lightning-fast vaccine development—including regulatory approval. Additionally, embedded subdermal tracking systems can ensure every person on planet Earth is up-to-date on their shots. Taken together, these innovations are rapidly converging on a long sought-after goal—an inescapable surveillance state, controlled by corporations, in which the global population is subject to continual medical experimentation."[150]

Is any of this feasible or is it all just a megalomaniacal pipe dream? "Big Pharma has an open ambition to generate endless mRNA vaccines using artificial intelligence… technocrats like Bill Gates and Robert Langer want human cattle to be tattooed with fluorescent nanoparticles to track their vaccine status, starting with the third world. It's easy to imagine the rest of us are next."[151]

As the WEF, Silicon Valley, and Chinese Communist Party have made clear, "[T]his is not a global conspiracy—these are publicly declared plans. AI-generated vaccines and subdermal tracking tech already exist, and they are rapidly improving. The germaphobic masses are now conditioned to submit to any technology deemed safe and effective. This terrified horde is also primed to insist that you submit too."[152]

COVID-19 scares and fears with false positive tests drove the government control to an entirely new level. We were told that to not vaccinate was socially irresponsible and anyone who dared question an experimental, untested vaccine was criminal and an anti-vaxxer. If anyone questioned that this vaccine was like no other, with experimental mRNA technology that alters genetics in the body, they were ridiculed. Doctors were no longer able to treat their own patients without government control and protocols. People became hostile to one another over masks, vaccines, and a myriad of other issues: six feet; no, three feet; cough in your arm; cough in a Kleenex; wear that dirty mask and cover your face between sips and bites on the airplane, but sit next to them the entire flight.

WAS THIS BIO-WARFARE AND PSYCHOLOGICAL WARFARE COMBINED TO CONDITION PEOPLE INTO GIVING UP THEIR FREEDOM AND "FREE WILL" AND LOOKING TO THE GOVERNMENT AND ITS AGENCIES ALONE FOR ANSWERS AND MANDATES ON HOW TO TREAT THEIR OWN BODIES? IT'S EASY TO LEAD IGNORANT MASSES THAT ARE DENIED TRUTHFUL REPORTING OR DISCOURSE AND DIALOGUE TO FIND THE BEST ANSWERS. THIS IS NORMAL IN TOTALITARIAN REGIMES WHERE ORGANS OF THE POOR ARE HARVESTED FOR THE RICH, BUT IN AMERICA?

Was this bio-warfare and psychological warfare combined to condition people into giving up their freedom and "free will" and looking to the government and its agencies alone for answers and mandates on how to treat their own bodies? It's easy to lead ignorant masses that are denied truthful reporting or discourse and dialogue to find the best answers. This is normal in totalitarian regimes where organs of the poor are harvested for the rich, but in America?

The history of psychology and psychiatry has a closet full of skeletons too. Check out the documentary *Psychology: Industry of Death.* We don't have to look far to find that various "diseases" of the mind are tied to creations of pharmaceutical origin. Unsuspecting parents and children have been their victims as well. A study of attention deficit disorder and children "referred" for analysis and medications is just the tip of the iceberg. But what has happened to children over the course of COVID with mental anxiety and suicides due to lockdowns and hopelessness, lost opportunities at school and sport's competitions, and social isolation has been staggering in comparison. What is the endgame of medical mandates, vaccinations, and vaccination passports that has denied doctors and patients their rights?

Dr. John Campbell shared a study from the British Medical Journal quoting philosopher Karl Popper as stating that "patients die because of the adverse impact of commercial interests in research agenda, universities, regulations, public relations, and propaganda placed over the priority of scientific integrity."

In another study from the British Medical Journal, Jon Jureidini and Leemon B. McHenry shared:

> The advent of evidence-based medicine was a paradigm shift intended to provide a solid scientific foundation for medicine. The validity of this new paradigm, however, depends on reliable data from clinical trials, most of which are conducted by the pharmaceutical industry and reported

in the names of senior academics. The release into the public domain of previously confidential pharmaceutical industry documents has given the medical community valuable insight into the degree to which industry sponsored clinical trials are misrepresented.

Until this problem is corrected, evidence-based medicine will remain an illusion. Regulators receive funding from industry and use industry funded and performed trials to approve drugs without, in most cases, seeing the raw data. What confidence do we have in a system in which drug companies are permitted to "mark their own homework" rather than having their products tested by independent experts as part of a public regulatory system?[153]

We have a pill for every ill and an injection for infection, but these are not concocted on scientific evidence but rather from a circular system that's highly profit motivated. The industry controls the research, and the scientific community receives funding from the pharmaceutical industry. Evidence based science and independent research are often ignored. The pharmaceutical industry controls research and operates on a publication basis. They suppress information and don't report adverse effects. Financial interests outweigh the common good. Doctors are given the protocols they must follow, and those protocols come from, you guessed it, the industry. It's a circle that has no checks and balances. Raw data is rarely released without court orders. Dr. Campbell says this is hypocrisy and we need to break apart research, funding, and the industry to bring integrity and prevention instead of merely profits.

The proposals for reforms include: "liberation of regulators from drug company funding; taxation imposed on pharmaceutical companies to allow public funding of independent trials; and, perhaps most importantly, anonymized individual patient level trial data posted, along with study protocols, on suitably accessible websites so that third parties, self-nominated or commissioned by health technology agencies, could rigorously evaluate the methodology and trial results."[154] They make the point that many who voluntarily participate in these studies risk their lives to do so, and integrity is integral to honoring their sacrifice and commitments.

In 2015, for their role in the discovery of Avermectin, which was subsequently chemically modified to a more effective compound called Ivermectin, as a highly effective antiviral, Satoshi Omura and William Campbell received Nobel Prizes.[155] There were doctors who used this anti-viral against COVID yet were met with incredible resistance, censorship, and cancellation. Why? Because the patent for Ivermectin had expired and there were no hefty profits to be made because of this. When doctors who were having tremendous success with Ivermectin or hydroxychloroquine petitioned for research since global trends showed the same, they were told there was no intention of conducting clinical trials. No profit, no trial, no protocol.

Self-preservation is a powerful instinct, and you can get people to do just about anything when they are afraid. In addition to medical manipulation of our lives depopulating societies across the world, I can't neglect to mention the number one killer of people—abortion.

As I mentioned in chapter 3, 62.4 million children have been murdered in the womb since *Roe v. Wade*, and abortion was the leading cause of death globally in 2021 with nearly 43 million unborn babies killed in the womb. These persons are not on this planet because they were killed in the womb!

We can see how fear in a crisis is used to drive people to do what governments and world organizations plan for society. The abortion industry grew more acceptable with the supposed "crisis" of overpopulation, driven in the 1970s with birth control pills sold alongside women's rights. I remember well my middle school classes in that era where teachers told us we would have to live in six foot by six foot by six foot cells by the time we reached adulthood because of overpopulation. Abortion was slipped right into the discussion as the answer. Never mind those unborn children: "They're just blobs of tissue." That is exactly what our schoolteachers told us, and the media as well, before the advent of ultrasound. "We must look out for ourselves and justify their deaths"—and when children hear teachers share these frightening ideologies, we believe. Adults believe too.

President Ronald Reagan said, "We cannot diminish the value of one category of human life—the unborn—without diminishing the value of all human life ... we cannot survive as a free nation when some men decide that others are not fit to live and should be abandoned to abortion or infanticide."[156]

The WHO has recently released new guidelines concerning abortion. Their propaganda sounds good to the leftist ear: "Comprehensive abortion care includes the provision of information, abortion management [including induced abortion and care related to pregnancy loss], and post-abortion care.[157] What do the new guidelines really call for? Abortion for minors at any age without parental consent, abortion through post-birth of the child, and governments to fund all abortion for any reason at any time. These babies' body parts are sold and delivered to medical research; and as we have learned recently, their organs and heads are used to humanize mice for research and development of medicines and products.[158] This is big business! I wonder how many women would abort their babies, instead of adopting them out to deserving families, if they knew that their babies would be used this way.

As set forth in Chapter 1, "the Fourth Industrial Revolution and Great Reset hinges on the creation of pandemics (either real or imagined) to usher in transhumanism and a system of mental, emotional, and physical control."[159]

A former Google CEO, also a World Economic Forum Young Global Leader, Eric Schmidt has gained influence over U.S. science policy and is chairing the National Security Commission. This is driving artificial intelligence and how it is used in science and health. Google controls 91.56 percent of all searches.[160] How does that affect the information you use to decide what is best for your body and health?

PROTECTING OUR
HUMANITY AND HEALTH

How do we manage to steer clear of the severe debilitating effects of tyrannical globalists, medical corporatism, and biohacking and live in health?

"The transhumanist ambition, implemented through technocratic policies, is to transform humanity through technology. Its delusional quest for perfection, however approximate—perfect health, perfect cognition, perfect machines. This ambition will never vanish. But like a devil chained up in the underworld, it can be contained.... The first step is public awareness. The second is a bold personal stance. The third is community action. The last and most enduring is the institutional protection of our rights, our privacy, and our bodily autonomy.... This struggle against the machine won't end until the last battery fizzles out. Prepare yourself for perpetual warfare. There can be no wishful thinking, but there's only one attitude to take—we will win this."[161]

As novel as the concept of transhumanism may sound, there is nothing new under the sun. Satan has tried to sow his seed into man's

SATAN HAS TRIED TO SOW HIS SEED INTO MAN'S DNA SINCE THE BEGINNING.

DNA since the beginning. Genesis reveals a similar plot in ancient days when fallen angels corrupted humans by having sexual relations that produced a race of giants called Nephilim. According to Genesis 6:

When human beings began to increase in number on the earth and daughters were born to them, the sons of God saw that the daughters of humans were beautiful, and they married any of them they chose. Then Lord said, "My Spirit will not contend with humans forever, for they are mortal; their days will be a hundred and twenty years."

The Nephilim were on the earth in those days—and also afterward—when the sons of God went to the daughters of humans and had children by them. They were the heroes of old, men of renown.

The Lord saw how great the wickedness of the human race had become on the earth, and that every inclination of the thoughts of the human heart was only evil all the time. The Lord regretted that he had made human beings on the earth, and his heart was deeply troubled. So the Lord said, 'I will wipe from the face of the earth the human race I have created—and with them the animals, the birds and the creatures that move along the ground—for I regret that I have made them." But Noah found favor in the eyes of the Lord.

—Genesis 6:1-8 (NIV)

Having no part in Satan's perverse plan, Noah walked faithfully with God and was esteemed by Him as righteous and blameless among the people of his time. So God warned Noah,

"I am going to put an end to all people, for the earth is filled with violence because of them. I am surely going to destroy both them and the earth. So make yourself an ark...."

—Genesis 6:13-14 (NIV)

Noah and his family were saved from the destruction of the flood and would be the last of Adam's DNA to survive in those days.

The human race had to be destroyed after angels had relations with humans and corrupted their genes. They were no longer humans made in the image of God but begat their own super race of giants and in their brute strength challenged God's creation. They had been recreated after the image of fallen angels instead of God. God had to destroy them for they had defiled His design and His divine image in man and woman. Otherwise, the human race would have been utterly destroyed.

Is this not what transhumanists attempt when they orchestrate ways to modify a person's DNA through "genetic editing" and "hacking" humans? Or to make them no longer male or female? Or even more chilling, when they claim that humans, like the *Nephilim*, can achieve immortality and "We don't need to wait for Jesus Christ to come back to Earth in order to overcome death. A couple of geeks in a laboratory can do it." No! Our DNA is our God imprint, and eternal life can only be found through Jesus Christ.

Most assuredly, a day is coming when God will give us a new glorified body that will restore all that was lost at the Fall when death entered, but transhumanism is Satan's counterfeit. We must not accept the counterfeit; we must never allow ourselves to be "hacked," "engineered," or mutated by the evil one.

In addition to doing all we can politically, morally, and prayerfully to stand against this darkness, we must follow the direction of the Holy Spirit to navigate through the propaganda, to discern what is actually happening versus what we are hearing. We cannot be blindly led, as we have uncovered. Instead, listen to God's voice and be wary of those touting agendas. Once you understand their endgame, the divisive and unsubstantiated claims and pressure become clearer. Taking responsibility for our bodies and self-governing our choices to stay free from health traps, just like debt traps, will make us prosper and be in health as our souls prosper.

TAKING RESPONSIBILITY FOR OUR BODIES AND SELF-GOVERNING OUR CHOICES TO STAY FREE FROM HEALTH TRAPS, JUST LIKE DEBT TRAPS, WILL MAKE US PROSPER AND BE IN HEALTH AS OUR SOULS PROSPER.

Dr. Avery Jackson in his book *The GOD Prescription*, "blends Scripture with Science to demonstrate the powerful impact that focusing on the tri-part person—spirit, soul (mind, will and emotions), and body—has on healing physical illnesses and injuries. In medical school, physicians are taught to investigate only the pathology of illnesses and diseases. The impact of spiritual and mental/emotional health on physical health is not typically investigated." Dr. Jackson provides empirical evidence, research results, and case studies of patients he has treated to demonstrate the significant connection among these three components."[162]

God created the body to heal itself. Our immune system is complex and miraculous. By learning how to take better care of our bodies, drink lots of water, exercise, eat right, and take natural supplements like Vitamin D and C, our immune systems and bodies can stay healthier and heal more quickly.

Does God heal today? Our daughter Amy has an amazing healing story that I had the joy of witnessing firsthand. She had a 13-pound tumor in her abdomen that twisted her spine, made her waist protrude, and created many digestive problems and pain. She grew discouraged with no medical answers after visiting several doctors. A surgery could have seriously impacted her future opportunities to have children. She began to seek God's Word for answers and to learn Scriptures about healing. Without surgery to remove the mass, Amy woke two weeks after receiving prayer to a completely new looking body. When she looked in the mirror, to her shock and her husband's, she looked radically different. The large tumor had disappeared while she slept. There was no explanation for it, except God did this after she specifically targeted her faith to receive healing from Him. I will never forget the call I received from her, in tears, as she rejoiced over her finding. I immediately jumped in the car and drove to her home. It was the most miraculous overnight change I have ever witnessed. We cried, laughed, and gathered our entire family together that evening to thank God, all of us in amazement. Her story and book have helped many to receive their healing too (amyfreudiger.com).

There was a woman in Scripture with an issue of blood that had a similar experience. Jesus spent most of His ministry healing all who were oppressed by the devil, for God was with Him. Scripture instructs us to, *"Lay hands on the sick and they shall recover"* (Mark 16:18, KJV).

James says,

> *"Is anyone sick among you? Then he must call for the elders of the church and they are to pray over him, anointing him with oil in the name of the Lord and the prayer of faith will restore the one who is sick."*
>
> —James 5:14-15a (NASB)

They will recover and be well, according to God's Word. It may be instantaneous or a recovering of one's health, but it is a promise from God. We are to mix faith with sound principles and receive what God says is ours. *"Beloved I wish above all things that you prosper and be in good health, just as your soul prospers"* (3 John 1:2, KJV).

Many churches no longer minister the healing covenant of God to their congregations or lay hands on sick persons expecting the sick person to be well. The laying on of hands is considered a basic doctrine in Hebrews 6. Instead of putting our trust in pills, vaccines, and surgeries, we must first put our trust in God, and He will direct us to the right answers and protocols for healing. "Healing is the children's bread." Churches and believers must return to biblical doctrines of healing that require trust in God and His power coupled with sound health practices. Check out the abundant healing stories from terminal cancer to MLS and in between at faithlifechurch.org.

Of course, better than receiving healing is walking in divine health! This is health physically, emotionally, and, most important, spiritually.

Receiving forgiveness and forgiving others helps us stay free from polluted thoughts and unhealthy meditations. If we meditate on His Word day and night, it will make our way successful. We choose to believe that health and healing are His will for us and then we act on those beliefs. Our bodies are the temple of God's Holy Spirit, and we must treat them with honor and respect for God. He can give us the power and direction to do so. "All things in moderation" goes a long way in maintaining health through diet, discipline, and discipleship. We cannot be out of control in a few areas without being considered out of control. Trying to eat foods that are as close to their natural state and unaltered as possible, exercising through walking and other activity, and getting proper rest (which means turning off the phone and TV to get true rest) go a long way in boosting our health. Find alternative sources to get information about your health besides the mainstream media that are bought and paid for by pharma. We cannot afford to give our health or our freedom to those who wish to abuse their power for profits.

EDUCATED TO BECOME LIKE THE TEACHER

As a youth leader for almost nine years, I witnessed the radical change of America's children on a smaller scale. It happened first in the cities and eventually spread to the rural areas. Typically, any difficult issues youth were experiencing were temptations to consume alcohol; occasionally, to lie to their parents; and rarely, to perhaps participate in sexual activity or view pornography.

I only had a couple of brief encounters with kids struggling with their sexual identity over 10 years. One of the young men in this situation did not grow up in our youth ministry, and he was already 16 when he shared that he was planning to experiment with homosexuality because he wasn't sure he was straight. He told me a teacher at school had encouraged him to try it so he would have "no regrets." No regrets?! I was shocked that the school was pushing kids to experiment with homosexuality. I was teaching our youth God's plan for marriage, with sexual intimacy to be saved for marriage, a holy covenant between a man and a woman for life. The contrast was sharp! I knew sexual promiscuity had increased over 30 years, but teachers pushing homosexual experimentation?

I tried to counsel this young man that he would certainly have regrets if he did experiment with homosexuality. I prayed with him and tried to help him. But honestly, I felt ill-equipped in some ways to counter the barrage of lies that were being pushed on him every day at school. Sadly, he slipped away, and when he was 18 and living as a homosexual, he came again to talk to me. He shared with me that he felt God had let him down. Then he went on to tell me that he had actually been introduced to homosexuality by a schoolteacher in junior high, who took several other young men with him away on "school trips" and engaged in homosexual activity with them. I was again shocked and begged him to go to the authorities and told him I would accompany him if he desired; but his shame was great, and he asked me to let him handle it in his own time. Other students were not subjected to the teacher since he had retired at that point.

I felt great sadness for this young, confused man, and shared God's love and forgiveness. I tried to help him see that God didn't let him down; the school and the teacher did! He had been abused, and these spirits involved in the abuse had confused and hurt him deeply. For years, his lifestyle broke his mother's heart. I felt great pain for her and regret for him.

After almost 30 years of pastoral counsel, I have found that children or adults who struggle with their sexual identity were usually molested and abused by someone older than them, often by an adult. Pedophilia is abuse, regardless of how our culture and the media try to justify and normalize it. One need not look far to see the double standard of organizations like Disney that purport to protect children while fighting legislation to protect children from being taught LGBTQ+ agendas in grammar school. The growth of this perversion has been astronomical in our highly sexualized culture as our nation grows further and further from God and our Judeo-Christian roots and feeds on occult entertainment. There is always a connection to the spiritual world and this behavior too. Lust is never satisfied, it gives way to more experimental behavior, and, eventually, often turns into serious sexual and domestic abuse. I have had opportunities to minister to those being abused by family or partners and seeking help. Shame and lies propagated by all seven mountains of culture keep people bound, but there is freedom in Christ.

"For everything in the world—the lust of the flesh, the lust of the eyes, and the pride of life—comes not from the Father but from the world" (1 John 2:16, NIV).

Fast forward to today… a decade from my youth leadership days, and a shift has happened that is beyond shocking. The problems facing youth have gone from typical, more innocent issues to extremely serious ones, especially for youth who did not grow up in the church. Youth leaders today are dealing with kids having multiple sex partners of both sexes; addictions to pornography; gender dysphoria; cutting; drugs; suicidal tendencies; prostitution; sex trafficking, arrested development; and youth carrying the weight of irresponsible adults, trying to raise their siblings while their mom and boyfriend do drugs.

Jesus said, *"The student is not above the teacher, but everyone who is fully trained will be like their teacher"* (Luke 6:40, NIV).

For the young man who turned to homosexuality, he was taught by his teacher. Children today are not just being exposed to gender fluidity and encouraged to experiment by the media, schools, and hospitals,

CHILDREN TODAY ARE NOT JUST BEING EXPOSED TO GENDER FLUIDITY AND ENCOURAGED TO EXPERIMENT BY THE MEDIA, SCHOOLS, AND HOSPITALS, BUT THERE ARE FULL-BLOWN CURRICULUMS GLORIFYING LGBTQ+ AGENDAS FROM KINDERGARTEN ON.

but there are full-blown curriculums glorifying LGBTQ+ agendas from kindergarten on. White House Press Secretary Jen Psaki told CNN's Chris Wallace that "she believes teachers should have the right to discuss gender identity with their pupils in grades as early as kindergarten."[163]

Drag queens read children storybooks in libraries, normalizing and encouraging this behavior. Kids are looking for love and acceptance, and celebrities are rewarding them with attention that all kids crave, especially those who are not getting it at home. Clubs with exciting names are developed, and teachers who themselves are involved in what were considered sexual deviancy disorders only 40 years ago are now mentoring children in these behaviors.

Children naturally look to adults to teach them the way to live. Children do not have the reasoning skills to discern good from evil or harmful or abusive behavior. Children are trusting. It is beyond horrific that innocent children with trusting hearts seeking direction are being abused in this way by teachers and by gaming and entertainment corporations. Stars like JoJo—and before her, Miley Cyrus of Hannah Montana—"come out" and lead devout child followers into their lifestyles and agendas.

School is no longer about reading, writing, and arithmetic but social engineering and political agendas. In 2020, Abigail Shrier, a parent and journalist with degrees from Oxford and Yale Law, wrote the controversial book *Irreversible Damage: The Transgender Craze Seducing Our Daughters*. In her book, Shrier's research revealed a "sudden, severe spike in transgender identification among adolescent, biological girls" in the 2010s. She attributes this to a social contagion among "high-anxiety, depressive (predominately white) girls who, in previous decades, fell prey to anorexia and bulimia or multiple personality disorder." Unsuspecting parents are waking up to discover their daughters have been persuaded by YouTubers, teachers, and therapists who push irreversible interventions—including double mastectomies, gender reassignment surgeries, and puberty blockers, which can cause permanent infertility.

With respect to schools, Shrier noted that the California Board of Education provides, through its virtual libraries, a book intended for kindergarten teachers to read to their students: *Who Are You? The Kid's Guide to Gender Identity* by Brook Pessin-Whedbee. This book for five-year-olds contends that "Babies can't talk, so grown-ups make a guess by looking at their bodies. This is the sex assigned to you at birth, male or female." The book continues, "These are just a few words people use: trans, genderqueer, non-binary, gender fluid, transgender, gender neutral, agender, neutrois, bigender, third gender, two-spirit...." While gender ideologues insist that books like Pessin-Whedbee's are merely presenting objective facts, as Shrier points out, it is clear that it is the hope that kids will pick a fun, "gender-creative" option for themselves."[164]

In November 2020, Target stores briefly stopped selling Shrier's book following criticism online but made it available for purchase again a day later. Chase Strangio, an attorney for the American Civil Liberties Union (ACLU), tweeted that "stopping the circulation of this book and these ideas is 100% a hill I will die on."

Recently, Shrier also wrote the article "How Activist Teachers Recruit Kids," exposing how activist teachers recruit kids after receiving leaked audio from a meeting of the California Teachers Association, the state's largest teachers' union.[165]

"Last month, the California Teachers Association (CTA) held a conference advising teachers on best practices for subverting parents, conservative communities, and school principals on issues of gender identity and sexual orientation," Schrier wrote. "Speakers went so far as to tout their surveillance of students' Google searches, Internet activity, and hallway conversations in order to target sixth graders for personal invitations to LGBTQ clubs, while actively concealing these clubs' membership rolls from participants' parents." To avoid parental opposition to the materials, these teachers openly disclosed to their audience that "Next year, we're going to do just a little mind-trick on our sixth graders. They were last to go through this presentation, and the gender stuff was the last thing we talked about. So next year, they'll be going first with this presentation, and the gender stuff will be the first thing they are about. Hopefully to mitigate, you know, these kinds of responses, right?"

"The Genderbread Person" is now a commonly used craft for teaching kids how to identify the various LGBTQ identities.[166] A website called thesafezoneproject.com has provided a free lesson plan to go with the free "Genderbread" activity sheet.[167]

The Genderbread Person v4

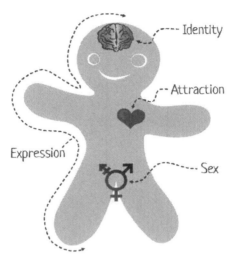

- - - - Identity

- - Attraction

Expression

- - - Sex

⊘ means a lack of what's on the right side

Gender Identity
⊘ ——————→ Woman-ness
⊘ ——————→ Man-ness

Gender Expression
⊘ ——————→ Femininity
⊘ ——————→ Masculinity

Anatomical Sex
⊘ ——————→ Female-ness
⊘ ——————→ Male-ness

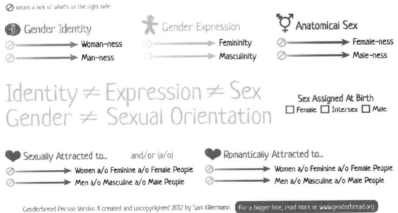

Identity ≠ Expression ≠ Sex
Gender ≠ Sexual Orientation

Sex Assigned At Birth
☐ Female ☐ Intersex ☐ Male

❤ Sexually Attracted to...   and/or (a/o)
⊘ ——————→ Women a/o Feminine a/o Female People
⊘ ——————→ Men a/o Masculine a/o Male People

❤ Romantically Attracted to...
⊘ ——————→ Women a/o Feminine a/o Female People
⊘ ——————→ Men a/o Masculine a/o Male People

Genderbread Person Version 4 created and uncopyrighted 2017 by Sam Killermann For a bigger bite, read more at www.genderbread.org

Similarly, "The Gender Unicorn," created by Trans Student Educational Resources ("TSER"), is being used to teach children about sex and gender identity.[168] Its creators distinguished the Gender Unicorn from "The Genderbread Person" because they "wanted to recognize genders outside of the western gender binary, which 'The Genderbread Person' does not. Not all trans people exist on a scale of womanhood and manhood." TSER facilitates and presents several workshops at conferences, events, schools, colleges, universities, and more.

This indoctrination of children is appalling, and the effects have life altering impacts: sterilization, mental illness, and suicide. Persons who transition have a 40 percent chance of suicide. This alone should scream this is wrong! Acceptance and education of these sexual behaviors have not helped children but instead have destroyed their innocence and lives. We must return to biology 101 and Jesus's declaration, *"Have you not read that he who created them from the beginning made them male and female"* (Matthew 19:4, ESV)?

The Scripture is very clear—not only has God "made them male and female," but in doing so, He sought godly children to come from their union. *"But did He not make them one? And why one? He seeks godly offspring"* (Malachi 2:15, NKJV).

The US has the world's highest rate of children living in single parent households. One fourth of children live with a single parent due to a decline in marriage rates and a rise in births outside of marriage. Compare this to China, where 3 percent live in single parent homes, and 4 percent in Nigeria. In Canada, the share is 15 percent. And adult children, ages 18-34, living with their parents in the U.S. is a whopping 27 percent! Is it possible that these young adults are also modeling what they have been taught about marriage from their teachers, mom, and dad?[169]

Millennials are making history by saying no to traditional marriage in record numbers—and they may be radically changing a centuries old institution. While traditional marriage has been on a downward trajectory for generations, with this group—the oldest now 40 years old—it appears to be in free fall. According to a Pew Research report, millennials are slower to establish their own households; more than

4 in 10 do not live with a family of their own. Many millennials are choosing to test-drive nuptials. Pew reports found that a significant share is living with a romantic partner.[170]

I consistently meet women my age who are sad that they have no grandchildren, and many say they have little hope of having any in the future because their adult children are choosing not to have children and instead of marrying are cohabiting. One mother lamented to me that she wished she had not prioritized career over family, over her daughter and son. It's easy to listen to the influences of celebrities and higher education and ultimately lose the best rewards in life.

Children are being barraged with sexual information, violent and sexual images, LGBTQ agendas, occult practices, and rebellious attitudes while missing healthy male/female marriage relationships at home. When you add to that the time spent on social media, TikTok challenges, comparing themselves to thousands of social media images, and the normal challenges of puberty, it's a lonely, lost world for children. Often, their parents, if they are there, are too busy to see their hurts and know their deepest, darkest pain and struggles.

These pains and wounds can have mortal consequences. Suicide is the number two cause of death of youth ages 15-19. Mental health issues among youth and even children have been drastically rising, but the lockdowns caused them to skyrocket. One in four youth said they had entertained thoughts of suicide in 2021.[171] Suicide rates among those aged 10-24 have increased 60 percent from 2007-2018 even prior to the lockdowns. These numbers should be a 911 to anyone observing the rate of unhappiness, depression, and mental issues among young people.[172]

I was recently approached by a nurse who reads behavioral hospital charts of children struggling with anxiety, suicidal thoughts, and other mental/emotional issues. She shared with me that she repeatedly observed these children almost always had similar experiences. They saw dark, wispy images or clouds, heard dark voices telling them to do wrong or take their lives. The children were dealing with demonic activity, but the medical professionals only medicated them and had no way of dealing with the spiritual issues and family issues that were the root of their problems. The medications did not seem to help. She shared with me that after suicide attempts, many of these young people are counseled that they may be in the wrong body and should consider gender transition. The hospital has an entire clinic run by those who have already transitioned to "help" these youth.

Why do parents go along with this? Some do not know until it's almost too late. They are told by doctors and psychologists, "It's better to have them transition than to commit suicide," as if those are the only two options. Even some clergy help them "transition" to their "new and improved" sexual identity, name, and pronouns in a rite of passage. Youth bind their sexual organs to their bodies to hide them until they can get mastectomies and castration. The tape wounds turn ghastly, and hospital staff must learn to care for their wounds. Can it get more shocking?

Is it possible that these children have been indoctrinated in school, by social media, celebrity culture, gaming, and entertainment yet starved of the security and love they need from parents, along with caring boundaries? Is the medical community profiting from the agendas perpetrated on children by adults with agendas in schools and medical boards, and the neglect of absent parents? Doesn't someone make money from the antidepressants, counseling, gender transition surgeries, pills, hospital stays, and suicide treatments? Obviously, I am not against educators or the medical community, but something is very wrong and has headed in a very dark direction. These children are simply emulating what they have been programmed to believe about life, themselves, their identities, and the world around them. We have failed them, but there is hope.

Jesus said in Matthew 18:6 (NIV),

> *"If anyone causes one of these little ones—those who believe in me—to stumble, it would be better for them to have a large millstone hung around their neck and to be drowned in the depths of the sea."*

"As youth grow and reach their developmental competencies, there are contextual variables that promote or hinder the process. These are frequently referred to as protective and risk factors.

The presence of, absence of, and various combinations of protective and risk factors contribute to the mental health of youth. Identifying protective and risk factors in youth may guide the prevention and intervention strategies to pursue with them. Protective and risk factors may also influence the course mental health disorders might take if present."[173]

RISK AND PROTECTIVE FACTORS FOR MENTAL, EMOTIONAL, AND BEHAVIORAL DISORDERS IN ADOLESCENTS

Domain: Individual

Risk Factors	Protective Factors
• Female gender	• Positive physical development
• Early puberty	• Academic achievement/ intellectual development
• Difficult temperament: inflexibility, low positive mood, withdrawal, poor concentration	• High self-esteem
• Low self-esteem, perceived incompetence, negative explanatory and inferential style	• Emotional self-regulation
• Anxiety	• Good coping skills and problem-solving skills
• Low-level depressive symptoms and dysthymia	• Engagement and connections in two or more of the following contexts: school, with peers, in athletics, employment, religion, culture
• Insecure attachment	
• Poor social skills: communication and problem-solving skills	
• Extreme need for approval and social support	
• Low self-esteem	
• Shyness	
• Emotional problems in childhood	
• Conduct disorder	
• Favorable attitudes toward drugs	
• Rebelliousness	
• Early substance use	
• Antisocial behavior	
• Head injury	
• Marijuana use	
• Childhood exposure to lead or mercury (neurotoxins)	

RISK AND PROTECTIVE FACTORS FOR MENTAL, EMOTIONAL, AND BEHAVIORAL DISORDERS IN ADOLESCENTS

Domain: Family

Risk Factors

- Parental depression
- Parent-child conflict
- Poor parenting
- Negative family environment (may include substance abuse in parents)
- Child abuse/ maltreatment
- Single-parent family (for girls only)
- Divorce
- Marital conflict
- Family conflict
- Parent with anxiety
- Parental/marital conflict
- Family conflict (interactions between parents and children and among children)

- Parental drug/ alcohol use
- Parental unemployment
- Substance use among parents
- Lack of adult supervision
- Poor attachment with parents
- Family dysfunction
- Family member with schizophrenia
- Poor parental supervision
- Parental depression
- Sexual abuse

Protective Factors

- Family provides structure, limits, rules, monitoring, and predictability
- Supportive relationships with family members
- Clear expectations for behavior and values

RISK AND PROTECTIVE FACTORS FOR MENTAL, EMOTIONAL, AND BEHAVIORAL DISORDERS IN ADOLESCENTS

Domain: School, Neighborhood, and Community

Risk Factors

- Peer rejection
- Stressful events
- Poor academic achievement
- Poverty
- Community-level stressful or traumatic events
- School-level stressful or traumatic events
- Community violence
- School violence
- Poverty
- Traumatic event
- School failure
- Low commitment to school
- Not college bound
- Aggression toward peers
- Associating with drug-using peers
- Societal/community norms favor alcohol and drug use
- Urban setting
- Poverty
- Associating with deviant peers
- Loss of close relationship or friends

Protective Factors

- Presence of mentors and support for development of skills and interests
- Opportunities for engagement within school and community
- Positive norms
- Clear expectations for behavior
- Physical and psychological safety

(Adapted from M.E. O'Connell, T. Boat, and K.E. Warner's *Preventing Mental, Emotional, and Behavioral Disorders Among Young People: Progress and Possibilities*, The National Academies Press, Washington, DC, 2009.)

Honestly, these risk factors and protective factors are not surprising as they can be found right in God's Word. This chart mentions religion as a favorable protective factor. Studies indicate youth with strong spiritual engagement, who attend church and church camps, and have a deep-seated faith are far less likely to be involved with drugs, alcohol abuse, or to have mental or emotional disorders or suicidal tendencies.

God has trusted parents to raise children with protection and love. When we stand before Him, it will not matter how much money we made or the things we acquired while on the earth or even how popular we became. Were we popular to our child? Did we love them enough to discipline them gently with patience?

HOW DID WE GET HERE IN OUR SOCIETY WHERE PARENTS HAVE BEEN PASSIVELY GIVING THEIR CHILDREN OVER TO THE BABYSITTERS OF ENTERTAINMENT, SMART PHONES, AND CELEBRITY PERSONALITIES WITH AGENDAS STRAIGHT FROM HELL?

How did we get here in our society where parents have been passively giving their children over to the babysitters of entertainment, smart phones, and celebrity personalities with agendas straight from hell? Who educated the teachers driving these agendas in schools and in medical communities?

Higher learning and college campuses have been infiltrated with anti-God, anti-democracy ideologies. The departure of our leaders and educators from a moral compass is destroying the fabric of family, faith, and financial integrity in our nation and its youth.

Since the 1960s, Leftists, Progressives, Socialists, and Marxists have migrated to and have taken positions in every level of public school and college education, including in the National Education Association (the national teachers union), public school teaching positions, public school administrator positions, college professorships, college department heads, college deans, members of Boards of Regents, and in government positions at every level of The Department of Education.

In 2007, four U.S. Communist groups formed an alliance in order to work toward taking control of the Democrat Party in California, and then in other states, with the ultimate goal of taking control of the National Democrat Committee. The long-term plan included the indoctrination of students at all levels of public-school education, and in colleges around the country, in order to convince millions of students that the Constitutional Republic had been a massive failure, while at the same time painting a positive image of Socialism. The goal was to gain the support of generations of naïve students with the expectation they would eventually help the Communists gain control of local, state, and the federal government. Their detailed plans are outlined in the Inside/Outside Project.[174]

"Give me just one generation of youth, and I'll transform the world."

—Vladimir Lenin

"Traditionally, for over 200 years, the curriculum in public schools and in state colleges was developed and controlled by local school boards and individual state Education Departments. In 2008, then Arizona Governor Janet Napolitano led a Common Core Task Force composed of commissioners of education, governors, corporate chief executive officers, and recognized experts in higher education. In December 2008, that Task Force developed what became known as the Common Core State Standards. Those state standards were then adopted by 45 states and the District of Columbia."[175]

There used to be a television commercial when I was young that said, "It's 10:00: Do you know where your children are [and who is influencing their behavior and beliefs]?" They will become like their teachers.

> *See to it that no one takes you captive through hollow and deceptive philosophy, which depends on human tradition and the elemental spiritual forces of this world rather than on Christ.*
> —Colossians 2:8 (NIV)

KNOWLEDGE WITH WISDOM: A BETTER WAY

The blessing in disguise of parents forced to home educate their children during lockdowns is that many parents reclaimed their responsibility for their children; and secondly, they got to actually see some of the hideous things being taught to their children. Some parents have continued to home educate after schools reopened.

Others have become activists and stood up against the teachers' unions and school boards that are propagating the agendas that are being force-fed to innocent children. This is a great and hopeful wake-up call, and I couldn't cheer these parents on enough. We knew just how serious things had become when parents' involvement in their children's education was deemed by the federal government to be "terrorist behavior, and the FBI was summonsed!" Parents, be parents and fight like heaven when it comes to your

WE KNEW JUST HOW SERIOUS THINGS HAD BECOME WHEN PARENTS' INVOLVEMENT IN THEIR CHILDREN'S EDUCATION WAS DEEMED BY THE FEDERAL GOVERNMENT TO BE "TERRORIST BEHAVIOR, AND THE FBI WAS SUMMONSED!"

children! Nothing, and I underscore nothing, will be more important to you at the end of your life besides your eternal destination of heaven.

Wisdom Is the Goal

"Wisdom is the principal thing; therefore, get wisdom: and with all your getting, get understanding" (Proverbs 4:7, NKJV). Wisdom is the knowledge and principles that establish truth, and understanding is good judgment on how to apply them. It doesn't matter how much education we have or how many pedigrees we have if we are not able to exercise wisdom and lack the character to live productive, good, and honest lives. Mental and moral foundations are more important than "book learning." Much of today's higher learning has to do with nonsensical studies that have no real world value or financial promise. The apostle Paul warned his spiritual son, Timothy, about this, and we should warn our youth too. *"O Timothy, guard the deposit entrusted to you. Avoid the irreverent babble and contradictions of what is falsely called 'knowledge'"* (1 Timothy 6:20, ESV).

It is a command from God to teach our children what He says about them, life, and His goodness.

> *"And these words that I command you today shall be on your heart. You shall teach them diligently to your children, and shall talk of them when you sit in your house, and when you walk by the way, and when you lie down, and when you rise."*
> —Deuteronomy 6:6-7 (ESV)

It's rarely emphasized, but the first part of Deuteronomy mentions these words shall be on your heart (and then you will talk about them). Our hearts will dictate what we say and how we lead. What's important to us will become the conversation of our day; and whatever we are doing, our priorities will show up. Regardless of if a parent has made it a priority to train their children in moral character, if they put their children in institutions for 7-9 hours a day, the institutions overpower their intentions. As we have seen, the problem with the education system is out of control.

The priority in the beginning of establishing a "school system" was to teach children the Bible. All lessons were taken from the Bible as a foundation for wisdom and understanding. Great names of history that shaped this nation had a strong knowledge of the Scriptures, if not personal relationships with Jesus Christ. Teachers were chosen for their knowledge of Scripture as well as skills.

I used to think of 1 Corinthians 15:33 (CSB), "*Do not be deceived: 'Bad company corrupts good morals'*" as referring to friendships, and it does. But it also refers to the people training our children. If their moral character is anti-God, then they will corrupt their students with the same spirits of deception.

The hand that rocks the cradle—not just rocks the cradle but educates and trains the brain—develops the heart and directs the soul. We are where we are today because of educating young people. Young people will form the world we will live in tomorrow. Today's issues in our nation are because of the education of youth. Youth become adults. Adults vote in leadership. Leaders shape policies and laws. Laws control the landscape we live in.

Your most powerful choices and freedoms are your vote or voice and the education of your child's voice. The enemy wants to silence both. Our nation is in the condition it is in because of the education system. A nation becomes what its people believe to be truth. The school system has been used to socially engineer agendas. Prayer and God were removed from schools in 1962. Since then, history has been rewritten, and God and the faith of our foundations has been removed from our American history. Youth have been programmed to accept tolerance over truth. They value tolerance. Talk to any young adult who was publicly educated, and you will have a hard time finding many who accept God's Word. They accept all manner of perversion as normal but reject God and think religion should be kept out of public life. It is tolerance over truth.

Three false areas that Israel adopted in their worship brought the destruction of their nation and every empire that has fallen: 1) Baal worship—pleasures and mammon; things and excesses, 2) Worship of Ashtoreth—sexual immorality and perversion, and 3) Worship of Molech—the offering of their children even to death. (See Judges 2:12-13, Judges 3:7, and 1 Kings 11:5-10.)

CHRISTIAN PARENTS ACT SHOCKED WHEN THEIR CHILDREN REJECT GOD—BUT WHAT DO THEY EXPECT WHEN THEY'VE TURNED THEIR CHILDREN OVER TO BE RAISED BY THE IDEOLOGY OF FALSE GODS?

These are exactly the same spirits operating in this age and propagated in the systems of our world.

Many parents have been conditioned that it's normal to offer their children to this ungodly educational brainwashing. Christian parents act shocked when their children reject God—but what do they expect when they've turned their children over to be raised by the ideology of false gods? If you examine the time the school system is indoctrinating students with social agendas over real educational skills and learning, it's no surprise we see these seriously negative outcomes in our youth.

Then Jesus told His disciples, *"For what will it profit a man if he gains the whole world and forfeits his soul? Or what shall a man give in return for his soul"* (Matthew 16:26, ESV)?

Clearly, there are certainly more important issues in life than careers and paychecks. Secularized learning that rejects God doesn't prepare anyone for the world, and especially to succeed in heaven's eyes or earthly relationships. Counsel from the wicked is poor counsel indeed. To increase in favor with God is to increase favorably with our families, businesses, and lives.

> *Blessed is the man who walks not in the counsel of the wicked, nor stands in the way of sinners, nor sits in the seat of scoffers; but his delight is in the law of the Lord, and on his law, he meditates day and night. He is like a tree planted by streams of water that yields its fruit in its season, and its leaf does not wither. In all that he does, he prospers. The wicked are not so but are like chaff that the wind drives away.*
>
> —Psalm 1:1-4 (ESV)

If we want to be prosperous and want the same for our children, we must make some radical changes. Jesus said, *"Very truly I tell you, no one can see God's kingdom unless they are born again"* (John 3:3, NIV).

To be born again is a radical change of life that realigns our priorities with God's, and it should impact radical change in the way we view our priorities, children, and education.

Sadly, I must state the public school system as it exists today can no longer be the method of choice to educate children. Christian schools or home education are no longer just optional. We discussed the why in the last chapter. The risks are too great. All parents, single or married, poor or rich or somewhere in between, have been given the same trust to train their children in the way they should go. If Christian schooling, then you must inspect what is being taught and be very engaged. By the time you provide transportation and preparation and help assisting with homework, the same time investment could have been used to home educate your children (maximum 2 to 2-1/2 hours a day is the average time and less in earlier grades). The remainder of their time can be invested in life skills and developing their specific gifts and callings (music, voice, athletics, business, arts, debate, politics, travel, computer, etc.). The time to explore and "do" is far better than simply using books. Social interaction is easy to supplement with church, home educational co-op groups, and life. Family life is regained, and the most important relationships are cultivated.

Parents should also be engaged in their state laws to drive bills that cause the money to follow the students of taxpayers, giving parents the right to spend that money at the school of their choice, creating a free-enterprise system that would force schools to listen to parents instead of teachers' unions when deciding what students learn. Bills like the one at backpackbill.com have begun to put the choice and dollars back into the hands of parents and students.

The Conviction to Educate Your Children

Home education doesn't mean we only protect children from harmful curriculums, but rather we as parents invest in their character and development through accompanying academics. We model a faith-based life and, therefore, educate our children in a biblical worldview. Life responsibilities are caught, and the two hours a day spent in books is taught. Whatever you're doing, you may involve your children. Real "life learning" is happening moment by moment, whether it's at the grocery store or the bank. Life becomes a field trip, and these students advance and learn more than any book affords. You may also tailor education to your time schedule, and if you have a business, even better. Involve them as much as possible. There are many curriculums and online learning opportunities and a thousand ways to accomplish the task. If you recognize the following as your guiding principles, you will succeed at training your children:

1) Recognize training our children is a responsibility from GOD—a calling!

2) Where He calls, He equips. If it's a calling, then there is equipping, a grace from God to carry it out placed on you that no one else can do quite the way you can as their parent.

3) If you disobey the call, there will be consequences that are greater than the price you would have paid to home educate or send them to a Christian school. You are training your children in life. What are your children being trained to believe and do?

4) Every day doesn't go perfectly, but neither does life! Even misses or messes can be great opportunities to learn for both parent and child.

5) Grow and learn together as God intended in a natural yet intentional way.

Many fear they are inadequate to educate their children, and yet as a parent, you taught them the toughest skills in life, to talk and walk. You did it quite naturally, and that is how all learning is best accomplished. You cared enough to show them the way and patiently instructed them how. These are the same prerequisites for home education.

Secondly, parents feel they lack time or resources, but you have both if you realize a small amount of time can accomplish great feats and low or no cost resources are all around you, a field or a brook. Famous stories of one of our founders, Abigail Adams, wife to one president and mother of another, say she home educated six children. Her very accomplished children became a statesmen, attorneys, doctors, and a President. How did she accomplish this? She developed their character, the wisdom, and understanding, the foundation to look to God to help them with the rest. Isn't that how we have learned is the best way to navigate life?[176]

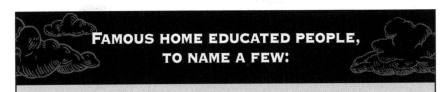

FAMOUS HOME EDUCATED PEOPLE, TO NAME A FEW:

GENERALS:
- Stonewall Jackson
- Robert E. Lee
- Douglas MacArthur
- George Patton

INVENTORS:
- Alexander Graham Bell
- Thomas Edison
- Wright Brothers: Orville and Wilbur Wright

PREACHERS & RELIGIOUS LEADERS:
- Joan of Arc
- Jonathan Edwards
- Charles Wesley
- John Wesley

PRESIDENTS:
- John Quincy Adams
- William Henry Harrison
- Thomas Jefferson
- Abraham Lincoln
- James Madison
- Franklin Delano Roosevelt
- Theodore Roosevelt
- John Tyler
- George Washington

SCIENTISTS:
- George Washington Carver
- Pierre Curie
- Albert Einstein
- Booker T. Washington[177]

Is College Worth It from a ROI Perspective?

"For which of you, desiring to build a tower, does not first sit down and count the costs, whether he has enough to complete it" (Luke 14:28, ESV)?

Is college the right option? The following statistics and costs demonstrate that some degrees weighed against the costs of college and loss of work time are not advantageous. Perhaps the biggest cost, shown in a study, is that roughly 70 percent of high school students entering college claiming to be born again abandon their faith after college. This is a cost that is too high to pay! When choosing whether college is the right option or alternatives—like apprenticeship, business ownership, Bible schools or Christian Universities, or online schools—in many instances, alternatives are the better choice.[178]

PERHAPS THE BIGGEST COST IS A STUDY SHOWING THAT ROUGHLY 70 PERCENT OF HIGH SCHOOL STUDENTS ENTERING COLLEGE CLAIMING TO BE BORN AGAIN ABANDON THEIR FAITH AFTER COLLEGE. THIS IS A COST THAT IS TOO HIGH TO PAY!

In October 2021, The Foundation for Research on Equal Opportunity published a study, "Is College Worth It? A Comprehensive Return on Investment Analysis."[179] Recognizing that most students elect to attend college in order to obtain better, more lucrative jobs, the report concluded that the return on investment ("ROI") varies vastly depending on the institution attended and academic programs studied. Specifically, the study concluded that:

The median bachelor's degree is worth $306,000 for students who graduate on time. But the median conceals enormous variation. Some fields of study, including engineering, computer science, nursing, and economics, can produce returns of $1 million or more. Others, including art, music, religion, and psychology, often have a zero or even negative net financial value. When accounting for the risk that a student will take longer than four years to finish college, or drop out entirely, median ROI drops to $129,000. Twenty-eight percent of bachelor's degree programs have negative ROI when adjusting for the risk of non-completion. If ROI is adjusted to reflect the underlying cost of education, not just tuition charges, the share of non-performing programs rises to 37%.

What are the average total costs of college? The cost of attendance ("COA") refers to the total cost of tuition and fees, books and supplies, as well as room and board for those students living on campus. COA does not include transportation costs, daily living expenses, student loan interest, etc. According to the Education Data Initiative, a team of researchers whose mission is to collect data and statistics about the U.S. education system, the ultimate price of the average bachelor's degree may be as high as $400,000.[180] Consider the following statistics as of January 27, 2022:

- The average cost of attendance for a student living on campus at a public 4-year in-state institution is $25,487 per year or $101,948 over 4 years.
- Out-of-state students pay $43,161 per year or $172,644 over 4 years; traditional private university students pay $53,217 per year or $212,868 over 4 years.

- While 4 years is the traditional period to earn a bachelor's degree, just 39% of students graduate within 4 years.
- Sixty percent of bachelor's degree earners graduate within 6 years, totaling an average of $152,922 for the cost of attendance.
- Students unable to work full-time stand to lose $40,612 in yearly income.
- Student borrowers pay an average of $1,898 in interest each year, and the average student borrower spends roughly 20 years paying off their loans.
- Considering lost income and loan interest, the ultimate price of the average bachelor's degree may be as high as $400,000.

Student Loan Debt Statistics[181]

- The collective debt of 44.7 million American student loan borrowers is $1.56 trillion.
- 30% of all adults take on some form of educational debt.
- 93% of those adults with outstanding debt have student loan debt.
- $32,731 is the national average individual student loan debt.
- The average student loan payment is $393.
- $85 billion of collective student loan debt is outstanding.
- 20% of people who owe student loan debt are behind on payments.
- 10.8% of student loans are in delinquency or default (90+ days overdue).
- Nationally, outstanding debt averages $22,500 per person.
- 30% of people with outstanding student loan debt had deferred loans prior to the onset of the COVID-19 pandemic.

- 23% of adults who borrow outside financial assistance use it to make payments on student loans.
- $404 is the average monthly amount householders under 40 spend on student loan repayments, which exceeds what the average family spends on monthly groceries.
- 96% of student loan borrowers report putting off at least one major life/financial milestone due to their student debt, e.g., home-buying, starting a family, and long-term savings.
- 68% of borrowers say their student loan debts are the cause of their financial struggle.
- 30% of all adults have incurred some type of educational debt.
- 54% of young adults who go to college graduate in some type of debt, usually student loan debt.
- College-educated adults under 30 owe more student loan debt than any other age group.
- College-educated adults over 60 owe the least amount of student loan debt.
- 73% of graduate degree holders under the age of 30 have outstanding educational debt.
- 68% of graduate degree holders aged 30 to 44 have outstanding educational debt compared to 48% of those aged 45-59.

Role of Apprenticeship and Other Alternatives

Unless the skill a student wants to perform requires a degree, many degrees offer no advantage to the worker. Business owners and salespersons fare better financially, so would the funds invested in school be better spent in business or investment? Hands-on skill in many positions is better than a degree. If you are planning on performing brain surgery, then yes, a degree is required. We need to rethink education and invest in skills rather than ideologies taught in universities. Apprenticeship may be the best investment of time and money for many.

> Apprenticeships put you to work immediately, and therefore you need to learn the required skills as quickly as possible. You are constantly exposed to the work environment every day, and this helps you to pick up the required knowledge for the job. University, however, provides a broader set of knowledge.
>
> As an apprentice, you are given the opportunity to learn by "doing" which can give you a richer and better understanding of the practical aspects of your role. Apprentices are constantly learning new skills on the job and have the opportunity to apply their learning every day.
>
> University prepares you for the workforce, but you normally wait years before you are able to apply your skills. University involves learning a lot of theoretical knowledge which can vary in applicability to your field. This is usually carried out in the form of lectures and reading and assessed through verbal and written assignments. Exams are also conducted for most units depending on what you study, and these form a large portion of your grade.[182]

Don't assume that the old adage, "Go to college and get a good job" applies today. We should prepare youth by giving them a strong foundation in God's Word, developing their character, alongside the basics of reading, writing, and arithmetic, and exploring science from a biblical worldview. The final step is apprenticeship, vocational, or higher education as their God-given giftings become evident. When we seek a vocation for ourselves or our children based strictly on money rather than God's calling, we are not seeking first the Kingdom of God, and it misaligns priorities. God knows the future, and He made each person with giftings and has a place for them to apprentice and to prepare them for their destiny. Life preparation starts in the home, extends to the classroom, manifests in life with consistent application, and ends in promotion. Financial rewards follow seeking first the Kingdom of God and "all these things are then added." Purpose is always more important than finances and will produce fulfillment, balanced living, *and* financial sufficiency.

GOVERNMENTS
GONE MAD

Since there is no freedom without responsibility, how do you take people's freedom? You get them to give up their responsibility, to no longer care, remove their purpose, and give them just enough rope to hang themselves. Remove men as protectors, remove women as nurturers, make children vulnerable, get youth addicted to drugs, and pay entitlements to fix broken people until the nation is broke. Enslave them to debt. Take their rights; establish a totalitarian state.

This is the short list of what has happened in America. We are in the last two steps. Take their rights. If we want to fix what's wrong, it goes back to taking responsibility, to caring and regaining our purpose, which can only come from God. It is immoral not to work. Scripture instructs us to work with our own two hands that we may have something to give. Further, it instructs that if a person won't work, they shouldn't eat. Whenever we give the government or anyone our responsibility, we lose freedom. There is no greater gift than freedom.

> For a democracy to be effective, the people must be disposed toward civic virtue and possess a certain moral standard.

Since the 1960s, the United States has been like a sick patient who cannot identify the cause of his affliction. Para-Marxist ideas have been deeply planted into American society and are spreading virtually unchecked.

After the unrest of the 1960s, the rebels who had pushed for revolution began entering academia. They infiltrated and corrupted the organizations that are crucial for the maintenance of the morality of Western society, including the church, the government, the education system, the legislative and judicial bodies, the art world, the media, and NGOs.

In 1966, a Columbia University sociologist couple, members of the Democratic Socialists of America, strategized a plan. The core concept was to bloat the public welfare system and push states into bankruptcy. They knew they could exhaust state funds by encouraging people to apply for benefits in huge numbers since the people receiving them would far exceed the available benefits. If states could be driven to the brink of collapse, the government could rescue them and reform the system, giving more control to the government and moving it toward a socialized system. This was implemented by the National Welfare Organization from 1966 to 1975, and the numbers of single parent families receiving benefits during that time rose drastically, from 4.3 million to 10.8 million. The number of people receiving benefits in New York went from 200,000 to 1.1 million over a 10-year period![183]

At the same time, the American family went into a tailspin. Divorce also doubled, and children, in many instances, became wards of the state.[184] As we demand that the government "pay" or "provide" for or nurture our children, the more they become the property of the one that feeds and cares for them. Parents handed over their greatest gift, their children, and the states have been all too happy to indoctrinate them using the teachers' unions controlled by socialists.

"...One of the forty-five communist goals is to 'capture' one or both of the political parties in the United States. The Communist Party saw that this could be achieved using a small number of people and organizing them to create 'crises' and 'revolutions' that could be used to the Party's advantage. Lenin once said that labor unions are 'the transmission belts from the Communist Party to the masses.' The communists found as long as they controlled labor unions, they controlled a large number of the votes. As long as they controlled the votes, they could make elected officials and lawmakers do their bidding. Ordinary workers are forced to join the labor unions in order to maintain their basic rights and interests, and thus they become the unions' pawns. An identical principle is at work when paying protection fees to organized crime syndicates."[185]

For too long, the average person would have rejected these notions as conspiracy or "that could never happen." This is mostly because we have lived in freedom so long, we take it for granted, like a marriage partner. We slowly give up a little at a time, so it's not so noticeable. Recently though, things are speeding up quickly, and people are taking notice! Lockdowns, demands, censorship, government in our face or on our face with masks, have opened eyes. One of the reasons we struggle to believe is we wouldn't think such evil, but we are certain that these influences are not natural.

"We know that we are from God, and the whole world lies in the power of the evil one" (1 John 5:19, ESV).

George Washington was sworn in at Federal Hall in Lower Manhattan. He said prophetically there: "The propitious smiles of Heaven can never be expected on a nation that disregards the eternal rules of order and right which Heaven itself hath ordained."

On 9/11, when the towers fell, a shock wave went from Ground Zero to Federal Hall, where cracks were opened up in the foundation of that historic building.

Coincidence or symbol of a metaphorical crack in the foundation of our nation?

According to the Congressional record, the first official act of the newly formed government in 1789 took place when the first-ever joint session of Congress with an acting President met for a time of prayer to dedicate the nation to God. And where did that take place? At St. Paul's Chapel, which stands at the corner of Ground Zero. At that time, the church actually owned the land where the Twin Towers eventually rose into the New York skyline—all on one deed. So, one of our nation's greatest tragedies—which indeed changed life as we know it—took place on the very ground where that nation was founded/consecrated.

The current entrance to St. Paul's is the opposite of where Washington and Congress would have entered. They would have gone in on the side that is now a courtyard, literally looking out on Ground Zero. This fits what Cahn believes to be a biblical principle: "The nation's ground of consecration will become the ground of its judgment."

In 2001, this little chapel was called "the miracle of 9/11," because it was one of the only buildings around Ground Zero not destroyed. How was that possible when much bigger buildings were taken down by the attack? Because it was saved from harm by a sycamore tree—the one that was uprooted, just as the sycamores in the Isaiah 9:10 terrorist attack. The tree absorbed much of the blow of flying debris."[186]

Isaiah 9 shares the judgment of Israel because of their sin:

... Who say in pride and in arrogance of heart: "The bricks have fallen, but we will build with dressed stones; the sycamores have been cut down, but we will put cedars in their place."
—Isaiah 9:9-10 (EVS)

Rabbi Jonathan Cahn, a friend, has shared many times in our church and in his books that God is trying to wake us up and warn us by what he calls "harbingers." He believes the sycamore tree at Ground Zero was a sign, a harbinger from a loving God, to warn and save the church of St. Paul's. At the location that our nation was consecrated to God, the Twin Towers fell, and the sycamore tree was cut down, protecting the place of our nation's consecration. And what did they plant in its place? A cedar tree! The cedar did not live. Anytime mankind tries to plant its own agendas instead of God's, we suffer death.

I have toured this small, peaceful chapel and seen the pictures of history, of those rescue workers who ministered to people in its walls. It became a symbol of hope that if we return and become consecrated to God, we can reclaim our spiritual heritage and nation.

"If all of this is indeed more than coincidence, as Cahn declares, then why? What is the basis for a comparison between ancient Israel and modern-day America? Cahn argues that in the history of mankind, only two nations have been founded upon biblical principles and specifically dedicated to the God of the Holy Bible—Israel and us."[187]

Interestingly, during the COVID challenges and the turmoil of the BLM and Antifa riots, in June of 2020, President Donald Trump held a Bible in his hand and declared faith would see us through the turmoil. As he stood in front of St John's church in Washington, D.C., after demonstrators had set fire to the church building the night before, his declaration noted that the church was lit on fire in the basement and that the Lincoln Memorial and the World War II Memorial were desecrated with graffiti. He also spoke of a man beaten to death by the protesting mob and the death of a black federal officer, Patrick Underwood. "These are not peaceful acts of protest. These are acts of domestic terror. The destruction of innocent life and the spilling of innocent blood is an offense to humanity and a crime against God," he said. Trump vowed to restore the rule of law and protect business owners who were suffering the impact of looting.[188]

The President was met with staunch criticism, driven by the media and even from the Episcopalian church. "The Rev. Mariann Budde, bishop of the Episcopalian Diocese of Washington, said Trump 'took the symbols sacred to our tradition and stood in front of a house of prayer in full expectation that would be a celebratory moment.' White House Press Secretary, Kayleigh McEnany said the President wanted to send 'a very powerful message that we will not be overcome by looting, rioting, by burning' and compared Trump's visit to British Prime Minister Winston Churchill's inspection of bomb damage during the London Blitz in World War II."[189]

Honestly, this is exactly the approach I believe our nation's founders, who met repeatedly in churches, would have taken, including Washington. Yet in today's climate, it was met with criticism of the police and the President, and with cries to defund the police and impeach the President resounding from actual clergy members. Many of us are shocked by governments and also by the churches embracing anti-biblical ideologies and agendas, violence toward the innocent, abortion, and LGBTQ. Jesus warned that if we are lukewarm, He would spew us out of His mouth. Churches do not have to engage in politics per se, but morality is mandated, and exposing anti-biblical actions are basic to the faith.

Sometimes, churches are confused about how to navigate the cultural storms and provide real answers. Many pastors bought into the BLM narrative with good intentions without examining the BLM website, which clearly laid out their objectives: to destroy the nuclear family and drive a Marxist system of government, as two of the three founders who identify as queer clearly stated.[190] Faced with these decisions myself, I researched their site, and it was clear this was an agenda to disrupt faith and family and to drive Marxism. It was there in broad daylight on their website, but pastors jumped on board to support and march with the Marxist ideology to destroy the family, of all ethnicities, without checking the foundations. I support that pastors wanted to stand with the Black community, but this was the antithesis of help. The nuclear family is the answer, not the problem. These same churches had done very little to give their church a biblical Kingdom worldview, and to confuse matters worse, they planned based on propaganda instead of facts, facts which appeared on BLM's site and in other media.

"In a recently surfaced 2015 interview, one of the three Black Lives Matter co-founders declared that she and another co-founder are trained Marxists." "Co-founder Patrisse Cullors told Cosmo that Assata Shakur is one of the leaders who inspired her. Shakur's real name is Joanne Chesimard, and she is wanted by the FBI as a domestic terrorist for murdering a police officer, escaping prison, and hiding in Cuba for decades."[191] Before getting a PR makeover, BLM's site claimed to "foster a queer affirming network and opposing the tight grip of heteronormative thinking." [In case you're wondering, heteronormative means "of, relating to, or based on the attitude that heterosexuality is the only normal and natural expression of sexuality."[192]] They oppose accepting as normal a mother and a father in a marriage. The organization vows to do the work to dismantle cisgender privilege" [Cisgender describes a person whose gender identity and sex assigned at birth are the same.] This is all leftist code for an anti-family agenda. BLM's co-founder said, "We disrupt the Western-prescribed nuclear family structure requirement."[193] Is this what pastors support? Or better yet, does the Word of God support it?

Corporations poured billions into the organization, and yet no Black communities will likely ever see the benefit of those funds. Be sure that Marxists organizing across the world will be the only benefactors. Pastors' support would go much further in proclaiming the Gospel in their local communities by building strong programs to teach people how to develop skills needed to succeed than funding organizations like BLM, whose monies end up making Marxist founders rich but not helping children who are hurting in its communities. Sadly, thousands of minority businesses were destroyed during the BLM and Antifa riots. This was exactly what Marxists prescribe—divide and destroy, then plunder.

When one area of the seven mountains doesn't particularly fill its role, another mountain steps into that area and must rise to accommodate the neglect. When parents don't assume their responsibility, they abdicate it to government. When churches don't stand up for biblical truth and get caught up in virtue signaling instead of the Kingdom of God, the Good News is not preached, and lives are not transformed. And just as wrong, people are led into lies and error because it is culturally popular, even if its intention is to silence religious freedoms. Make no mistake, Marxism has always been an enemy to the true Gospel of Jesus Christ.

> **WHEN PARENTS DON'T ASSUME THEIR RESPONSIBILITY, THEY ABDICATE IT TO GOVERNMENT. WHEN CHURCHES DON'T STAND UP FOR BIBLICAL TRUTH AND GET CAUGHT UP IN VIRTUE SIGNALING INSTEAD OF THE KINGDOM OF GOD, THE GOOD NEWS IS NOT PREACHED, AND LIVES ARE NOT TRANSFORMED.**

The Kingdom of God is established on justice. God is just, and Jesus is the great equalizer. There is neither Jew nor Greek, male nor female... or any other ethnicity that holds a higher position in the Kingdom. Equality is basic to the Kingdom. There are only two kingdoms. Either we are with Jesus or against Him. One gathers, the other scatters. All ethnicities are expressions of a loving Father God who gave us beautiful expressions of Himself in our uniqueness. We are not to be divided. People are people, and we all have the same needs, regardless of our skin tone. The Equality Act and similar legislation attempt to equate skin color with sin. It is an insult to the Black community that evildoers attempt to manipulate the struggle for civil rights with LGBTQ rights. Sadly, there are those who embrace sinful sexual behavior and use whoever they can to drive their agenda to force those who believe the Bible to hire transgenders and homosexuals at their ministries.

Our fight must be for the truth of God's Word and His established order of equality, freedom, and family. Media and our courts have confused and exasperated justice. People have lost any trust in media or the courts to rule on behalf of law and side with truth or equality. Villains are glorified and justified as "misunderstood" in Disney's portrayals. It's no longer right versus wrong or truth versus a lie. In this way, children are confused as to how to live life and whether there are any absolute values. They reject the Word of God because they have been trained to do so, because it does offer values that are not wishy-washy. You can't do your own thing or define your own rules and follow Christ. Rooting for the villain is how media leads our culture into compromises and lawlessness. And pastors who don't clearly take a stand with God's truth do the same.

Recall at America's dedication:

Washington's warning was, if we would begin to depart from God, He would remove His blessings, His prosperity, and His protection from our nation. After Washington's address, the government, the House, the Senate, and America's first President traveled on foot to Saint Paul's Chapel. No one knows exactly what was said inside, but we do know the entire government was on their knees praying and consecrating this nation to God. In the chapel, there is also a plaque above Washington's pew with the words *"Almighty God, we make our earnest prayer that you will keep the United States in Holy protection."*[194]

"America's first Presidential Inauguration—that of President George Washington—incorporated seven specific religious activities, including [1] the use of the Bible to administer the oath; [2] affirming the religious nature of the oath by adding the prayer "So help me God!" to the oath; [3] inaugural prayers offered by the President; [4] religious content in the inaugural address; [5] civil leaders calling the people to prayer or acknowledgement of God; [6] inaugural worship services attended en masse by Congress as an official part of congressional activities; and [7] clergy-led inaugural prayers."[195]

We have wandered far from these principles, and the further we have moved from God, the rottener things have become. *"God is not mocked, for whatever one sows, that will he also reap"* (Galatians 6:7b, ESV). This applies to nations as well. God cannot bless us anymore than He could Israel when she chose to reject Him and take up the idol worship of the land. We must pray for America and act.

RECLAIMING THE GOVERNMENT

"In America, the law is king."

—Thomas Paine[196]

The apostle Paul petitioned his government by demanding his rights as a Roman citizen when he was about to be flogged. "Is it legal for you to flog a Roman citizen who hasn't been found guilty?" When those in authority recognized he was a citizen with rights, they immediately withdrew. For too long, we have trusted others with our destiny and rights. Pleasure and convenience can be the theft of standards and morality. We must know our rights as citizens in God's Kingdom and our nation and speak up. As a citizen of America, we should use our vote and petitioning power and contact state lawmakers since they are the ones who make laws in our state and local governments. These are our rights as citizens. A lawmaker remarked, "We don't fear paid lobbyists or even average citizens, but we greatly fear mama-bears; grand-mama bears are even more fierce."[197]

Your citizenship as a believer is in the Kingdom of God. Even though we are not of this world, we are in it, and the government you and I live in does make a difference! I have traveled the world and observed the empty faces, cold and lifeless, of those shuffling through the streets of communist countries and dictatorships. The people have little hope and no dreams, as reflected on their hollow faces.

We ministered in a nation that had imprisoned several pastors for five years. They were released and eventually given an opportunity to host a meeting to teach people about family and finances. The Bible was allowed as one of the sources of information for the trainings. Positive presentations of the country, with great appreciation, accompanied the teachings to assure the government that the Christ-centered meetings honored the opportunity. Thousands of young people filled the large auditorium and fervently worshiped God. Freedom to worship in a setting that had never been allowed in their lifetime caused a response like none I had ever witnessed.

Those who have come from pain and suffering have an appreciation of freedom. Governments may attempt to oppress and even martyr church members, but they cannot remove the human spirit when the Kingdom of God invades the hearts of men, women, and children. *"It is for freedom that Christ has set us free. Stand firm, then, and do not let yourselves be burdened again by a yoke of slavery"* (Galatians 5:1, NIV).

God's Kingdom and laws supersede all governments. The Scripture is clear that God instructs us to obey the laws of the land, pray for those in leadership, and "render to Caesar" what belongs to him. It is also clear that we are to render to God what is His and not to allow Caesar, or government, to take that which belongs to God. What doesn't belong to government is your worship or to be coerced to violate your conscience or moral or religious convictions that are based on Scripture. Nor are we to allow our voices to be silenced when it comes to sharing the Kingdom of God. This is clearly illustrated in the disciples' rejection of governmental demands made of them to stop preaching the Gospel. Peter and the other apostles were brought before the Sanhedrin (the council).

> **ULTIMATELY, WE WILL STAND BEFORE THE THRONE OF GOD AND GIVE AN ACCOUNT FOR OUR LIVES AND CHOICES, AND SO WILL EVERY DICTATOR, DESPOT, TYRANT, AND GOVERNMENT LEADER.**

> *"We gave you strict orders not to teach in this name," he said. "Yet you have filled Jerusalem with your teaching and are determined to make us guilty of this man's blood." Peter and the other apostles replied: "We must obey God rather than human beings!"*
> —Acts 5:28-29 (NIV)

We ought to obey God rather than men. Paul possessed the same boldness in declaring,

> *"I care very little if I am judged by you or by any human court; indeed, I do not even judge myself. My conscience is clear, but that does not make me innocent. It is the Lord who judges me."*
> —1 Corinthians 4:3-4 (NIV)

Ultimately, we will stand before the throne of God and give an account for our lives and choices, and so will every dictator, despot, tyrant, and government leader.

Our Founders did not intend that congressional leaders or the President would become professional politicians. Those who served were to devote time to government service and then return to their civilian lives to live under the laws they had passed. Unfortunately, politicians have made a career of passing laws from which they seem exempt. Term limits would go a long way as a solution to ensure those who serve have accountability.

Likewise, campaign financing needs overhauled to prevent the ones with the most money from being the only political contenders. Additionally, many politicians must borrow large amounts from private individuals or give corporate favors to finance their campaigns. This becomes a conflict of interest and too often directs their vote instead of what is best for the American public. Politicians answer to their debtors and contributors more than their constituents. In this way, PACS, donors, and indebtedness become a controlling factor in electing officials. The borrower becomes a servant to the lender. Lobbyists and corporations direct votes and buy votes and legislators.

Lobbyists and nefarious individuals and governments use their influence to entertain, buy, or blackmail candidates caught in compromising situations at parties or gatherings hosted with the intent to entrap politicians. We need not search far as recent years' headlines are crowded with scandals and abuses, from Epstein and his sordid associations and sex trafficking island to Democrat Congressman Eric Swallwell's involvement with a Chinese CCP spy. Our leaders, many compromised, have given American interests away to benefit their own lives, foundations, and other nations. Honest ones are attacked so viciously that many good people want little to do with government service. We must change this to protect our legal system.

In the last few years, the mandates and demands of government have caused a public outcry across the world. We have spoken to leaders across the globe, and each time we hear, "At least you have a Constitution!" Thankfully, we do! There is a very large difference between countries that have democratic governments and America, that exists as a Republic and has a Constitution. We must know the difference and our rights or they will be taken from us. "We the people" are protected by the Constitution and given rights that are greater than our President, Congress, or officials. It is not a majority rule! We must wake up and realize the Constitution is in danger of being dissolved. Popular talk shows hosts, like "The View" hosts, have called for its removal, as well as *The Atlantic's* article, "Do We Really Need the Constitution?" I offer a resounding "Yes, we do—to protect us from tyrants!" Without it, whatever party is in position, their votes rule. And that is dangerous, as we have witnessed.

> "DO WE REALLY NEED THE CONSTITUTION?" I OFFER A RESOUNDING "YES, WE DO—TO PROTECT US FROM TYRANTS!" WITHOUT IT, WHATEVER PARTY IS IN POSITION, THEIR VOTES RULE. AND THAT IS DANGEROUS, AS WE HAVE WITNESSED.

Make sure you grasp the following and teach it to your children. Reclaim the rule of law, not mob rule or allowing the media's shenanigans to trick and deceive our nation as Satan did in the Garden of Eden, stealing freedom and replacing it with tyranny.

RECLAIM THE RULE OF LAW, NOT MOB RULE OR ALLOWING THE MEDIA'S SHENANIGANS TO TRICK AND DECEIVE OUR NATION AS SATAN DID IN THE GARDEN OF EDEN, STEALING FREEDOM AND REPLACING IT WITH TYRANNY.

The Constitution is the supreme law of the United States of America. In fact, it is the longest surviving government charter in the world. The Constitution has withstood the test of time "because its framers wisely separated and balanced governmental powers to safeguard the interests of majority rule and minority rights, of liberty and equality, and of the federal and state governments."[198] This founding document sets forth the national framework of our government from the creation of the three branches of government to its 27 amendments. The fact that the Constitution itself created a government of the people, by the people, and for the people is demonstrated in its first three words—"We the People."

In advocating for the ratification of the Constitution, Alexander Hamilton wrote in "The Federalist No. 33":

> But it is said that the laws of the Union are to be the SUPREME LAW of the land. But what inference can be drawn from this, or what would they amount to, if they were not to be supreme? It is evident they would amount to nothing. A LAW, by the very meaning of the term, includes supremacy. It is a rule which those to whom it is prescribed are bound to observe. This results from every political association. If individuals enter into a state of society, the laws of that society must be the supreme regulator of their conduct.[199]

The Rule of Law—which is integral to the Constitution—is the keystone principle "under which all persons, institutions, and entities are accountable to laws that are publicly promulgated, equally enforced, independently adjudicated, and consistent with international human rights principles.[200] The Rule of Law limits the powers of a government pursuant to its constitution "to prevent dictatorship and protect the rights of the people."[201] Even the United Nations has acknowledged the Rule of Law and defined it almost identically:

> A principle of governance in which all persons, institutions and entities, public and private, including the State itself, are accountable to laws that are publicly promulgated, equally enforced and independently adjudicated, and which are consistent with international human rights norms and standards. It requires, as well, measures to ensure adherence to the principles of supremacy of law, equality before the law, accountability to the law, fairness in the application of the law, separation of powers, participation in decision-making, legal certainty, avoidance of arbitrariness and procedural and legal transparency.[202]

The Constitution has assigned the responsibility to the courts to interpret the Constitution's meaning, as well as the meaning of any laws passed by Congress. "The Federalist No. 78" states that if any law passed by Congress conflicts with the Constitution:

> The Constitution ought to be preferred to the statute, the intention of the people to the intention of their agents. Nor does this conclusion by any means suppose a superiority of the judicial to the legislative power. It only supposed

that the power of the people is superior to both; and that where the will of the legislature, declared in its statutes, stands in opposition to that of the people, declared in the Constitution, the judges ought to be governed by the latter rather than the former.[203]

The importance of the Rule of Law is perhaps best reflected in the oaths taken by all federal employees, including the President, Supreme Court Justices, and members of Congress. According to the Constitution, Article II, Section 1, Clause 8 [emphasis added]:

Before he enter on the Execution of his Office, he shall take the following Oath or Affirmation: I do solemnly swear (or affirm) that I will faithfully execute the Office of President of the United States, and will to the best of my ability, ***preserve, protect and defend the Constitution of the United States***.

Similarly, United States Supreme Court Justices take the following oath:

I, _____, do solemnly swear (or affirm) that I will administer justice without respect to persons, and do equal right to the poor and to the rich, and that ***I will faithfully and impartially discharge and perform all the duties incumbent upon me as _____ under the Constitution and laws of the United States***. So help me God.[204]

Other than the President, this oath is now taken by all federal employees:

> I, _____, do solemnly swear (or affirm) that *I will support and defend the Constitution of the United States* against all enemies, foreign and domestic; that I will bear true faith and allegiance to the same; that I take this obligation freely, without any mental reservation or purpose of evasion; and that I will well and faithfully discharge the duties of the office on which I am about to enter. *So help me God.*[205]

The American system of government is not one of majority rule. The Rule of Law maintains that fundamental constitutional freedoms, particularly freedom of religion, speech, equal treatment, and due process of law are deemed so important that not even a majority should be allowed to change them. Further, the Rule of Law embodies the principle that all people and institutions are subject to and accountable to law that is fairly applied and enforced. No one is above the law. Not the President, not Justices on the Supreme Court, and not the members of Congress.

Rights given by God:

> We hold these Truths to be self-evident, that all Men are created equal, that they are endowed by their Creator with certain unalienable Rights, that among these are Life, Liberty, and the Pursuit of Happiness—That to secure these Rights, Governments are instituted among Men, deriving their just Powers from the Consent of the Governed, that whenever any

Form of Government becomes destructive of these Ends, it is the Right of the People to alter or to abolish it, and to institute new Government, laying its Foundation on such Principles, and organizing its Powers in such Form, as to them shall seem most likely to affect their Safety and Happiness.[206]

The Constitution and Declaration of Independence were inspired by God, as demonstrated by the same biblical principles:

> *Now the Lord is the Spirit, and where the Spirit of the Lord is, there is freedom.*
>
> —2 Corinthians 3:17 (NIV)

> *So if the Son sets you free, you will be free indeed.*
>
> —John 8:36 (NIV)

> *It is for freedom that Christ has set us free. Stand firm, then, and do not let yourselves be burdened again by a yoke of slavery.*
>
> —Galatians 5:1 (NIV)

> *In him and through faith in him we may approach God with freedom and confidence.*
>
> —Ephesians 3:12 (NIV)

> *I will walk about in freedom, for I have sought out your precepts.*
>
> —Psalm 119:45

> *You, my brothers, were called to be free. But do not use your freedom to indulge the flesh; rather, serve one another humbly in love.*
>
> —Galatians 5:13 (NIV)

But now that you have been set free from sin and become slaves of God, the benefit you reap leads to holiness, and the result is eternal life.

—Romans 6:22 (NIV)

Live as free people, but do not use your freedom to cover-up for evil; live as God's slaves.

—1 Peter 2:16 (NIV)

"I have the right to do anything," you say—but not everything is beneficial. "I have the right to do anything—but I will not be mastered by anything."

—1 Corinthians 6:12 (NIV)

There can be no freedom without responsibility. We must be involved to remain free to worship God without harassment from government and to raise our children with our parental rights protected. The preservation of our freedoms cannot be taken for granted or placed in the hands of those who do not honor God or His Word. It is our God-given right and duty to vote for candidates who best reflect the will of God and His Word. We need to know what is going on and to stay informed. Look at voter's guides, and make calls or email your legislators. It's easy to find them at senate. gov and house.gov. Local government is extremely important, and voting for or against issues in your state can determine how your community lives and what wrong behavior is held back or permitted. Fair and honest elections are crucial to our republic. Volunteering to be poll workers and holding authorities in check, again, is our responsibility.

We are called to pray for our nation and to speak our voices for righteousness. The threats to our Constitution have never been greater. Get involved in government. Run for office or support someone who is running. The local government and school boards are extremely important. What happens in the local community impacts the nation. We must stop taking freedom for granted and · reengage the culture in this most important mountain, next to faith and family. It's time to shine our light from sea to shining sea.

MEDIA CONTROL, CENSORSHIP, AND SEX

It's all in the words used! Words have power, and they can acquit, condemn, accuse, and justify. They can paint beautiful pictures to make a murderer seem justified or a saint seem like a swindler. They can be spun to sell swampland and form opinions. One of the tactics of our spiritual adversary is to use words to accuse the innocent and acquit the guilty; to harm people with evil and then point the finger of blame at God. The goal is to confuse the truth and make it hard to determine the good guys from the bad guys. If there is any group who has dealt in misinformation, lies, propaganda, and suppression of the truth, it has been the media.

And today, that media mountain doesn't stand alone, but it includes the mountain of arts and entertainment. In the past, the arts could exist without the media. But no longer! The media is now the engine that entertainment travels through. In the guise of entertainment, political agendas and cancel culture are driven by celebrities, athletes, and even comedians, and comedy isn't funny anymore. And journalism has become more like entertainment than fact-based investigative journalism. COVID lockdowns caused many performance arts to shut down or take to the Internet for performances and viewings. Cancel culture has been driven by the joint efforts of the arts and media by controlling the industry in a monopoly like fashion.

"The media industry covers a wide variety of areas—advertising, broadcasting and networking, news, print and publication, digital, recording, and motion pictures—and each has its own associated infrastructure." The top companies are: Apple ($2.74 trillion), Disney ($238.21 billion), Comcast ($213.75 billion), Netflix ($152.77 billion), AT&T ($140.11 billion), and Sony ($114.10 billion).[207]

Additionally, Internet and social media giants control information, news, and even what information pops up in searches. "Google has dominated the search engine market, maintaining a 92.47 percent market share as of June 2021."[208] Want to exclude information or ideas from opinions? Control the flow of available information, and you can control the narrative. From brainwashing with slick marketing campaigns to slapping those on the wrist who don't line up with "their" rules—rules that allow terrorist groups to post but censor the sitting President of the capital of the free world—media is responsible for the words that sell the story.

Their words market organizations that kill millions of babies in the womb, with names like "Planned Parenthood." They create words that stir emotions coupled with human stories to drive their beautifully crafted words, like equity, inclusion, diversity, kindness, love is love, and ascribe new meaning to these words. Margaret Sanger's Planned Parenthood didn't sell as well when it was called "American Birth Control League" and dubbed the sterilization movement. It needed a PR makeover, and, voila, Planned Parenthood was the new name. Those peddling bondages have learned to craft words to convey warm fuzzies with their messages.

We are shocked daily to find out that information we were assured was simply conspiracy theory or misinformation over the past five years not only had validity, but also because it had validity, it was suppressed. Those who tried to share this "forbidden" information in public discussion, on social media, and on other media formats were called conspiracy theorists or, worse, "terrorists" and had their accounts banned and their information silenced. Even seemingly conservative news outlets like Fox News interrupted and abruptly shut down Senator Newt Gingrich for using George Soros's name on the network in September 2020:

> …Gingrich argued that money provided by the billionaire progressive activist Soros was helping to fuel riots in multiple U.S. cities throughout the summer following the police killing of George Floyd in Minneapolis.
>
> "Progressive district attorneys are anti-police, pro-criminal, and overwhelmingly elected with George Soros's money. And they're a major cause of the violence we're seeing because they keep putting the violent criminals back on the street," Gingrich said Wednesday.
>
> "I'm not sure we need to bring George Soros into this," said co-host Melissa Francis.
>
> "I was going to say you get the last word, Speaker," Faulkner said.

"He paid for it. I mean, why can't we discuss the fact that millions of dollars ..." Gingrich said before co-host Marie Harf injected.

"No, he didn't. I agree with Melissa. George Soros doesn't need to be a part of this conversation," Harf said.

"OK. So, it's verboten," Gingrich replied.

"OK. We're going to move on," Faulkner said.[209]

This embarrassment at Fox caused a huge backlash resulting in an apology from Faulkner.

Whoever pays the bills controls the narrative, whether it's pharmaceutical ads that run during programming or billionaires who inadvertently pay to shape culture, politics, society, or themselves into the image they desire.

WHOEVER PAYS THE BILLS CONTROLS THE NARRATIVE, WHETHER IT'S PHARMACEUTICAL ADS THAT RUN DURING PROGRAMMING OR BILLIONAIRES WHO INADVERTENTLY PAY TO SHAPE CULTURE, POLITICS, SOCIETY, OR THEMSELVES INTO THE IMAGE THEY DESIRE.

In 2016, the shock of President Trump winning against Hillary Clinton created a backlash from the Obama Administration and Mark Zuckerberg of Facebook, along with other marketers who began to shadow ban and censor accounts to control the narrative and ultimately influence the election outcomes of 2020. They took it a step further and even paid for mail-in ballot boxes akin to a money laundering scheme, infecting the nation's election under the guise of "fair elections." What's fair about an election that had more ballots come in than persons living in districts? Never mind truth, the word "fair" made it fair to cheat.

When it came to the Russia Hoax, they hid any messages that questioned whether the Clinton campaign was potentially involved in creating a dirty dossier for political gain. Then former Congressman Devin Nunes was one of the first to be shadow banned by Facebook as he tried to bring the truth forward about the Russia Hoax and the dirty dossier, attributing its origin as bought and paid for, fabricated by the hires and hacks at the Clinton campaign for political gain.

Conversely, when the Hunter Biden laptop from hell filled with horrific sexual images and connections between "Joe Biden and foreign governments receiving favors through Hunter" story was revealed, it was quickly silenced by mainstream media outlets and social media. Anyone who attempted to share the information was censored, including congressional leaders and conservative media outlets—all just before the election. It was labeled misinformation, yet the information was clearly there if anyone was allowed to see it. CEO Devin Nunes said, "We're in the middle of a propaganda war here, and you can't win a war without basic communications architecture, of any kind, whether it be a kinetic war or a propaganda war."[210]

Revelations from Special Counsel John Durham's recent investigations show the Clinton campaign gathered information on Donald Trump prior to the election and then as a sitting President in the White

House and should probably yield the award for the biggest criminal enterprise in our lives if not American history. It's certainly bigger news than the Russian collusion story that turned out to be a hoax. The Clinton campaign, dirty cops, and people with government contracts mined the sitting President's data, and, of course, the media was also tremendously complicit in driving the words that convince.[211]

"The legal watchdog group Judicial Watch obtained documents that show the unnamed technology experts referenced in the Durham probe worked for the Pentagon's Defense Advanced Research Projects Agency from 2016-2021. That division of the Defense Department is responsible for developing new military technologies. This revelation means the government contractor hired by the Clinton campaign continued to work for the government through the entirety of the Trump administration."[212]

The conspiring together of so many organizations and government agencies, politics, and the media is shocking and should send chills up the spine of any freedom loving American. This far exceeds the Nixon campaign's Watergate scandal, yet the mainstream media continues to suppress and hide this and more information from the public.

There can be no freedom without freedom of speech. We may expect these types of activities in communist countries and banana republics—but this in America? Seventeen FBI agents were fired as a result of the Durham investigation, and we continue to see more indictments, yet the media killed and buried such a major story and "trumped up" other accusations against so many without a thread of evidence.

The movie, *The Plot Against the President* details the hideous attack against our sitting President. John Durham has followed the money and uncovered bad actors from Clinton attorneys, Michael Sussman of Perkins and Coie, Fusion GPS, and a host of others involved in infiltrating the Trump campaign and the White House. Will justice make it to the top of those who are ultimately responsible? If not in this life, the next for sure.

Personal attacks waged against Congressman Nunes and his family resulted in Nunes stepping down from Congress and helping to form and lead an alternative social media platform, Truth Social to combat big tech control of information. Sadly though, the media has the power to destroy a person's life, there seems to be nothing that is taboo any longer, and truth doesn't matter to weasels.

We are in an information war, and the increase of technology has made this a techno-war. A war is underway, but many do not know that it is a war of propaganda to steal our freedoms and move us toward the New World Order. A fire is lit in one corner of the world to distract us from seeing the real fire under our noses. A bone is thrown in an opposite direction to get us to chase that story. And while running there to look, we are unwittingly losing territory to those who have been crafting a plan, for many years, to steal our freedom of speech. We are constantly being baited by the political operatives and the media. Their motto of "Never waste a crisis" has turned to "Create a crisis and then milk it for all

> **A WAR IS UNDERWAY, BUT MANY DO NOT KNOW THAT IT IS A WAR OF PROPAGANDA TO STEAL OUR FREEDOMS AND MOVE US TOWARD THE NEW WORLD ORDER.**

its worth." Propaganda and tactics used to fight this information war are detailed in a lecture given by Jennifer Carnevale as follows:

> While war is primarily fought on a battlefield, there are also battles fought in people's minds, known as psychological warfare. The violence of war is one thing, but what about another form of warfare that you can't even see? This is the act of psychological warfare.
>
> Psychological warfare is a broad term, but in all documented cases, the concept uses actions intended to reduce an opponent's morale or mental well-being. The aim is to use manipulative tactics to intimidate or persuade a person or people. This process is usually employed through propaganda… ideas or statements that are false or exaggerated and deliberately spread to influence the masses. The goal of psychological warfare is to intentionally use propaganda to manipulate another and break down their will without using physical force.[213]

To get a clearer picture, let's take a look at some techniques that have been used throughout history.

Psychological warfare uses fear to break down the psychological well-being of an opponent. Here are several techniques that can be used to spread psychological uncertainty, fear, and terror.

> The news is a large information source that all can tap into. Whether it's government run or independently owned, the news has the ability to spread whichever information it chooses. By infiltrating a news source, a population could be tainted by volatile information.

Threats of violence, restrictions of freedom, and control can be made to instill fear in the people. These could be empty threats or threats with true intention. Whatever the case, threatening a group or groups of people can psychologically damage the recipients over time, putting them in a state of constant fear, anxiety, and terror....

A false flag is when a group releases false information or carries out a fake terror attack to instill fear in people. However, the blame is put on another group or organization to gain control over the masses and shift opinion.

While it may not seem like it, films, music, and books can act as tools for psychological warfare. The messages in the media can rewrite history from a new perspective and/or put new ideas in the minds of the populous.[214]

The media's handling of COVID-19 with silencing and censorship of doctors across the world is another story in the chapter on the mountain of health and medicine. Needless to say, these same propaganda techniques were employed to drive fear, make emergency orders, and create laws that will have implications for years to come.

What happened to free speech and real investigative journalism? Our ideas, discussions, and even our faith have been censored and shadow banned by social media companies, YouTube, Facebook, Twitter, and Google searches. I know. I have been shadow banned and received strikes on my YouTube account with warnings to remove my account. The suppression of free speech is real and really dangerous.

Journalism has been replaced with what an ex-CNN executive described as Infotainment, leading to his resignation:

> A 25-year CNN executive has joined Project Veritas as an executive producer. During an exclusive interview released last week, Patrick Davis explained why he left CNN after giving "blood, sweat, and tears" to the network. He told Project Veritas founder James O'Keefe a wide range of issues pushed him to leave CNN but stressed the FBI raid against the homes of Project Veritas journalists was the final straw.
>
> "Do you know what made me decide to come here? It was the FBI raid," Davis explained. "I thought that it was the biggest abridgment to the First Amendment probably in maybe the history of this country. For the FBI to go blowing into the doors of journalists, it was unheard of."
>
> Davis, who previously worked at CNN's Washington bureau, said journalism has become more infotainment than real news, and there is a strong need to return to ethical reporting. He believes it's time to get back to the basics of journalism while noting media outlets need to tell the news without a spin. He added, "Americans can decide for themselves what to think."[215]

We have seen how media has the power to control and manipulate information flow and impact politics and free speech, but these same outlets also have the capability to utilize strong messaging to feed appetites, influence people to make decisions, purchases, commit immoral actions, and explore new ideas about sexuality, family, marriage, and especially impact children.

For instance, the rise of messaging about "equity" and LGBTQ+ across the globe has been driven by media, politics, and educational institutions coupled with the medical community to create an alarming number of young people who are now identifying as gender diverse. Many churches and parachurch ministries also embraced these ideologies claiming to represent "Jesus's tolerance." Did Jesus tolerate sin? No. He died for it and told us to go and sin no more.

"The number of young people who are gender-diverse—including transgender, non-binary, and genderqueer—may be significantly higher than previously thought, according to a new study. Researchers in Pittsburgh found that nearly 1 in 10 students in over a dozen public high schools identified as gender-diverse—five times the current national estimates. Gender diversity refers to people whose gender identities or gender expressions differ from the sexes they were assigned at birth, according to the American Psychological Association."[216] [217]

Why are more young people turning to gender diversity? They have been indoctrinated by adults in media, medicine, and education to do so. Several mountains of influence joined forces in a universal move to create a united voice to drive the populous to embrace and explore gender diversity, catching parents and many opposing educators and medical professionals off guard. Once in place, the machine of media shamed any voice that dare question whether this was in the best interest of young people. (See Chapter 12: Educated to Become Like the Teacher). Serious ethical considerations of the sterilization of children and the impacts of mental and physical health were silenced by the shunning of social media platforms and eventually treated as hate speech.

Even according to an LGBTQ advocate's study in 2020, "40% of LGBTQ respondents seriously considered attempting suicide in the past 12 months, with more than half of transgender and nonbinary youth having seriously considered suicide."[218]

Another study found that the transgender population is "at a higher risk of a variety of mental health problems compared to members of the non-transgender population."[219] According to this study, "Especially alarming, the rate of lifetime suicide attempts across all ages of transgender individuals is estimated at 41%, compared to 5% in the overall U.S. population." Compared to the general population, adults who have undergone sex-reassignment surgery continue to have a higher risk of experiencing poor mental health outcomes. Notably, "sex-reassigned individuals were about 5 times more likely to attempt suicide and about 19 times more likely to die by suicide." Why is the mainstream media not revealing these devastating outcomes?

Sadly, Google and other search engines deliver information that is controlled so real facts and data are harder and harder to find. The fact-checking services are their own hires and subsidiary companies. Brainwashing is the terminology that comes to mind, which is "the process of pressuring someone into adopting radically different beliefs by using systematic and often forcible means."[220]
To see the lack of "equity" and diversity or free speech wrapped in a cloak of inclusivity, just read the YouTube or Facebook guidelines.

Where is the "equity" or protection in silencing conservative alternative viewpoints while allowing others with a far more damaging impact on youth and adults to flourish? The wide acceptance of pornographic sexual imagery in movies, games, music lyrics, videos, and even the streaming of beatings and murderous acts on social media by individuals illustrates our culture's depravity. TikTok challenges have resulted in deaths of children, severe disabilities, and damaging ideologies indoctrinating kids. The picture of what we are experiencing as a culture is captured in Romans 1:26-32 (NIV):

> *Because of this [their rejection of truth], God gave them over to shameful lusts. Even their women exchanged natural sexual relations for unnatural ones. In the same way the men also abandoned natural relations with women and were inflamed with lust for one another. Men committed shameful acts with other men and received in themselves the due penalty for their error.*

> *Furthermore, just as they did not think it worthwhile to retain the knowledge of God, so God gave them over to a depraved mind, so that they do what ought not to be done. They have become filled with every kind of wickedness, evil, greed and depravity. They are full of envy, murder, strife, deceit and malice. They are gossips, slanderers, God-haters, insolent, arrogant and boastful; they invent ways of doing evil; they disobey their parents; they have no understanding, no fidelity, no love, no mercy. Although they know God's righteous decree that those who do such things deserve death, they not only continue to do these very things but also approve of those who practice them.*

Media platforms are influencing behavior and planting seeds of immorality through explicit content and reaping a harvest of data and billions while leaving behind broken lives of followers, and especially children. Another real danger to women and children is the stalking of victims and sharing of content involving children on these outlets.

"The vast majority of online child exploitation reports were found on Facebook, according to new data from the National Center for Missing and Exploited Children's (NCMEC) CyberTipline. The study identified over 20.3 million reported incidents related to child pornography or trafficking (classified as 'child sexual abuse material') on the social media site. By contrast, Google cited 546,704 incidents, Twitter had 65,062, Snapchat reported 144,095, and TikTok found 22,692. Facebook accounted for nearly 95 percent of the 21.7 million reports across all platforms."[221]

MEDIA PLATFORMS ARE INFLUENCING BEHAVIOR AND PLANTING SEEDS OF IMMORALITY THROUGH EXPLICIT CONTENT AND REAPING A HARVEST OF DATA AND BILLIONS WHILE LEAVING BEHIND BROKEN LIVES OF FOLLOWERS, AND ESPECIALLY CHILDREN.

Additionally, platforms like TikTok have challenges that encourage kids (and adults) to emulate disgusting and dangerous behavior. The latest of numerous shocking videos to show up on social media is perhaps the most tragic. In August 2020, a man livestreamed his apparent suicide on Facebook. Since then, the suicide video has gone viral on TikTok and other social media platforms. Youth already facing depression, anxiety, and other mental disorders took their lives as a result of the suicide that became a challenge. Suicide is the number two killer of youth and young adults between the ages of 10-34.[222]

Harvesting of data is another danger that many are not aware of. Clicking to accept terms which no one reads grants social media companies the right to take your data and use it in ways you may be unaware of. If you use the video-sharing platform TikTok, you may be feeding information to the Chinese Communist Party (CCP) intelligence services, warns Casey Fleming, a cyber security expert and CEO of the strategic advisory firm BlackOps Partners.

In 2020, then "U.S. Secretary of State Mike Pompeo warned user data is sent to China. 'It's not possible to have your personal information flow across a Chinese server,' he warned during a British media interview, without that data 'ending up in the hands of the Chinese Communist Party,' which he characterized as an 'evil empire.' TikTok is firmly in the sights of the Trump administration, and they're not letting up."[223] [224] [225]

Peter Schweizer's book *Red-Handed: How American Elites Get Rich Helping China Win* looks at how Microsoft, an American company, aided and abetted the Chinese military.

Previous books by the six-time *New York Times* bestselling investigator and Breitbart News Senior Editor-at-large Peter Schweizer has previously exposed the corrupt dealings of the Clintons, the Bidens, and other members of the American ruling class.

From *Red-Handed:*

> By 2010, Microsoft had taken another step in its tightening association with the Chinese government. The company set up a research laboratory in China to work on artificial intelligence (AI) with a Chinese military university, an essential area of research that would have huge implications for the economy and on the battlefield. Microsoft even

started taking in interns from the People's Liberation Army at its Asian research facility.

According to the book, Microsoft also allowed PLA officials to monitor chats on Skype that might be used for organizing protests and other dissident activity in the country.[226]

The gaming industry is perhaps the most dangerous media because of the interactions with sex and violence as a participant. Want to kill or rape a woman, kill a cop, or act out sexual fantasies of any and all types? Games give the opportunity to become anything you want. The game, Last of Us II, killed the male lead character from Last of Us I and introduced a lead trans-lesbian character as the killer and new lead.[227]

The newly launched Metaverse, Zuckerberg's new empire, is taking role-play to a new level.

Researchers found that users would mimic their virtual avatars in real-life—fashion, demeanor, and, yes, behavior. If a user were to consistently make their avatar act bad, these behaviors could possibly translate to real life. Dangerous in the metaverse could mean dangerous in the real world.

The metaverse has been around for a long time but is now only coming into the mainstream. It's easy to dismiss abuse in the metaverse because "it's not real." However, we forget how it can potentially impact the real world. While the metaverse is not a physically real place, the humans shaping it are.[228]

These avatars created by users have the ability to attend strip clubs and engage in abusive and graphic sexual interactions. They can assault, rape, and harm other's avatars. They can also stalk them and engage in creepy behavior just as in the "real world." This poses a serious danger to people exposed to their bad behavior online, and also it mentally reinforces in the abuser the role of abuser and the gratification of feeding unhealthy appetites and behaviors that eventually will most likely play out in real life. This holds true for gaming in general.

If Facebook happened to be a human being, where would he/she/they currently be? Most likely in prison… for a very long time. The company's transgressions are too numerous to list. But Facebook is not human; it's a company, and a very profitable one at that. In fact, it's now one of the most profitable companies in the world. Facebook's market capitalization has recently surpassed the $1 trillion mark.

When we think of Facebook—more specifically, Facebook, Inc.—we tend to think of a social media platform that is somewhat dated. However, it is important to remember that this multiheaded hydra is a conglomerate that owns 78 different companies, including WhatsApp and Instagram. In other words, Facebook is much more than cat videos and conspiracy theories. Spearheaded by Mark Zuckerberg, a champion of smoked meats, Facebook, Inc. is a well-oiled machine. Its power is undeniable, and this power is growing. As *Fortune* magazine recently noted:

> "Facebook, it appears, can't be hurt—not by major ad buyers boycotting its service, not by state and federal investigations, and not even by a pandemic."

The COVID-19 pandemic may have brought the world to its knees, but Mark Zuckerberg, Facebook's CEO, hasn't felt the effects. Last year, he had a measly net worth of $82 billion; today, it's above $130 billion. Now, with Zuckerberg attempting to create his own metaverse, expect his value—and his power—to increase substantially.

THE METAVERSE

A blending of the words "meta," which means beyond, and "universe," the metaverse combines elements of the physical world and merges them with virtual spaces. American writer and author Neal Stephenson coined the term in 1992. Two decades later, no longer confined to the realms of sci-fi, the metaverse is almost upon us.

In this brave new world, the lines between physical reality and digital domains will become increasingly blurry. Nonfungible tokens (NFTs) and cryptocurrencies are already part of the metaverse experience, but going forward, in the actual metaverse, they will be combined with you, the user. Although we currently live, communicate and shop on the Internet, once the metaverse comes into existence, we will very well live our lives in the Internet. We will even be able to obtain once-illusive luxury fashion thanks to designers like Louis Vuitton, Dolce & Gabbana, Cavalli, and Tommy Hilfiger, all of which have invested in NFTs and the metaverse to produce virtual fashion and shopping experiences.[229] Elon Musk wants to transport us to Mars, but Zuckerberg wants to transport us to, and place us in, the Internet. Literally.

In a recent interview to The Verge, Zuckerberg described the metaverse as an "embodied Internet, where instead of just viewing content—you are in it." We will be tenants in Zuckerberg's ever-expanding house. Rent will be paid in the form of data. This is not a comforting thought. As Wired's Toby Tremayne noted, big tech firms like Facebook have "become walled gardens increasingly centralized and controlled by corporate interests." Facebook already "owns WhatsApp, Instagram, and Oculus," which gives "them ownership of our friends, our behavior, our gait, eye movement, and emotional state." Soon, if Zuckerberg has his way, Facebook, Inc. will have even greater control over our lives. That, I argue, should comfort no one but Zuckerberg.[230]

The highly sexualized content in every form of media no longer seems to shock, as Super Bowl halftime looks more like a sex occult ritual, and movies, gaming, and now the metaverse are replete with unbridled sexual images, and not just suggestive but interactive images. What would have been considered in years past as hard-core pornography is mainstream. This strongly plays into the family failure witnessed in culture. We become the images we feed into our minds. There is a spirit/soul (mind, will, and emotions) connection to the body. Our minds can be tricked into believing propaganda, and it will have a brainwashing effect on our lives, health, and our children. Engaging in immoral behavior, whether with an avatar or in real life, creates brokenness and addictions. Jesus said, "If a man (person) looks on a woman with adultery in their heart, it's the same as if they committed it," and this applies to media and the metaverse, whether we acknowledge it or not.

May God Himself, the God of peace, sanctify you through and through. May your whole spirit, soul and body be kept blameless at the coming of the Lord Jesus Christ.

—1 Thessalonians 5:23 (NIV)

What words and images are we tolerating to rule our lives for convenience or to feed our egos? How are those image makers recreating life, and are we willing to lose our freedoms to let them entertain and inform us? If they can bully or control any person or our free elections, they can control all of us. This is precisely the problem. Congress has done little to nothing to hold these social media companies accountable for fear of losing their own accounts and status. We need to raise our voices and vote with our money. Hopefully, we aren't too late.

THINKING OUTSIDE
THE PROPAGANDA

These media giants may be huge, but we do have power if enough of us choose to wield it. They have managed to swallow any smaller competition, but we can take heart that the bigger they are, the harder they fall. Disney recently flexed its entertainment muscle to stop a bill in Florida designed to protect children third grade and below from being taught about LGBTQ at school. Sound reasonable? Not to Disney. A Disney exec vowed to put 50 percent minority and trans characters in its upcoming "entertainment," and to mirror it in hiring standards. Its website promises that 50 percent of regular recurring characters across the Disney universe will come from underrepresented groups. This is all part of Disney's Reimagine campaign… "We no longer say ladies and gentlemen, boys or girls." We say, "dreamers of all ages."[231]

"Parents are outraged over Disney's pushback on the Florida parental rights law: Leave the kids alone. Parents around the country are pushing back on Disney after it publicly denounced a new parental rights law in Florida which bars teachers from discussing sexual orientation or gender identity in kindergarten through third grade.…"

"Disney publicly denounced the legislation after it was signed into law when Disney exec Bob Chapek released a statement saying it should never have been signed into law."[232] Disney is opposing its core consumers, parents. Many are deleting Disney+ and opting not to take their children to its parks.

Maybe Disney needs reminded that the LGBTQ population only represents 4 percent of the world's population, and parents represent far more of its support system. Media and entertainment companies like Disney want the representation of LGBTQ characters to be 30-50 percent of their programming. Why? These are the values of the entertainment industry execs, and employees must obey or face discrimination. Streaming platforms like Netflix have likewise done away with all ratings systems, exposing viewers, especially children, to pornography, violence, and filth without any warning. It's interesting that I hear more complaints, "There are so many options and yet nothing to watch."

WE MUST STAND UP TO THE OVERSEXUALIZED CANCEL CULTURE AND REFUSE TO SUPPORT THEIR BULLYING WITH OUR TIME AND FINANCES. WE MUST RECOGNIZE THE PROPAGANDA WAR. WE NEED TO TAKE THE APPROACH: GO WOKE, GO BROKE.

We must stand up to the oversexualized cancel culture and refuse to support their bullying with our time and finances. We must recognize the propaganda war. We need to take the approach: Go woke, go broke. I read a book about propaganda techniques in middle school. It stuck with me because it was my first awareness that not everything I heard or saw was factual and that there were people with agendas that were neither honest nor trustworthy. Those are hard lessons to learn as a young person with great trust in authorities, government, schoolteachers, doctors, and longstanding institutions. Among these institutions are the legacy media outlets that have told us what to believe and how to think. In times past, we at least had freedom to read, write, and think for ourselves. Something has drastically changed, yet there is a tidal wave of pushback like never before.

There is hope, as we have seen thousands of new media voices emerge, from conservative voices to counterculture. Many of these voices are bringing faith and family values back into current events' discussions. It has caught the attention of the media elite and social media giants, resulting in a war of censorship. The harder tech giants have pushed their censorship, and legacy media have parroted the same narratives from network to network, the more people are waking up and rising in solidarity against their control.

One of the battles that has ensued deals with section 230 and repealing the protection it provides big tech companies.

"Section 230 is a provision of the 1996 Communications Decency Act that protects companies that host user-created content from lawsuits over posts on their services. The law shields both Internet service providers, like AT&T, Comcast, and Verizon, and social media and internet platforms, like Facebook, Twitter, and Google."

"Section 230 isn't blanket protection. There are exceptions for federal crimes or intellectual property claims. A company could still be held accountable if it knowingly allowed users to post illegal content."

Many argue that is hard to prove with the incredible amount of muscle these tech companies garner.

"The law provides social media companies with sweeping protections that let them choose what content they restrict, and how. This means social media platforms can't be sued for taking down content or leaving it up."

However, this gets tricky since these platforms have monopolizing financial power!

"Most of the problems around Section 230 involve which posts social networks allow to stand and which ones they remove."

"Democrats are most concerned about getting big social media companies to take down hate speech, harassment, disinformation, and terrorism-related content. Democrats have even accused the companies of using the liability protections as a means to profit from the lies spread on their platforms."

"Republicans allege that social media companies censor conservative viewpoints. This is a narrative Trump used in the lead-up to the 2020 presidential election when Twitter and Facebook began slapping warning labels on his posts for containing inaccurate information."[233]

In Democrats' minds, they want more censorship of posts controlling speech. Their goal is to hold Facebook accountable for posts they deem as false information. But who becomes the guardian of truth? Hasn't a democracy always had the freedom to share ideas and let people decide what to believe or the best course of action for themselves?

If The New York Times is the guardian of truth, then judge this article in the New York Times by Kevin Roose on February 5, 2020 criticizing an alternative media outlet, The Epoch Times: "Late last summer, YouTube users began noticing a surge of ads for an obscure news outlet called The Epoch Times. One ad touted an exposé of 'Spygate,' a baseless conspiracy theory alleging that President Barack Obama and his allies placed a spy inside President Trump's 2016 campaign."[234]

Or was it a baseless conspiracy theory? Special Counsel John Durham's filings I shared earlier would indicate not so. The Epoch Times was far closer to the actual story than The New York Times, boasted as the world's largest newspaper outlet. This is the problem with censorship. When the powers that be decide what the public has a right to hear, and what is truth or not, there must be "a controller" of that narrative. And as we have seen, there are agendas and

WHEN THE POWERS THAT BE DECIDE WHAT THE PUBLIC HAS A RIGHT TO HEAR, AND WHAT IS TRUTH OR NOT, THERE MUST BE "A CONTROLLER" OF THAT NARRATIVE. AND AS WE HAVE SEEN, THERE ARE AGENDAS AND INFORMATION THAT IS FORBIDDEN BECAUSE IT IMPACTS FINANCIAL EMPIRES AND POWERFUL ELITES.

information that is forbidden because it impacts financial empires and powerful elites.

There is legislation to revoke Section 230 from social media companies. They're not tech alone—they're media, news, and information—yet Section 230 gives them the protections of a utility company, much like a phone company. But these companies are handling more information exchanges and weighing in on those exchanges by manipulating algorithms, search engines, and fact-checking (with questionable results), and certainly by removing people's posts and ads.

The definition of media is "the main means of mass communication (broadcasting, publishing, and the Internet) regarded collectively.[235] Social media companies are publishing and operating at the very least as editors and should fall under the same guidelines as other media outlets with added rules to protect people's privacy and data. Republican Senator Josh Hawley has taken up this fight, and others are in lawsuits concerning social media companies' impact on their lives. The Supreme Court needs to hear these cases and protect our free speech while holding big tech accountable.

We Cannot Allow Our Voices to Be Silenced

During the COVID-19 hysteria, major doctors across the world were censored by big tech, and information doctors shared about protocols or success with alternative treatments other than the accepted "protocol" of big pharma (ventilators, Remdesivir, and a few others) was sharply censored. Google searches and media outlets favor their media darlings that fit the World Health Organization and Bill Gates's vaccine narratives. Searches bring up the content they want you to see, and conservative voices are missing in those searches. They literally control what we see and believe through monopolizing the search engine.

People are pushing back! Alternative voices emerged stronger as citizens witnessed the discrepancies in government commands and the media's complicit role in driving the demands. They went too far, and citizens began to loathe them for their power plays. Nothing recently has moved our nation like the wake-up calls we have experienced in the last few years.

We need alternative voices in the media, and fortunately, it is beginning to happen. Get your news somewhere else besides the mainstream legacy media—that is now left stream! Alternative media is soaring if we can keep cable companies and networks from "cancelling" these media. The Epoch Times newspaper, The War Room with Steve Bannon, Joe Rogan, One America News, the Daily Mail, and many others have emerged. "One America News Network is a conservative news site that was started by libertarians and conservatives. This site focuses on news stories affecting the United States and is one of the largest websites on the Internet and broadcasts on cable. The site features actual reporting, cutting-edge political analysis, and intuitive commentary on trending stories. Among its strengths are its ability to provide factual and balanced news.

There has been a fight to stop OAN by removing their cable contracts and "canceling them," but conservatives are fighting back and recognizing that we can collectively pool our resources too. You can find them at oan.com and on national providers as well as on international carriers in the United Kingdom, Trinidad, Puerto Rico, Germany, Latvia, the Caribbean, and Canada. Newsmax is another that has risen in prominence.

These are reportedly the top conservative outlets: The Daily Wire, The Blaze, OAN, Newsmax, The Federalist, National Review, Breitbart, Zero Hedge, Townhall, The Federalist, Washington Examiner, World Net Daily, Joe Rogan (language), Gab Trends, Washington Free Beacon, Life Site News, The Daily Signal, Drudge Report, Free Republic, American Thinker, Red State, Gateway Pundit, Flashpoint, my program, *Drenda on Guard*, and more![236]

How to Take Back Control of Our Lives and Get Back Our Autonomy

We must redirect our dollars to organizations and businesses that are not insulting and stealing our freedoms. If we allow convenience and pleasure to drive our decisions, we will lose them. The great news is that many are rethinking their media choices and the businesses they support. Amazon is very convenient, I admit, but those packages delivered to our doors support causes and agendas and have consequences, especially to local businesses. Several buy conservative sites have sprung up to give consumers choices as to where their money goes and who gets support.

> ...simply complaining is not enough. We must find viable alternatives and then support those companies. So what are those conservative companies? I'm sure there are more, but these have stood up to ridicule and those who would attempt to shut their doors:

Mike Lindell's My Pillow, Goya Foods, Hobby Lobby, Cracker Barrel, Cintas Corporation, Gab, Parler, Reginery Publishing, Daniel Defense, Home Depo, Bass Pro Shops, Sheetz, Sturm, Ruger & Co, Las Vegas Sands Corp., The Daily Wire.[237]

Companies that support censorship and radical Marxist organizations are dangerous to our freedoms. They're banking that most people will tolerate their Marxist goals because they aren't willing to lose their services.

According to genzconservative.com, here's a list of twelve companies you should definitely boycott: 1) Facebook; alternatives are MeWe, Gab, Gettr, and The Happy Life Social, 2) Bank of America; use instead credit unions or state chartered banks in conservative states, 3) JP Morgan Chase (has stopped business with conservatives and de-platformed them), 4) Netflix (normalizing pedophilia); replace with Rumble, or even Hulu is better, 5) Google (threatens and de-platforms conservatives); replace with Duck Duck Go, 6) Disney (voice of CCP); download Minno, a Christian app for children; watch old Disney DVDs, 7) NBA (allowed Chinese instructors at their camps to abuse children); replace with playing ball with your son or daughter or friends, 8) Apple (pro-China, anti-American, and refused to release evidence of terrorists); replace with Samsung, Spotify, 9) The NFL (woke, anti-American); replace with college football or golf, 10) Levi Strauss (outspoken against second Amendment), 11) Nike (anti-American).[238] There are many others, but these have the largest impact.

In a free world, supply and demand would cause most of these companies to financially suffer to the brink of collapse, much like what we have observed with CNN recently, bought out in a sharp decline. But when you control the narrative as a monopoly, it is hard for justice to be accomplished. This is in fact the problem. We must continue to raise our voices to fight the censorship of ideas and especially those that affect our freedom of religion.

Retribution may be happening at some of the networks, finally. Media corporations and personalities have seen huge shake-ups. The departure of Jeff Zucker from CNN just on the heels of other CNN scandals involving Chris Cuomo and his producer are just the beginning. "A major investor, John Malone has signaled he believes the network, which is on the cusp of launching its new streaming service, became too explicitly liberal. And all the change has led some of the top anchors and correspondents to question the networks' leadership vacuum and wonder where it's headed."[239] Notably, CNN's streaming service failed within a month of launching. There is a sifting and shaking happening all over the world. Evil is being exposed, and people are waking up. It's in the eleventh hour, but it's not too late.

It's not enough to find fault with the industry. We need innovators to create alternatives in entertainment also—like the Dry Bar Comedy app (clean comedy), which is experiencing a boom. *The Chosen* movie series became the most successful crowdfunded media project in history and has captured the viewership of multimillions all over the world.[240] Live performances and community theatre need to re-embrace the arts with an approach of beauty and talent. Churches especially need to engage the arts and overcome evil with good! There is a hunger for relaxing and enjoyable entertainment that engages creativity and values decency that a majority of Americans share, and if we weren't censored, perhaps more of us would be aware of the need and demand.

Freedom is granted by God's Word. Freedom is granted by our Constitution. Jesus used military terms throughout Scripture, and even with the word ecclesia, meaning "to transform or take over, impacting every area," when He referred to His church. The fight we find ourselves in is good versus evil. Communism is evil. In our fight to stand up to evil, we are fighting against foes on foreign soil and cowardice in our own country... An evil that justifies and even glorifies killing babies in the womb and after birth... An evil that wants to control us through division... An evil that corrupts children and distorts their bodies. Retreat can't be an option in the face of such evil. We must fight or die and contend for the faith as good soldiers. We are given freedom by God and freedom in our Constitution and the Bill of Rights:

Bill of Rights
Amendment 1 reads:

> Congress shall make no law respecting an establishment of religion or prohibiting the free exercise thereof; or abridging the freedom of speech, or of the press; or the right of the people peaceably to assemble, and to petition the Government for a redress of grievances.

If we are not willing to take this mountain, who will? The world is watching to see what we will do, for we are the only nation with such a Constitution. It has withstood, but it can only continue to stand if we stand up for it.

FAMILY FALLOUT!

Our family took an RV trip through Alaska in an attempt to add a few more national parks to our bucket list created by our 12-year-old daughter (since every twelve-year-old needs a list). We arrived at Denali National Park to see the beautiful Mount McKinley. But it was a dismal overcast, cloud-filled day. There was no mountain in sight. Feeling a bit dejected, we prayed for it to come out, and nothing seemed to happen. What a disappointment. We ate our pan-fried salmon dinner and parked alongside the barren highway to sleep for the night.

The next morning, a beautiful beam of sun cascaded across our camper wall and woke us, seven family members stirring with a touch of hunger. As we slipped out into the lovely morning air, with birds singing and dew covering the ground, we looked up. To our astonishment, there was the most amazing, beautiful, partially snow-covered, spectacular mountain peak we had ever seen, huge in all its glory. The sun made the enormous mountain glisten golden. Mount McKinley didn't disappoint, and we were beyond thrilled. The morning seemed new, and that day, we felt anything was possible.

Family is often like that. We fail to see the beauty in the pressures of the day-to-day. There are disappointments, trials, conflict, and lots of work. Later in life, we begin to realize the real gold and the greatest beauty is family. It is the tallest of mountains next to the mountain of the Lord.

Life began in a beautiful Garden in the creation of God, and the highest order of God's creation was male and female, man and woman. "Male and female He created them." God began with a family. The decision to disobey God's direction brought problems to the couple and their family. When confronted by God, Adam would blame his wife and God, "This woman You gave me told me to eat, so I did." Their son Cain would murder his brother Abel, consumed with jealousy and sibling rivalry. Their beautiful life turned dark, cloudy. The beginning of God's desire for a family quickly turned into a disappointing experience.

God began with a family, and I believe His last order of business will begin with an awakening of family. "God will turn the hearts of the Fathers back to the children." I have documented in two of my other books—*She Gets It!: The 11 Lies that Hold Women Hostage* and *Nasty Gets Us Nowhere: Women and Men Succeeding Together*—how men and women have fallen out of love and the disastrous impact it has had on marriage, and ultimately children. In the Garden, God gave the first man and his companion and wife, Eve, everything they needed for life. Through an act of disobedience, Adam listened to the

> **GOD BEGAN WITH A FAMILY, AND I BELIEVE HIS LAST ORDER OF BUSINESS WILL BEGIN WITH AN AWAKENING OF FAMILY.**

deceptive lies Satan told to the woman; and she used her influence to convince him that there was more than what God was giving them. Those famous words of Satan, the enemy, "Did God really say?" are familiar to us all, regardless of what we face in life. There's always a temptation to do it "our way" or the way it was planted in our heads as a "good idea" by marketers, celebrities, educators, governments, and others who want our money and influence.

The strong family values of the 40s and 50s gave way to the sexual rebellion and promiscuity of the 60s, followed by the drug culture and "if it feels good, do it" philosophy of the 70s and 80s, developing a strong divorce culture. Perhaps the women's movement of the 70s was a rebellion from the hurts many women experienced as their husbands left them for younger women coupled with the messages of free sex in the 60s. It was supposed to give women equal pay for equal work, power, and freedom but resulted in more dissatisfaction for women, and family brokenness became the norm. The promiscuity of the sexual revolution was spun as freedom and fulfillment. Satan knows how to sell a just cause like equality and couple it with poisonous actions that destroy lives.

Sin is the problem. Selfishness is that sin. Whenever people have sexual intimacy with someone, it's a spiritual act that makes the two become one, not just in the natural or physical way but spiritually as well. Sex is much more than physical; it's spiritual too. When people become sexually involved with someone, spirit to spirit, everything they possess is united or bound to that partner. God intended this for deep intimacy that would bind two people for life in marriage. This is why Scripture warns us to stay away from the harlot. "Her house is the way to hell, going down to the chambers of death." They will destroy you. Spiritual entities possess the souls of sinful individuals, and sexual union causes these spirits to possess and transfer into souls that sexually "become one" with them. Most marriages and sexual unions aren't whole because they started in disobedience.

What does this transference of spirits look like? Look at the confusion that people, especially children, face today. It is manifesting in plural pronouns for individuals, non-binary declarations, name and sex changes, sexual immorality and derision, transgenderism, sex change surgeries, sterilization, suicide, and death. These are indoctrinations of the state, educational, and medical communities at work while absent parents working long hours to pay back their indebtedness abandon their children. The foundation is weak. Pornography, affairs (both imagined and acted on), pressures, and the cares of life choke out the love and light of the beauty of family.

Why did God make the two one? Because He sought a godly seed (children). Satan divides a home because he, too, is after the godly seed. Parents must wake up to the dangers and reclaim their parental rights given from God to direct their children in the way they should go, not the way the state wants them to go. We must confront evil head-on, especially when it impacts the most vulnerable of society.

How do we remedy the problems? One word, men. We need more good men. Men of God who are willing to love their wives and children are the greatest cure and, unfortunately, are in tremendous shortage. If men model what a loving husband and father looks like, good women will follow, and children will too. Men are the catalysts we need to right the wrongs, defend the home, and drive out the darkness and clouds. When men rebel against God, so do women;

and children rebel against parents. Our decisions always affect those under our leadership. We desperately need a revival of men to turn their hearts back to their wives, and especially to their children. I can think of no greater place to impact the culture than this mountain and no greater force than that of a father. Most of the brokenness in the culture could honestly be healed by a father, a good father. And men cannot be good without God.

WE NEED MORE GOOD MEN. MEN OF GOD WHO ARE WILLING TO LOVE THEIR WIVES AND CHILDREN ARE THE GREATEST CURE AND, UNFORTUNATELY, ARE IN TREMENDOUS SHORTAGE. IF MEN MODEL WHAT A LOVING HUSBAND AND FATHER LOOKS LIKE, GOOD WOMEN WILL FOLLOW, AND CHILDREN WILL TOO.

God gave Adam and Eve another son after the loss of their son to death. His name was Seth, and the lineage of Jesus Christ came through him. When it appeared all was gray and cloudy, God sent His answer to cause the Son to shine and majesty to break forth in the world. A beautiful mountain appeared, the mountain of the Lord. We beheld it, and it was glorious.

No mountain surpasses this one! Family has been wounded, but miraculous healing is possible. Women and children are yearning for godly men who represent our Father.

Train up a child in the way he should go; even when he is old he will not depart from it.

—Proverbs 22:6 (ESV)

Therefore a man shall leave his father and his mother and hold fast to his wife, and they shall become one flesh.

—Genesis 2:24 (ESV)

Your wife will be like a fruitful vine within your house; your children will be like olive shoots around your table.

—Psalm 128:3 (ESV)

And if it is evil in your eyes to serve the Lord, choose this day whom you will serve, whether the gods your fathers served in the region beyond the River, or the gods of the Amorites in whose land you dwell. But as for me and my house, we will serve the Lord.

—Joshua 24:15 (ESV)

He must manage his own household well, keeping his children under control with all dignity [keeping them respectful and well-behaved].

—1 Timothy 3:4 (AMP)

TEAMWORK, DREAM WORK

We need strong marriages and homes to save America! Children need the security and love that strong marriages bring. Gary and I are very different in personality, as most marriage partners tend to be. Opposites do attract. Additionally, men and women's brains are actually physiologically wired different. With our differences, we are better people with a better life together because of our marriage. Our children are also better for our differences. The hope is that as we follow Christ with all our hearts, our better qualities and character will be developed in our children—and the balance of *"two are better than one, because they get a good reward for their labor"* will happen in our children (Ecclesiastes 4:9, NKJV). We need the help of each other to carry the weight and invest, *"For if either falls down, his companion can lift him up; but pity the one who falls without another to lift him up"* (Ecclesiastes 4:10, CSB)! Single parents can also engage with God and get "help" and instructions to raise up their children by His principles. Involve them in the family of God through church and activities which help support your efforts in the absence of a spouse.

Commitment to God and commitment to our marriage have helped us to weather life's storms and fight for our marriage… And a whole lot of prayer and communication! Conflict happens in every marriage, and the strongest of families must learn to communicate to resolve the conflict with understanding. Understand each other's side by putting yourself in their shoes. Selfishness asks, "How will this affect me?" Love asks, "How will this affect them?" Know when to let things go. Peace can be better at times than having to be right. We can learn to communicate with humility instead of proving we are right and they are wrong. No one wins that game! We must know the times to back down. Pick your moment, and decide what is most important. Men are singular in focus, so if you try and talk to them when they're focused on something else, it's useless. And women are not always going to see the logic only; they can sense more behind the curtain with their super sensitive perception skills. We have to work toward success with one another instead of attacking our differences. Children are watching and learning from our behavior, commitments, and priorities.

The top five key findings of a survey concerning children's ministry completed by ministry-to-children.com showed that:

> Childhood is when most people find Jesus. No matter who does the survey, one fact is overwhelming. Once a person reaches adulthood, accepting Christ becomes increasingly rare. Evangelism is most effective in the childhood and teenage years. 2/3 of Christians came to faith before the age of 18. 43% came to Christ before the age of 12. Less than 1/4 of current believers came to Christ after the age of 21; and secondly:

Parents have the most impact on them. Every parent has the God-given privilege of teaching children how to live. We should not be surprised that young people often come to Jesus thanks to a loving mother or father.

- Parents were named by 50% of our readers as a help in their coming to Christ.
- Half of children who come to Christ are led by their parents.
- 24% of our readers listed other family members as a factor.

Thirdly, children's ministry matters. The role of parents does not exclude or diminish the mission of the church. Jesus set the course for all congregations that bear His name when He said, "Let the little children come to me."

The Bible offers many strong examples supporting the importance of children in the life and mission of the church. This starts with relationships. Our survey found children's ministry and Christian peers are an important factor in how people find Jesus.

- 29% of our readers said children's ministry (or a children's ministry leader) helped them come to Christ.
- 26% listed other children—i.e., friends—who were Christians as a factor.

We serve because Jesus loves kids. When we surveyed our

leaders on the state of children's ministry, we asked them to describe what motivates their service.

Christ's love for children was the overwhelming leading answer.

- 86% responded that Jesus loves kids.
- 23% felt the church or pastor was depending on them.
- 23% recalled their own salvation as a child for motivation."[241]

Thankfully, there are those in the church who value ministry to youth and children and serve them. A vibrant church must place a strong value on reaching the youngest of these but not the least.

Children who have spiritual influences are far less likely to get involved with addictive substances or have depression or suicidal tendencies. "Young people who regularly attend religious services and describe themselves as religious are less likely to experiment with drugs and alcohol," according to a new study.

The study of 195 juvenile offenders was done by researchers at Baylor University's Institute for Studies of Religion, the University of Akron, and Case Western Reserve University School of Medicine. It appears in the journal *Alcohol Treatment Quarterly.*

Juvenile offenders in the study were referred by a court, mental health professional, or physician to a two-month residential treatment program and were assessed by researchers at intake and discharge through interviews, medical chart reviews, drug screening, and reports by youths, parents, and clinicians.

Study findings, which support a growing body of research, suggest that young people who connect to a "higher power" may feel a greater sense of purpose and are less likely to be bothered by feelings of not fitting in, according to researcher Byron Johnson, Ph.D., Co-director of Baylor's Institute for Studies of Religion.[242]

Parents are busy, and life keeps getting busier; it seems like the pace is speeding out of control. I am often asked, "How do you keep up and do all that there is to do?" One of the keys in my life—and I believe for yours—is to discern the times and choose according to the season. Ecclesiastes says, "*To everything there is a season.*" For almost nine years, I was able to work as our church's youth leader, helping my own teens to grow in Christ while helping other teens and investing in God's Kingdom. Not only was I able to spend time with my children and help others grow in the process, but I also grew; and it became an experience that would help define some of the next stages of my life. Was it sometimes hard or demanding of my time? Yes, you can be sure! Was it worth it? Absolutely. I didn't lose this time with my children by pursuing my own ambitions. I incorporated opportunities to invest in them while enjoying using my gifts too.

I see the fruit of my investment in my adult children, in other youth, and in my own spiritual growth. Many years before, I had resigned from coaching a girls' basketball team because our children were small and the time commitment would detract from our growing, young family. It was not the right season. The return was simply not worth the time away from our young children. It's choosing the right priority in the season. It's not that you can't have it all—you just can't have it all at the same time!

What are you doing with this season and with the time you have? Each season has definite and important requirements that lay a foundation for the success of the next one. I encourage moms to invest in your children while they are young instead of pursuing full-time vocations or ministries, yet take some time to use your gifts along the way. You won't miss the quickly evaporating small window of opportunity with them, and it will make the following seasons of life be built on a more solid foundation.

I ENCOURAGE MOMS TO INVEST IN YOUR CHILDREN WHILE THEY ARE YOUNG INSTEAD OF PURSUING FULL-TIME VOCATIONS OR MINISTRIES, YET TAKE SOME TIME TO USE YOUR GIFTS ALONG THE WAY.

Engage in activities in the season that will give you the most time with your children, to steer and train them. Time spent investing in their character, hearts, and modeling the Kingdom of God for them in everyday life yields incredible returns.

Pastors and leaders, we must partner to fight the enemies of our youth and protect their hearts. If your church is not aggressively targeting reaching this generation of young persons, you must begin to do so immediately. We have lost time, but it is not too late to turn the tide. When youth have an experience with God and His power, it's addictive, and His touch can transform. Create an atmosphere for God's power to manifest, and be actively engaged in youth and family ministry in the church. The principles of transformation that change adults change young persons too.

Our children were busy alongside us in ministry, and that gave them purpose and time with us. They caught our passions because they become like the ones "teaching them," primarily us. If moms and dads and pastoral leaders are children's main companions and teachers, instead of educational ideologies, youth do not have to succumb to the world's temptations around them. Our children did not rebel against us or God, five out of five. We aren't that good, but God's ways are!

I want to share some hopeful testimonies from our youth pastor and daughter-in-love Alecia:

> I've been involved in youth ministry as a youth leader and pastor for almost 13 years. I've seen 12 classes graduate, married multiple couples that have come out of our youth group, and have watched them walk into owning businesses, having children, and many other of life's milestones. I'm no greenhorn. It's easy to look at the culture around you and become discouraged. The rampant sin and blatant disregard for righteousness is disheartening, especially if you have no connection to this generation.
>
> I can tell you from firsthand experience that the upcoming generations are amazing. They are creative, compassionate, strong, brave, and are looking for an opportunity to change the world. They have strong convictions and are not afraid to jump out there to defend others. This generation's biggest

struggle is you and me. The world puts everything they have into reaching the new generations, money, time, strategy, people, and creativity! Meanwhile, many of us in the body of Christ look down on young people and use excuses as to why we do not disciple them.

I've seen teens and those in their young twenties saved, delivered, set free, and healed! But more importantly, I've seen those same teens turn around and lead their friends into the same salvation and deliverance they experienced. I've taken 30+ teens on a missions trip with other missionaries, and they could not believe the power and authority they walked in. I've had those same kids disappear and almost miss busses because they were scouring villages to make sure there wasn't one person who didn't get to hear the Good News of the Kingdom or receive healing. I've seen kids delivered from witchcraft literally going home from camp and burning "magic" books.

I've worked with high schoolers who would rather spend hours in worship than play video games or hang out in the world. They'd rather hang out at my house until 1:00 a.m. talking about the Bible than go to a bar. They look for opportunities to share Jesus. This isn't one person's life or just one-off, random events. This is a daily occurrence for me. While I am a youth pastor, and I have the privilege of working with young people daily, it isn't as rare as you think if you would just take the opportunity to talk to some of them. Obviously, there are sad stories, and I've seen my own share of destroyed lives, but there is more hope in these young people than you may know. They are just looking for someone to believe in them, love them, listen to them, and pour into them.

This generation is on fire and hungry for God. I have been personally challenged by this generation in my own faith too many times to count. I want to challenge parents, pastors, young adults, and anyone else reading this book: Open up your life to these next generations. Get involved in your local youth group, encourage them any chance you get, pray for them, and pray for all the youth pastors. We need it.

God has given all of us gifts of time, talent, and energy! Passion fuels energy!

I'm not as energetic about something I don't want or want to do. I can feel exhausted, but if I receive a call from one of our adult children to go somewhere or do something, I am immediately motivated. We will invest in our priorities, where we have a burning desire for something, someone, or a lifestyle. To change our culture and reach youth, we must get a burning desire to draw them into a vital relationship with God.

We must also get involved with the fight to protect them legally and spiritually from those in

THE ENEMY KNOWS HOW TO CORRUPT INNOCENCE, BUT PARENTS WHO ARE ON GUARD CAN LAUNCH COUNTERATTACKS BY BEING THERE FOR THEIR KIDS AND CHURCHES AND CAN POUR TIME AND RESOURCES INTO CREATING AN ATMOSPHERE FOR THE MIRACULOUS.

government spheres who would attempt to harm them with indoctrination that steals their innocence and purity. The enemy knows how to corrupt innocence, but parents who are on guard can launch counterattacks by being there for their kids and churches and can pour time and resources into creating an atmosphere for the miraculous. When youth have an experience with the power of God and draw close to Him in relationship, their hearts are touched, and it changes everything.

We have many stories of young people learning how to apply Kingdom principles and experiencing God's power at work. They are drawn into worship and search the Scriptures to find more from a living and breathing relationship with Him.

Darcy's Story

When Darcy was nine and a half years old, she told her parents that she wanted a horse. Their neighbors at the time had bought a horse for their grandkids, and Darcy loved that horse. Her father wasn't sure about the horse thing. In his words, he was "a city boy" and knew nothing about horses. He tried talking Darcy into a dirt bike instead, but Darcy was sold on getting a horse. She told her dad that Pastor Gary said that the Lord could move the heart of a king (Proverbs 21:1) and stated that she would not only be praying for a change of heart for her Dad but also that she was going to pray and give financial seed for a horse! Talk about some confident, childlike faith! How could her dad say no? After all, he had encouraged and supported what they heard about every week at church.

On April 4th, Darcy gave the church $20 as a faith seed for a horse, but not just any horse. "I sowed for a bay mare, which is a color and a gender, so I was very specific. And I wanted her to be lovable, ridable, trainable, and healthy." A friend called them not too long afterwards, looking to get rid of her horse, and it was exactly the perfect horse, exactly what Darcy had sowed for! In her very first year, Darcy joined a club and participated in speed events, which she walked away from with many trophies.

She moved into a new class from there that was centered around showmanship, jumping, and other equestrian specialties. In her second year, she went to the state fair, where she was competing against people who had spent $25K - 50K on horses. Meanwhile, Darcy got her horse for free based off of a seed she had sown, and I must mention that neither she nor her beautiful mare had the same amount of training that the other competitors had. Regardless of these facts, Darcy knew that God was going to help her get first place at the state fair. When the judge got up to announce the winning competitors, she told everyone that this had been one of the most competitive classes she had ever seen at the state fair, and that placing anywhere in the top 10 would mean you performed very well. They started at 10th place and worked all the way up to 1st place, which ended up being Darcy! To this day, she serves God and has seen His hand at work in her life in many other ways.

Darcy experienced provision from God for a dream she desired. It looked impossible, but she discovered that with faith, all things are possible.

How does it change a young person's life to encounter God in their needs, wants, and deepest longings? Dreams do come true, not by wishing upon a star but by following the One who made them. This is the understanding children need to be raised with. Their allegiance is developed by their influences. Darcy's parents have been wise and careful to protect her heart and surround her with godly examples.

Chinue shared with me how being involved in a vibrant youth ministry has helped her not just to see spiritually but also physically:

> XM Youth and XM camp have changed me and marked me in so many ways. I don't think I would have done most of the things I'm doing now if it wasn't for my leaders and youth pastors who are on fire for God and always pointed me to what He says. The year 2017 was a lot for me, but one of the highlights that year was XM camp. That year, I got my eyes healed! It was the last night of camp, and I don't remember every detail of that night, but I do remember asking Pastor Alecia to pray for my eyes so I wouldn't have to wear glasses anymore. And after she was done praying, she said she saw God taking off my glasses and putting them on Himself. After that, I took off my glasses and left them off. I went outside and just started singing and thanking God. After a little while, I realized I could see completely fine, and I could even see things far away easily. I still thank God to this day, and He has changed my life in so many ways!

When young people understand there is a God who loves them physically and emotionally, they have hope and answers that are not offered in pills, alcohol, or one-night stands.

Autumn shared this:

> I was never a bad kid, and I never have dealt with anything
> super serious like abuse, depression, porn, or anything like
> that. A few years ago, I had this sore on the bottom of my
> foot. I played basketball at the time, and I was constantly
> hard on my feet. Around this time, I had issues exercising
> self-control, and I would get angry easily. After getting sick
> and tired of being sick and tired, I decided I wanted to get
> prayer for this sore on my foot. I went to Pastor Amy after a
> First Wednesday service, and she prayed for me. She told me
> that before she was able to be healed, she had to let go of self-
> hatred. She also explained to me that there are things that can
> block our healing from taking place if we do not deal with
> them. And for her, it was self-hatred. So, after we prayed, I
> went home and thanked God that I was healed. And every
> time my foot would hurt, I would thank God for my healing.
> I also started to pray that my anger would leave. And it did.
> About two weeks after I prayed with Pastor Amy, my foot
> was healed and I was no longer angry either. I am changed.

We must develop a vision for our families and then pursue that
vision as our highest priority next to our relationship with God. The
churches' purpose must become a huge part of the mission to teach
how to develop strong families and the principles of discipline, love,
example, and faith with Jesus at the center of family life to succeed.

There are many opportunities in life, but we must choose to say no
to the ones that will harm us or our families. The Bible tells us this
about Jesus:

He departed and went into a remote place. And searching for Him, the people came and tried to prevent Him from leaving them. But He said to them, "I must preach the Kingdom of God to other cities also, for this is why I was sent."

—Luke 4:42-43 (MEV)

If we want our families and churches to thrive, we must focus our time, talent, and energy on why we were sent. If you are a parent or leader, that's your children and family—the right things!

Our greatest accomplishments and joy are in our family, our children; and the foundation we laid is priceless. Everything else is nothing compared to that. I feel when we stand before God, the highest attainment will be our family, for it created a ripple effect into every other sphere of influence.

(See *The Mystery of Marriage* Bible study by Gary and me and my *The New Vintage Family: A Vintage Look at the Modern-day Family* for a more extensive marriage and family study.)

THE TRUTH SETS
US FREE

Confronting Evil

For the past several years, we have taken our children and grandchildren on a family trip to be refreshed and draw closer together. It's an enjoyable time, but it seems more difficult than ever to find family friendly entertainment and environments that are restful. I was swimming and then was sitting in the family hot tub with my young grandsons and a couple of granddaughters as they came from the pool. A woman in her early thirties (I'm guessing) came to our hot tub from the adult pool/hot tub wearing a barely there thong swimsuit. I tried to greet her pleasantly, but she didn't respond. I didn't want to make the children stay away from the hot tub or not enjoy their vacation. I supervised, not trusting her to be alone with them as they darted back and forth between the pool and the hot tub.

Using her phone to record herself (with my grandchildren in her background), she started dancing provocatively and licking her lips (probably making a TikTok). She then lay on her stomach, bent over on the side of the hot tub, with her completely exposed backside within a couple of feet of my young grandson's face. The only part we could see of her then was her derrière: all of it up close and personal! I was shocked. My grandkids looked at me shocked too. It was up to me to make a decision to protect them from obscenity or pass it off as no big deal. Why should I allow her obscenity? Why should we tolerate this indecent behavior and allow it to drive us out and force us to leave? Since her music was louder than my voice, in a split second, I splashed the only visible part of her to get her attention! When she turned to look, I confronted her about exposing herself to children and told her it was inappropriate. I warned her that if she didn't stop, it would be necessary to call the hotel management. After all, she could move back to the adult pool/hot tub.

We are called to love people but not to placate the devil and the spirits that attempt to operate against us or others. Has the church vacated areas of influence as the devil moved into them instead of taking a firm, respectful stand for right versus wrong? When we surrender these areas, they are taken over by dark forces. We have forfeited our influence and let the enemy occupy. For the last decade, we have heard so much about tolerance that we have allowed evil actions, especially against children, to go unchecked. We are not called to tolerate wrongdoing but to expose the deeds of darkness. These deeds are motivated by more than flesh and blood—by powers and principalities. They manifest in people and their actions. Sometimes, we can have conversations and plant seeds of truth, and other times, we must be bold in confronting blatant evil for the sake of others and the person too.

Conviction of wrongdoing is the beginning of recognizing wrong behavior. If we are never confronted or never confront wrongdoing, there is no conviction of wrongdoing. I have been confronted on numerous occasions in my life, and it left a stinging mark that I had done something wrong. It was the beginning of me turning to God's way and eventually changed my heart and actions.

After praying, I had no doubt that this woman needed confrontation, and my grandchildren also needed to know this was unacceptable behavior. Both the boys and girls needed to know there was something very wrong about her obscene, sexualized behavior. She got up, laughed at me, and sashayed away. I knew it was spirits mocking us through her behavior.

When I told my husband what happened, he said she had been conjuring demons previously. I certainly felt that presence, which explained why she wanted to be in our hot tub instead of the adult one. It was clearly a demonic manifestation. I prayed under my breath for her several minutes. I noticed that any time a male came near her, she turned her backside to them, making sure to offer a show. The spirits in her wanted attention. As a woman, I was in a better position to confront her. I was cordial but firm. Had she offered any opportunity or sorrow, I would have been in a position to minister to her. I did go to bed praying for her and hoping I had handled it correctly. A minister friend affirmed my response and helped me to see the absolute importance of correcting this for the children and exposing the deeds of evil.

When I say to the wicked, "You shall surely die," and you give him no warning, nor speak to warn the wicked from his wicked way, to save his life, that same wicked man shall die in his iniquity, but his blood I will require at your hand. Yet, if you warn the wicked, and he does not turn from his wickedness, nor from his wicked way, he shall die in his iniquity; but you will have delivered your soul.

—Ezekiel 3:18-19 (NKJV)

Sin is defined as "all wrongdoing" (1 John 5:17). Its origin is in rebellion against God. Satan is its father, the father of lies. All sin begins with a lie and the deception that there are no consequences for wrong behavior. But there are, and consequences destroy lives, the lives of innocent people, and ultimately the life of the rebel. Its outcome is heinous crimes against children, the defenseless, the elderly, and the most vulnerable in society. Sin should offend; we should not compromise its impact, hide that it's happening, or think it will go away. Sin does not stop unless confronted. God set up the Ten Commandments and created laws to protect people. These laws are the foundations of order. Without laws, there are no standards of right and wrong. Without a standard, people do what pleases them at the expense of harming others. Without law enforcement, lawlessness will abound. Lives, and eventually the life of a country, will be destroyed, and freedom will be stolen.

James 5:20 (ESV) says, "...*Whoever brings back a sinner from his wandering will save his soul from death and will cover a multitude of sins.*"

When I was an unsaved teen, someone confronted me about a situation that was wrong. At the time it bothered me, but it also convicted me that they rejected my actions. That rejection called my behavior into question, which ultimately led to my conversion to Christ Jesus.

There is no conversion without conviction. Conviction comes when we hear the truth. Then, it is the person's choice to rebel or to turn to God in humble correction. The believer is responsible for upholding what our Father says is true and just, regardless.

Jesus did not embrace sin. He reached out to sinners, but He drove out demons. If people allowed Him, He set them free from devils. He cast out devils, setting people in their right minds. He confronted people with the truth about their sin and then told them to "Go and sin no more." God loves people so much that He made a way of escape from sin and corruption in this world. We are to pray for people, that the spirits blinding them will be removed so they can hear the truth and be set free. When an opportunity exists, we should be open to being led by the Holy Spirit to speak truth with love to them. Love must be tough at times.

We are not to compromise children or give in to devils that want to harass or demoralize innocence. There is such a cultural emphasis on tolerance preached in churches that protecting the innocent has been completely forgotten. Jesus had very strong words about those who cause one of these little ones to stumble: *"It would be better for him if a millstone were hung around his neck, and he were drowned in the depth of the sea"* (Matthew 18:6, NKJV).

It is a far more loving thing to confront someone and let them know the outcome of their actions now while they have time to change than to "tolerate and coddle evil" and allow them to spend eternity in hell. And even worse, to take the innocent with them!

We can see in Isaiah 5:20 (NKJV) that it brings woe, which means great sorrow or distress, to those who choose this: "*Woe to those who call evil good, and good evil; who put darkness for light, and light for darkness; who put bitter for sweet, and sweet for bitter!*" Great sorrow or distress comes to the life of someone who perverts life and confuses evil with good.

There was a woman in John 4 whose life was filled with sorrow because of her choices. She was drawing water at a well when Jesus spoke to her. Jesus confronted her lifestyle of sexual sin and broken relationships. It's important to note that He treated her with respect. She was shocked that this man, a Jew, would speak to her at all. She wasn't accustomed to this. Many customs and attitudes in the culture forbade this. She was a Samaritan, looked down upon by Jews, and a woman, and not just a woman but a woman of ill repute. After conversing with her, He asked to meet her husband. She said, "I have no husband." Jesus confronted her with the truth, saying, "The truth is you've had five husbands and the one you're living with now is not your husband." She was astonished at His knowledge of her life and His authority to speak the truth. I'm sure His words convicted her to receive change, and she did.

Truth carries authority, and love penetrates the soul. The woman called Him a prophet and went into town to invite everyone who would listen to come and hear Jesus. She said, "Come hear the man who told me everything I ever did." If Jesus would have refused to confront her sin, she would not have trusted and received Him, or experienced a transformation. He cared enough to confront her lifestyle, and she was moved to receive Him. It was His boldness to confront her along with His willingness to receive her that brought her into God's plan for her.

Authority carries responsibility with it. Without truth, there is no real authority. It is truth that delivers a soul from the bondage of a lie. Open rebuke is better than secret love (Proverbs 27:5). Why must we expose evil? To protect the innocent and to separate right from wrong as an example to the young. It is to call the person's action or evil activity into question for their sake as well and to bring them to a place of decision between their choices and God's commands. How can others recognize and reject evil if no one is willing to expose darkness so they may know their trust is rooted in evil instead of God?

> **AUTHORITY CARRIES RESPONSIBILITY WITH IT. WITHOUT TRUTH, THERE IS NO REAL AUTHORITY. IT IS TRUTH THAT DELIVERS A SOUL FROM THE BONDAGE OF A LIE.**

Jesus did not scream at her or reject her because of her sin, but He also did not leave her in it and fail to have a discussion with her. Love isn't love if it doesn't want to *"gently instruct those who oppose the truth"* (2 Timothy 2:25, NLT). Her life had left her broken, unloved, and destitute. She didn't draw water with the other women because she was known for her behavior. "Even a child is known by his doings, whether they are right or wrong." Jesus knew and yet cared enough to have a conversation with her. Everyone else had conversations about her. Real love will reach past sin to help the person ensnared by it but will not embrace sin as acceptable.

The Age of Tolerance

Often, we believe that it is not nice to tell people the truth about wrongdoing. We want them to feel loved and accepted, and in an attempt to do so, truth is usually compromised. We harm them more by not engaging them in dialogue and helping them to understand what is helpful and harmful to their lives. It takes more courage to speak the truth in a spirit of love than it does to dismiss their actions completely and leave them in the harmful behavior that perpetuates their brokenness.

THE LUKEWARM GOSPEL OF "COME AS YOU ARE AND LEAVE AS YOU CAME" WILL NOT HELP PEOPLE BE TRANSFORMED. WE SHOULD INVITE ALL TO COME, BUT ONCE WE HAVE A CONVERSATION, WE CAN'T PRETEND THAT THEIR LIFESTYLE IS ACCEPTABLE IF IT VIOLATES GOD'S WORD.

The lukewarm gospel of "come as you are and leave as you came" will not help people be transformed. We should invite all to come, but once we have a conversation, we can't pretend that their lifestyle is acceptable if it violates God's Word. Many believers are silent because they fear rejection from people more than they have a respect for the Lord and a desire to protect from wickedness. *"Have nothing to do with the deeds of darkness but rather expose them"* (Ephesians 5:11, NIV).

Jesus was tougher on political and religious leaders who claimed to have the answers but didn't do anything to help people with their problems. Those who have been given more authority have a stricter judgment. Jesus confronted the Pharisees, who had been given both religious and political leadership, for their hypocrisy, calling them "whitewashed tombs"! "Who warned you to escape the coming judgment?" He exposed them as "of their father, the devil," and turned over their money changers' tables in the temple. He also called them a brood of vipers! These political and religious leaders were hypocritical in their judgment. Jesus also called Herod, a political religious leader, a "fox," which is translated in Hebrew as a jackal, an unclean animal. Too often, we hear the words "judge not lest you be judged" tossed around to shut down any confrontation of sin. The context is "not to judge hypocritically." The Word of God must be the standard of right or wrong, not a person's appearance or wealth or position. John 7:24 (KJV) says, *"Judge not according to the appearance, but judge righteous judgment."*

People choose whether to "acknowledge their sin that they might be saved." Conviction comes through confrontation. Either way, it will trouble them that someone clearly cared enough to confront their sinful behavior that's not only harming them but also the innocent. Perhaps our culture would not have deteriorated to this place if there had been those who were willing to speak truth to sin, to protect the innocent children or bystanders. If we witness a crime, we hopefully will intervene if it is in our power to do so. What about the crime of stealing innocence from children? Our protection of these little ones must be greater than our complacency and excuses.

Many leaders use evangelism as a reason to be silent. It's fine if you chose to lay aside your personal offense of lawlessness or indecency to reach an offender, but when their choices violate the innocent, conscience, or shed innocent blood, it is not acceptable to be silent. It is no longer a higher priority or choice to reach them; it becomes foremost to protect the law and those harmed by their lawbreaking transgression.

There are times to mind your own business, minister to a person in sin, confront evil, and even turn over tables of adulterous religion to protect the purity of faith in God. All of these are biblical scenarios in an effort to bring "His will to Earth as it is in heaven." We must pray and ask for discernment on how to minister truth. The goal is to expose darkness (ultimately Satan), restrain lawbreakers, stop evil and evildoers from harming the innocent, and to bring justice and restoration from God and His Kingdom.

We are witnessing what happens when the role of law enforcement is squelched in the natural realm. Crime rates rise and evil abounds. Children are killed in the streets, and drug abuse is rampant. There are consequences for the removal of law enforcement, and there are consequences when God's leaders and people do not address sin in the church or wickedness in the culture.

Psalm 94:16 (ISV) says, "*Who will rise up for me against the wicked? Who will stand for me against those who practice iniquity?*"

The hypocrisy of religion and evil is that it will strain at a gnat and swallow a camel. This was the hypocrisy of the political and religious leaders of Jesus's day as well. We have seen mandates for people to wear masks in major cities, but prostitution is legal in those same cities. Lawbreakers are turned back out on the streets. Even murder is treated with a lighter sentence than lesser crimes. In Oregon, people were fined for not wearing a mask, but drugs like heroin were legalized.[243] Which is more harmful to people? A church in our area stated its beliefs boldly on a sign: We believe in equity, love is love, etc.—but in their seven beliefs, not one mentioned we believe in God or Jesus or the Bible! This is what happens when restraint is gone: The Holy Spirit operating in believers is removed from church and society. He that restrains is removed (the Holy Spirit) before God's judgment is poured out in the end of days, but unfortunately, some churches have already removed His presence by choice.

This has become an age of tolerance, which is actually a minimization of sin, calling good evil and evil, good. The moral compass of the culture is broken, and those who would dare try to repair it become archenemy number one. Unfortunately, not only is the moral compass of evildoers broken, but the standard of the church has also moved in the same direction.

THIS HAS BECOME AN AGE OF TOLERANCE, WHICH IS ACTUALLY A MINIMIZATION OF SIN, CALLING GOOD EVIL AND EVIL, GOOD.

We are salt, and we are light. I believe that as the salt, we are called to season. If you have a wound, salt poured into a wound burns, but salt purifies, cleanses, and preserves. It may hurt, but the truth heals a wound when it's brought into the light. We are called to expose darkness, bring light to tough topics, cleanse the infection, and preserve truth so a person and a society can heal.

Truth sets people free. Are there no more truth bearers? Or do we only have left soft churches that embrace the way (sin) of Balaam, tolerate Jezebel spirits, and sexual sins? Jesus addressed these in the Revelation of the seven churches and the last days (Revelation 1-4). We can see the towns of Sodom and Gomorrah as another example. Was this not the same God we preach that judged these cities for their sexual sin? Throughout humankind, God has judged sin-consumed cities and cultures. It was the responsibility of the prophets to warn them of their sin and show them a way of repentance. The New Testament has more warnings about sinful behavior than any other category of passages. Are churches and believers honest enough with their faith to warn people that the wages of sin is still death? Truth sets us free, believer and unbeliever alike.

FREEDOM IN THE BATTLE

While playing with my sweet three-year-old, curly-haired granddaughter, Journey, she asked me if I was ever going to be a granny. "Well, to some people, I'm already a granny," I said with a laugh. To clarify what she meant, she said, "No, you know, when your neck does this." She proceeded to make a long V protrusion under her neck, like a triple chin. I laughed and said, "I'll try not to get that, but you'd still love me if I did, right?" She said, "No, I like your neck the way it is." I laughed even more. I determined I will not let my chin triple for my granddaughter's sake!

Now, I can't stop myself from getting older, but I do have control over how I get older! There are things we have control over and some things we do not, but we can certainly make the very most of our lives, our impact, and choices. We can't always stop the battles from originating, but we can determine how we fight them. We can choose, "As for me and my house, we're going to serve the Lord." We must remember that our lives and times are in God's hands. He created us for such a time as this, and nothing catches Him by surprise. The events around us can be unsettling, yet we must choose to be happy, to live the best life we can in spite of the difficulties. We live once in this life, and each day, the choice to follow God's plans and stay true belongs to us, regardless regardless of what others choose. We must consistently lay our swords down and sit at the feet of our Victor, the One who is faithful and true, and be reminded the battle is the Lord's.

You can't control everything or everyone around you, or all the headlines across the world, but you can control you and how you react and respond. You can control what you will do in your sphere of influence where you have impact. You can pray and petition heaven in faith and believe God for truth, restitution, and reformation. Then, you can do your part. Men and women have done so throughout history. You can choose whether to let go of your dreams, whether to quit on God and yourself. We all have things we want or need to quit, but we must not quit making the right decisions and doing the right things, even in a world of chaos—especially then.

There are past mistakes, hurts, and hardships we need to release to God within life's ups and downs. I picture myself waterskiing and remind myself to remember that when I fall down, it's best to let go of the rope! Otherwise, it's a very bumpy ride and may even drown me in care or sorrow. We need to develop a life balance of letting go of the rope. We need to let go of pressure and learn to cast the world's problems and our own on God. First Peter 5:7 (NIV) says, *"Cast all your anxiety on him because he cares for us."*

As I discuss in my *Better Than You Think* and *Better Than You Feel* books and workshops, we must let go of guilt, regret, bad habits, wrong beliefs, negative self-talk; and we must let go of this world's cares, its troubled times, and simply rest in God. Rest in the Lord. There are things to never let go of like the value, foundations, and principles of the Kingdom of God! There are some things you need to let go of or quit, but never let go of your faith in God.

During our first conference on finances, my husband, Gary, taught what became "Your Financial Revolution." Many were introduced to our ministry through it. Eventually, it went across the globe! What you may not know is our ministry board told me just before Gary spoke the opening evening of the conference that we were $11,000 short in the checking account. This was 25 years ago, and we were a far smaller ministry. That seemed like a tremendous amount then! We had a part-time bookkeeper, and we were investing our monies from our personal business, trying to get things off the ground. I asked the board not to share this with Gary right before he delivered the words that would become his signature message. I rightly identified this as an attack to discourage us. The timing was a sure giveaway!

We cannot afford to allow ourselves to be tossed around by situations and circumstances. Forces of darkness will attempt to manipulate the world's spheres and people. It's best to focus on what God said and ignore the distractions.

ONCE YOU RECOGNIZE THAT YOUR BEST DAYS ARE AHEAD, YOUR GREATEST PLATFORM IS USUALLY PRECEDED BY SPIRITUAL WARFARE AND CHALLENGING CIRCUMSTANCES.

Once you recognize that your best days are ahead, your greatest platform is usually preceded by spiritual warfare and challenging circumstances. You learn to resist those temptations to tuck your tail and run. There's an old saying, "It's always darkest before the dawn." It's not just a cliché.

That evening, I recognized the years we struggled and the ground we had gained personally were being challenged in the public arena. The enemy did not want us to take this new territory, and he certainly didn't want us to share freedom with others! With every new ground you take, there will be opposition. Once you win the battle on a personal level, it's imperative to help someone else fight their battles! As you do, you will encounter another level of warfare, but it yields a more satisfying victory.

Alone in our office, I prayed a simple prayer and asked God to come through for us that evening. I said, "I will not manipulate, or pressure, or beg anyone. I will simply trust you tonight." (I did throw in that I would never doubt Him again if He helped us, lol.) Our typical Wednesday evening offering was $1,500 or less, so $11,000 was a long shot. I asked Gary, "May I receive the offering in service?" He said, "Sure!" I had my faith engaged for what I knew was needed. Twelve thousand dollars came in that evening! That seemed like an impossible feat. I didn't make the need known or use any pressure whatsoever. I asked for and received the amount we needed in prayer, and it came to us. I was excited to see that the very principles we were teaching others not only worked in our personal finances but also in the ministry's! I told God I would never doubt Him again!

Circumstances come to steal your vision and destiny right before the takeoff of your dreams. As with a plane, the most challenging time is the takeoff. There must be enough speed to overcome the weight and drag for the law of lift to raise the vision. A pilot can't choke just beforehand or he will miss the lift and perhaps crash. What if? What if I would have panicked and gave way to fear? What if I would have begun to get upset and blamed God or someone else? What if we would have compromised what God told us to do because there was a price?

Don't let go of your dreams! As a young couple, we wanted to have the financial freedom to proclaim God's Word. We purposed to own a business that would fund ministry and to build a great marriage and family that would honor God. Our dream was to have freedom to see the world, build a great home, and change the world for Christ.

I had a dream in college of broken women, and I was helping to bring them into freedom and healing, and of rescuing children from evil. I have always been passionate about uncovering the enemy's lies concerning marriage and family. My desire has always been to help people see that God's plans for their lives are good and that He alone can produce happiness and peace.

Your vision may look very different than ours, but whatever comes, don't let go of the vision, the God-breathed destiny He gave you! I have been there, when we were hurting, and it looked like God's promises were far off! When our funds were so low, I remember asking if we could afford to buy our kids Happy Meals at Christmas. Otherwise, we purchased the kids a 39 cent burger and a water, and we could almost never eat at a sit-down restaurant.

The same pressure we had in the beginning of our ministry held true beforehand when starting our business. We basically just squeaked by, trying to learn the financial services business and starting our young family. We were always one setback from failing and sometimes had to have help from family.

After several years of this, we felt God instruct us to move to Ohio. That day, Gary came in from his usual jog and told me we were moving. I said, "I know, but where?" God had been stirring in me the same impression that we were moving. He said, "God spoke to me while I was praying, and we are to move to Ohio." Gary had grown up in Ohio, and I really wasn't surprised that God would take him there to be a witness to family who didn't know the Lord. As I prayed about this, God also confirmed to me that we would move to Ohio and do our end-time work. Because we had God's direction on this, I thought that when we arrived there, everything would be easy, but it was just the opposite. Not only were we starting all over in a new area, but we also had debt that we had incurred for several years just trying to survive. My husband got very discouraged trying to establish our business all over, now with a family of two children and another one on the way.

We were renting a twin single apartment that we struggled to make rent on, and even groceries were scarce. One evening, wishing we had enough money to eat out, I got an idea! If we could just scrape together enough money for one adult meal to split, I had two free children's dinner coupons for a spaghetti chain located downtown. Mind you, we had not even been downtown yet and didn't know our way around. We went through pockets, old handbags, couch cushions, and the car and finally managed to search out enough pocket change for one dinner and a tip for service. We drove downtown after stopping to convert our change to bills at the grocery store. Upon arriving at the restaurant, we quickly found that our wait would be over an hour! The kids were getting tired, and we were all so hungry that we decided we would leave. The coupons expired that day, and we opted for fast food instead. Not exactly what I had expected!

On our way out of the big city, a rock concert let out, and the streets were filled with people. Gary nervously drove, watching and trying to navigate through hundreds of people crossing the dark streets, yelling and singing. In all the commotion and on unfamiliar streets, he missed a red light in a triple block of lights right in front of an officer, who quickly pulled us over.

Gary was summoned to the officer's car, while our small children began to cry in fear that the police were taking Daddy away. I reassured them and prayed, unsure myself that he wouldn't be arrested. Because on top of running the light, we had been financially unable to pay off our car in Oklahoma, so we could not get an Ohio title. Ohio required a title to get a new license tag, but Oklahoma had a title-holding law, so we were in a catch 22 with no way to obtain new car tags.

Gary was released from the officer's car but was given two tickets to pay, and we cried on the drive back to the suburb where we lived. Stopping for fast food, we sat silent and defeated. I have never forgotten that night because it was one of the lowest points I can remember. I have never felt more like quitting. It was a painful evening, but we didn't quit on our dreams.

Eventually, we became financially free, built multimillion-dollar companies, and went on to pastor a large, thriving multi-campus church with media outlets all over the world. Our five children are serving God today because they witnessed the transformation of our lives.

Recognize that when you make incredible strides, win battles over debt or sickness, the world's giants are not going to leave you alone forever. We have seen many deliverances and the hand of God help us get freedom in every way imaginable, but once we take that ground, we must defend it to stay free.

The Hebrews broke free from Pharaoh and his bondages of slave labor, political, and religious persecution. It was an act of God's deliverance, following intense plagues, that Pharaoh released them. Once he did, he regretted it. In Exodus 14:5 (NIV), he and his officials recanted:

> *When the king of Egypt was told that the people had fled, Pharaoh and his officials changed their minds about them and said, "What have we done? We have let the Israelites go and have lost their services!"*

The enemy always makes a second play for you after you have been delivered from Egypt (the world's system). Whether you have been healed, experienced financial breakthroughs, been delivered from sinful actions, reclaimed your family and children, or tasted truth and victory of any kind, there is a battle you must fight after the battle you've won. You can't simply gain ground and rest on your past. The truth sets you free, but continuing it keeps you free! The same God that got you out of the messes of yesterday expects you to stay true to the relationship today. Our human nature tends to be attentive when we need help, thankful when we receive it, and over time, to forget where we came from and just how much God has done for us. Perhaps no one has seen this like a pastor!

To the Hebrew children, it appeared briefly that they had been delivered from Pharaoh, but:

> *So he had his chariot made ready and took his army with him. He took six hundred of the best chariots, along with all the other chariots of Egypt, with officers over all of them. The Lord hardened the heart of Pharaoh king of Egypt, so that he pursued the Israelites, who were marching out boldly.*
> —Exodus 14:6-9 (NIV)

As Pharaoh approached, the Israelites looked up, and there were the Egyptians marching after them. They were terrified and cried out to the Lord.

The enemy uses fear to paralyze and then to move back into any area where we have gained freedom. The temptation is to return to old patterns and to revert back to old belief systems, living in Egypt's ways of yesterday.

The people, when faced with reappearing problems that they had assumed were conquered, became fearful and blamed their leader. They blamed God, blamed Moses, blamed someone instead of squaring their shoulders and facing the real enemy, Satan and his messengers. As long as we compromise and co-exist with a bully, we will always live with him. Blaming won't change it. Only God and His Word that freed us before will keep us free.

They said to Moses, "Was it because there were no graves in Egypt that you brought us to the desert to die? What have you done to us by bringing us out of Egypt? Didn't we say to you in Egypt, 'Leave us alone; let us serve the Egyptians'? It would have been better for us to serve the Egyptians than to die in the desert!"

—Exodus 14:11-12 (NIV)

Resist the temptation of the enemy to blame leaders and others for your problems. This is a diversion and won't bring freedom or keep you free. The Israelites regretted that they believed! I've seen people do this. It's easy to make the right choices on a sunny day, but what happens when the warfare returns? How do we deal with our fears and frailty tempting us to return to the patterns of the world we grew up in?

Moses answered the people, "Do not be afraid. Stand firm and you will see the deliverance the Lord will bring you today. The Egyptians you see today you will never see again. The Lord will fight for you; you need only to be still."

—Exodus 14:13-14 (NIV)

God will remind you of who you are called to be coupled with an admonition not to fear! I was once attacked by two ferocious pit bull dogs running toward me from about 100 feet away. There was no one nearby to help me. I was alone. In that moment, I had to make a choice to stand! To stand still when they were charging full force at me, baring their teeth and snarling. It was a frightening moment, but as I stood, they stopped short of the attack. Be still and stand. "When you have done all you know to do, stand." Stand in faith. Stand in truth. Stand in a position of victory and freedom. You will see the perpetrators of evil no more once you defeat them and refuse to allow them to ever enslave you again.

"Then the Lord said to Moses, 'Why are you crying out to me? Tell the Israelites to move on" (Exodus 14:15, NIV).

The Lord says to you today, "Stop crying! Move on!"

I have been through the toughest situations, but once I stopped crying and looking at my distress, I heard the voice of my Father, who I know loves me. He strengthened me to stand and use my authority against my spiritual enemy and stop his assault. God told Moses the same! *"Raise your staff and stretch out your hand over the sea to divide the water so that the Israelites can go through the sea on dry land"* (Exodus 14:16, NIV).

> **I HAVE BEEN THROUGH THE TOUGHEST SITUATIONS, BUT ONCE I STOPPED CRYING AND LOOKING AT MY DISTRESS, I HEARD THE VOICE OF MY FATHER, WHO I KNOW LOVES ME. HE STRENGTHENED ME TO STAND AND USE MY AUTHORITY AGAINST MY SPIRITUAL ENEMY AND STOP HIS ASSAULT.**

The apostle Paul was in a similar situation. He had Judaizers following him wherever he preached. They taunted him, mocked him, and at times even beat him up. Paul sought deliverance from God three different times, but the Lord said, "My grace is sufficient for you." In other words, I have given you a grace to walk out your ministry, to run your race in the midst of persecution, in the midst of enemies, in a crooked and perverse generation. I have given you the power to stand and to continue to fight the good fight of faith, to Fight Like Heaven!"

God will instruct you on what to do when you face problems, which usually come through the pharaohs of life. Our Father will give us counsel by His Spirit on the inside of us. He says, "Do what I tell you, and go through!"

God instructed Moses on what He would do and what Moses needed . to do. Remember, we have our part, and God has His.

> *"I will harden the hearts of the Egyptians so that they will go in after them. And I will gain glory through Pharaoh and all his army, through his chariots and his horsemen. The Egyptians will know that I am the Lord when I gain glory through Pharaoh, his chariots and his horsemen."*

> *Then the angel of God, who had been traveling in front of Israel's army, withdrew and went behind them. The pillar of cloud also moved from in front and stood behind them, coming between the armies of Egypt and Israel. Throughout the night the cloud brought darkness to the one side and light to the other side; so neither went near the other all night long.*
> —Exodus 14:17-20 (NIV)

The same Holy Spirit who led you will stand between you and the enemy that desires to hit you a second time!

> *Then Moses stretched out his hand over the sea, and all that night the Lord drove the sea back with a strong east wind and turned it into dry land. The waters were divided, and the Israelites went through the sea on dry ground, with a wall of water on their right and on their left. The Egyptians pursued them, and all*

> *Pharaoh's horses and chariots and horsemen followed them into the sea.*
>
> —Exodus 14:21-23 (NIV)

I have seen the hand of God lure evildoers into a trap and then spring it on them to catch them in their misdeeds. He is God, and His Word reminds us, "He laughs at the wicked." They will not outsmart God or His plans for your life. As long as we refuse to abandon God, He will not abandon us. Moses trusted God and obeyed Him, and God performed the Word He had spoken. God is still performing His Word on your behalf.

> *During the last watch of the night the Lord looked down from the pillar of fire and cloud at the Egyptian army and threw it into confusion. He jammed the wheels of their chariots so that they had difficulty driving. And the Egyptians said, "Let's get away from the Israelites! The Lord is fighting for them against Egypt."*
>
> —Exodus 14:24-25 (NIV)

When we obey and stand on God's promises, He throws our enemy into confusion!

> *Then the Lord said to Moses, "Stretch out your hand over the sea so that the waters may flow back over the Egyptians and their chariots and horsemen." Moses stretched out his hand over the sea, and at daybreak the sea went back to its place. The Egyptians were fleeing toward it, and the Lord swept them into the sea.*

The Lord will give you an action plan! God opened a window, in this case a sea, and provided a way of escape for God's children.

*The water flowed back and covered the chariots and horsemen—
the entire army of Pharaoh that had followed the Israelites into
the sea. Not one of them survived. But the Israelites went through
the sea on dry ground, with a wall of water on their right and on
their left. That day the Lord saved Israel from the hands of the
Egyptians, and Israel saw the Egyptians lying dead on the shore.
And when the Israelites saw the mighty hand of the Lord displayed
against the Egyptians, the people feared the Lord and put their
trust in him and in Moses his servant.*

—Exodus 14:28-31 (NIV)

Regardless of wars, rumors of war, evildoers, mockers, censorship, shaking, rocking, shifting, pestilence, or any other issue, remember "Nothing can separate you from the love of God in Christ Jesus!" Trust God with your dreams and visions, and He will give you the power, the grace, to do what He told you, the Word He gave you. Put your faith in Him and confidently expect to win whatever battle rears its head. Trust God's Word to you is true and His plan will not harm you but bring good to you all the days of your life. This is your moment! It is no accident you are here! You must make up your mind to break fear and doubt! Philippians 1:28 (NASB) says, *"And in no way be alarmed by your opponents—which is a sign of destruction for them, but salvation for you, and that too, from God."* Pray for courage! Fight like heaven and take your life back.

LIVING ON GUARD

I am a bit of a rock hound. Since childhood, I have enjoyed collecting rocks and nice stones. Once, my loving husband carried a very large rock, a crystal geode, on his shoulder almost a mile back to our campsite for me. I have petrified wood in my yard from another journey. If you pan for gold in one of the 12,000 Alaskan rivers, in order to separate gold from sediment or dirt, you must shake the deposits in a pan. Sediment will be sifted out and washed away, but gold, because it is a weightier substance, will stay intact and sink to the bottom. You discover the gold through the shaking and sifting.

> *"This is what the Lord Almighty says, 'In a little while I will once more shake the heavens and the earth… I will shake all nations, and what is desired by all nations will come, and I will fill this house with glory,' says the Lord Almighty."*
> —Haggai 2:6-7 (NIV)

Glory is weighty. God's glory withstands the shaking and fills the temple. You and I are the temples of the Holy Spirit. As distractions and trivial matters are shaken from us, the glory fills our lives. This is where we are in these days! The glory of God, His presence, resides on the inside of each person who knows Him. When this shaking occurs in the world, the gold will be separated from the sediment, and it will bring forth His glory, the magnificence of what is His.

> *"The Lord knows those who are His,"* and *"Everyone who confesses the name of the Lord must turn away from wickedness."*
> —2 Timothy 2:19 (NIV)

This is not church as usual! We have come through shaking, and everything will continue to shake until the return of the Lord.

THIS IS NOT CHURCH AS USUAL! WE HAVE COME THROUGH SHAKING, AND EVERYTHING WILL CONTINUE TO SHAKE UNTIL THE RETURN OF THE LORD. "NORMAL ISN'T COMING BACK; JESUS IS."

"Normal isn't coming back; Jesus is." We must be anchored to the only Rock that can help us stay firm in the storms and shaking, knowing that the sun will come out once this season is fulfilled. Meanwhile, we have this hope as an anchor for our soul, firm and secure. It is impossible for God to lie (Hebrews 6:18-19). It will become evident where we have invested and placed our treasure and trust in these times. For those who love Him and are called according to His purpose, they will come through this fire and be sifted to become pure gold. God's glory brings miracles, peace, and joy.

There was a woman in 2 Kings 4 who was unable to have children. She was married to a man of affluence and able to afford many things, but that didn't answer her longing for a child. She was curious to hear the word of God, so she invited a prophet, named Elisha, to eat in her home. She heard the Word of God during his visits. Then she spoke with her husband to influence him to build a room onto their home for the prophet to stay in when he was in town. In this way, she housed the glory of God and all He was doing in the earth. The prophet wanted to bless her for this generosity. He prayed and prophesied to her that she would hold a son of her own in her arms a year from then.

In a year, she held the promised son, and he grew into a young boy. God's glory always brings impossibilities to reality! Then an attack came against God's gift. One day while working with his father in the fields, the boy grabbed his head in pain and fell. They took him to his mother, and he died in her arms. The once joyful mother lost her dream, her son. The future could have seemed lost. But instead of despair, she kept speaking, "It is well" through the ordeal and returned to the prophet Elisha to tell him what had happened. She looked to Elisha and the Kingdom of God because she had built her trust there. After coming to the prophet, she shared her situation. Elisha went to the young man and prayed over him with life and breath, and he came back to life.

Sometime later, Elisha instructed the woman to take her son and go to another land while a famine ravaged the land of Israel for seven years. She left all she had, and she and her son went away for the seven years. Upon returning after the famine, she went to the king to ask to reclaim her abandoned property. The Holy Spirit orchestrated a divine strategy to restore the woman's losses. The king was listening to her very story, read from Elisha's diaries by his former assistant, in the moment she entered his presence. God had already prepared the way for her to receive back what had been lost. The king ruled to have the matter investigated and to return her house and lands, along with the seven years of harvest lost while she was gone!

This is an amazing example of how God moved in a sphere of influence to favor someone who trusted in Him. Hers had been a journey of faith. The earth curse world's system of sickness tried to take her vision; the world's system of famine tried to take her provision, but God provided her with a family, vision, and provision. The kingdom that we have trusted in will be the kingdom we rely on when in need and having difficulties. When we face troubles in life, we will turn to the system that is our priority. She had prioritized God's Word and mission in her life, and it was from there that she received help in times of sorrow.

God provided for her in Shunem and then took her away to escape the coming famine. He restored to her all that the enemy sought to take from her, her family and her finances. But she had developed her trust in God's system. She was not pulled into fear but stood on truth. "It is well," she said. That is the voice of faith in God. The system she had trusted in became everything to her. In the midst of trouble, she turned to the Word she had fed on in her house and the Word that had occupied her house. It became her everything, her answer.

God took her away for seven years, and then she returned to reoccupy her possessions and even to receive what she had missed, because she trusted God as her source in the good and the challenging times. Her heart was established in God's Word more than disaster, more than famine, more than the government. The Kingdom she trusted had power over both.

In the Garden, Adam and Eve ate from the Tree of the Knowledge of Good and Evil instead of the Tree of Life, from the enemy's fickle system instead of God's abundance. We, too, have been trained in things that are contrary to God's Word. In this hour, we must especially recognize this and let the truth, what God says, train our senses to discern between good and evil.

The enemy knows how powerful you are as a born-again, new creation in Christ, especially as you are filled with His Spirit and manifest His glory. Satan is trying to keep us off of God's path through hurts and deception. I find it interesting that Scripture warns us in the last days the love of many will grow cold because of the hardness of their hearts. Wrongdoing and not forgiving offenses hardens hearts. We can discern the will of the Lord for our lives and families if we talk to God in prayer and keep our hearts in a place of tenderness toward Him. We must stay in God's Word and pray in His Spirit to sift wrong from our hearts. Abhor what is evil, and cling to what is good (Romans 12:9).

We need help to discern our own hearts. "The fear of the Lord is the beginning of knowledge." What is that fear of the Lord? For me, it is to fear being without His presence more than anything else. Proverbs 2:1-5 instruct us to, "Search for God's wisdom as hidden treasure." It's an attitude, not just an understanding. When Cain and Abel offered their sacrifice, Cain had a wrong attitude toward the Lord. It wasn't what he gave; it was how he gave, with a hard heart and a wrong attitude. This is a head versus heart attitude. Our hearts must be trained to want to be like Jesus more than anyone or anything we see in the world. Jesus said, "If you're not for me, you're against me." Our heroes can't be stars or villains. Our goal cannot be to obtain popularity but rather to become like Him!

If we meditate on the Word of God day and night, it makes our way prosperous. Proverbs 2:6 (NIV) says, "*The Lord gives wisdom,*" and Jesus said, "To you it has been given to know the mysteries of the Kingdom of God!" There is so-called wisdom of the world coming at us from all directions, from universities, from media, from entertainment, but we decide where we will align our hearts. If God's wisdom isn't treasured, it won't be revealed to us. We must seek it as treasure and have an attitude that it is life itself. Guard your heart with all diligence for in it is life, all the issues of life (Proverbs 4:20-23).

If people try to achieve the blessings that come with the fear of the Lord through the wisdom of the world, it will not work that way! The deception of the life of celebrity culture ends badly; we need only to look at the outcomes. The greatest names in stardom end up bankrupt, and their families are wrought with pain, brokenness, divorce, suicide, and murder.

We cannot spend more time with social media, news, movies, entertainment, and gaming than we spend with God and in His Word and expect to have the wisdom and blessings of God. We will trust in the system we have developed in our lives. What are we giving our primary attention to? It will impact our hearts and direct the course of our lives. We must impact and influence the culture but not allow it to direct

WE CANNOT SPEND MORE TIME WITH SOCIAL MEDIA, NEWS, MOVIES, ENTERTAINMENT, AND GAMING THAN WE SPEND WITH GOD AND IN HIS WORD AND EXPECT TO HAVE THE WISDOM AND BLESSINGS OF GOD.

our belief system or our actions when they are contrary. We must build a bridge to reach people in the spheres of influence, but we can't compromise God's Word to do so.

This is the story of the wise and foolish virgins in Scripture preparing and waiting on the marriage supper. The ones who were not attentive to their spiritual lives did not have oil for their lamps when the bridegroom came and wanted to borrow it from others. They said, "No, we will not have enough for ourselves. Go get your own!" Everyone must get their own oil, have their own relationship with God through the Holy Spirit (the oil). Your mother or father's relationship will not buy your oil. It must be your own. Work out your own salvation with a fear of the Lord. "Seek Him while He may be found."

> *Let not mercy and truth forsake you.... Write them on the tablet of your heart. And so find favor and high esteem in the sight of God and man. Trust in the Lord with all your heart and lean not on your own understanding; in all your ways acknowledge Him, and He shall direct your paths. Do not be wise in your own eyes. Fear the Lord and depart from evil. It will be health to your flesh and strength to your bones. Honor the Lord with your possessions, and with the firstfruits of all your increase; and so your barns will be filled with plenty.*
> —Proverbs 3:3-10a (NKJV)

This covers health, fitness, finances, and success, not just our church attendance or faith. Proverbs 4:20-22 (NLT) say, *"My child, Pay attention to what I say ... they [my words] bring life to those who find them, and healing to their whole body."* We don't want to secularize or compartmentalize our faith. God's Word speaks to every mountain in life, with instructions, and gives us authority to speak to the mountains that attempt to create havoc against our faith.

Jesus said, "If you say to this mountain, 'Be removed and cast into the sea,' and do not doubt in your heart, it shall be done for you." We have authority in these spheres when we keep ourselves from worshiping at the tree of their knowledge. What we compromise to gain we will ultimately lose. Although we want to use our God-given authority to reach the people in every sphere, we cannot let cunning and crafty plans pull us into their lifestyles.

Power, money, and sex are the "Big Three" areas Satan uses to tempt and attack men and women, and there is no exception for those who love God. People struggle to navigate these powerful desires, displayed in mountains of influence that draw us into the temptations of the world's system. We have seen the fallout of men and women of God who compromised and destroyed their lives and ministries. We must not drown while trying to save those in trouble. We have seen ministers build lives of incredible outreach and inhabit these spheres only to lose everything in a brief moment of indiscretion or pain. The world will entice those who have influence to fall into the same trap of Satan, being wise in our own eyes and forgetting it is the Lord who gave us the power to get wealth to establish His Kingdom, not ours.

It looks innocent and exciting in the movies, but unfaithfulness to a spouse and sexual appetites being out of control ruin lives. Proverbs 5:8-12 warn those getting involved in adultery: It will take your honor and all that you make. In the end, you will be consumed with disease. "Oh, how I hated discipline! If only I had not ignored all the warnings!"

These strong words remind us to share our sexual intimacy with our spouse only. You will be satisfied and intoxicated with her love.

This only happens if we guard our lives from other messages that tempt us to look outside our marriage, God's provision for intimacy. Pain seeks pleasure, and when we feel pain, we must run to God and our spouse. Otherwise, the world is all too ready to offer a counterfeit.

A culture that no longer protects children is set for destruction. In the last 40 years, our culture has sent a very clear message to children, "You don't matter." Toy stores like ToysRUs and the original FAO Schwarz are things of the past, and even children's clothing stores have almost disappeared. Yet pet superstores abound. Americans spend over $100 billion a year on pets, which is more than the combined GDP of the 39 poorest countries in the world.[244] [245] [246]

> **A CULTURE THAT NO LONGER PROTECTS CHILDREN IS SET FOR DESTRUCTION. IN THE LAST 40 YEARS, OUR CULTURE HAS SENT A VERY CLEAR MESSAGE TO CHILDREN, "YOU DON'T MATTER."**

A school superintendent was petitioned by students to put litter boxes in school restrooms to accommodate kids identifying themselves as "furries." When the superintendent's potential plans were reported at a recorded school board meeting, the video went viral, sparking parental outrage and public disgust. Predictably, the superintendent denied the allegations as fake news, but the genie was already out of the bottle.[247] These children believe they are dogs, cats, or other pets. And why wouldn't these children want to be animals? The culture has more esteem for its pets than its children. The culture has departed from truth and sent the message: Truth is relevant, and you can be anything you want to be, even an animal.

As citizens of the kingdom of Earth and the Kingdom of heaven, we must pray, "Your will be done on earth as it is in heaven." We are to possess Earth and bring heaven's peace, joy, provision, healing, and values into culture, every mountain, and carry the Kingdom of God wherever we go, demonstrating truth with power. God's Word is truth coupled with God's presence, His power manifested through you. We accept Jesus's commission in Mark 16:17-18 that tells us to take action:

> "In My Name, they will cast out demons. They will speak with new tongues. They will take up serpents; and if they drink anything deadly, it will by no means harm them. They will lay hands on the sick, and they will recover."

It's always a David versus Goliath scenario, lest we get discouraged. The religious authorities in Jerusalem sent priests to ask John the Baptist who he was. He told them plainly, "I am not the Christ." And when they asked if he were the Prophet, he said "No!" Finally, they asked, "Who are you then? We have to give an answer to the ones who sent us. Tell us who you are!" John answered in the words of the prophet Isaiah, "I am only someone shouting in the desert, 'Get the road ready for the Lord'" (John 1:8-9).

Yes, Jesus is coming again, and we must pave the way.

> *Do not let your hearts be troubled. You believe in God; believe also in me. My Father's house has many rooms; if that were not*

so, would I have told you that I am going there to prepare a place for you? And if I go and prepare a place for you, I will come back and take you to be with me that you also may be where I am. You know the way to the place where I am going.

—John 14:1-4 (NIV)

The disciples asked Jesus when He would set up His Kingdom. In Mark 13:28, Jesus reveals the conditions that precede His return, and He gives them an indication of the timing. We know the season but not the day or hour:

"Now learn this parable from the fig tree: When its branch has already become tender, and puts forth leaves, you know that summer is near. So you also, when you see these things happening, know that it is near—at the doors! Assuredly, I say to you, this generation will by no means pass away till all these things take place. Heaven and earth will pass away, but My words will by no means pass away.

But of that day and hour no one knows, not even the angels in heaven, nor the Son, but only the Father. Take heed, watch and pray; for you do not know when the time is. It is like a man going to a far country, who left his house and gave authority to his servants, and to each his work, and commanded the doorkeeper to watch. Watch therefore, for you do not know when the master of the house is coming—in the evening, at midnight, at the crowing of the rooster, or in the morning—lest, coming suddenly, he find you sleeping. And what I say to you, I say to all: Watch!"

—Mark 13:28-37 (NKJV)

Our role is to preach the Kingdom of God and refuse to back down to cultural pressure to compromise what God says is right or wrong. Too many faith and religious leaders are taking their cues from the world's standards instead of God's. Younger faith leaders need to be aware that they have most likely been trained in Marxist ideologies in media, schools, and propaganda. If the Bible has a different viewpoint than the culture, Scripture commands us to come out from among them and be separate. We need the Holy Spirit to give us understanding and discernment. Scripture teaches us that in the last of times, if the days were not shortened, even the very elect would be deceived. Deception and offense are signs of the last days. Let's stay the course and keep free from deception.

We must protect our own hearts from error; protect our children from error; protect our churches from error, especially from wolves in sheep's clothing; arm ourselves with truth, and share it with whoever will listen. It doesn't take an entire army to defeat Goliath, just someone who will believe God's Covenant and challenge Goliath.

Ephesians 5 clearly instructs us how to live in the last of days.

> *...No immoral, impure or greedy person—such a person is an idolater—has any inheritance in the kingdom of Christ and of God. Let no one deceive you with empty words, for because of such things God's wrath comes on those who are disobedient. Therefore do not be partners with them.*
>
> *For you were once darkness, but now you are light in the Lord. Live as children of light (for the fruit of the light consists in all goodness, righteousness and truth) and find out what pleases the*

Lord. Have nothing to do with the fruitless deeds of darkness, but rather expose them.

—Ephesians 5:5-11 (NIV)

Be very careful, then, how you live—not as unwise but as wise, making the most of every opportunity, because the days are evil. Therefore do not be foolish but understand what the Lord's will is. Do not get drunk on wine, which leads to debauchery. Instead, be filled with the Spirit.

—Ephesians 5:15-18 (NIV)

Be filled with God's Spirit. There is peace in God's Spirit. There is joy in God's Kingdom. There is direction, provision, and vision. We stay filled with God's Spirit by meditating on His Word, staying anchored in the storm to what He says instead of the storm. We have an incredible future ahead and promises that are worth fighting for to stand on. Jesus said He would never leave us nor forsake us. Let's not forsake Him in the name of cultural influences. Friends or fellow believers may, but if we stand with God, He will stand with us. Just as there are two kingdoms at war, there are two eternal destinies— heaven or hell. Each will be rewarded according to their decision.

That's why we must fight like heaven! When I spoke with a publisher about this book, he said, "Fight like heaven" and "Get the hell out of here!" I guess he's right! We need to drive hell out of people's lives and help them find heaven. And when this Gospel of the Kingdom is preached to every nation, we will get out of here.

Women, men, and children of every background, God has called us to take up the truth and speak it with real love, love that doesn't compromise truth but builds a bridge to share it, for it is only truth that sets us free.

Be on guard! When you see these things, look up. Your redemption is nearer than ever.

EPHESIANS 2:6-7 (NIV):

"And God raised us up with Christ and seated us with him in the heavenly realms in Christ Jesus, in order that in the coming ages he might show the incomparable riches of his grace, expressed in his kindness to us in Christ Jesus."

EPHESIANS 6:10-12 (NIV):

"Finally, be strong in the Lord and in his mighty power. Put on the full armor of God, so that you can take your stand against the devil's schemes. For our struggle is not against flesh and blood, but against the rulers, against the authorities, against the powers of this dark world and against the spiritual forces of evil in the heavenly realms."

EPHESIANS 6:13-15 (NIV):

"Therefore put on the full armor of God, so that when the day of evil comes, you may be able to stand your ground, and after you have done everything, to stand. Stand firm then, with the belt of truth buckled around your waist, with the breastplate of righteousness in place, and with your feet fitted with the readiness that comes from the gospel of peace."

EPHESIANS 6:16 (NIV):

"In addition to all this, take up the shield of faith, with which you can extinguish all the flaming arrows of the evil one."

EPHESIANS 6:17 (NIV):

"Take the helmet of salvation and the sword of the Spirit, which is the word of God."

ZECHARIAH 4:6 (NIV):

"So he said to me, 'This is the word of the Lord to Zerubbabel: 'Not by might nor by power, but by my Spirit,' says the Lord Almighty."

JOSHUA 23:10 (NIV):

"One of you routs a thousand, because the Lord your God fights for you, just as he promised."

DEUTERONOMY 3:22 (NIV):

"Do not be afraid of them; the Lord your God himself will fight for you."

JOSHUA 1:9 (NIV):

"Have I not commanded you? Be strong and courageous. Do not be afraid; do not be discouraged, for the Lord your God will be with you wherever you go."

2 CORINTHIANS 10:4 (NIV):

"The weapons we fight with are not the weapons of the world. On the contrary, they have divine power to demolish strongholds."

2 CORINTHIANS 10:5 (NIV):

"We demolish arguments and every pretension that sets itself up against the knowledge of God, and we take captive every thought to make it obedient to Christ."

LUKE 10:19 (NIV):

"I have given you authority to trample on snakes and scorpions and to overcome all the power of the enemy; nothing will harm you."

1 JOHN 4:4 (NIV):

"You, dear children, are from God and have overcome them, because the one who is in you is greater than the one who is in the world."

ROMANS 8:37 (NIV):

"No, in all these things we are more than conquerors through him who loved us."

1 TIMOTHY 6:12 (NIV):

"Fight the good fight of the faith. Take hold of the eternal life to which you were called when you made your good confession in the presence of many witnesses."

JAMES 4:7 (NIV):

"Submit yourselves, then, to God. Resist the devil, and he will flee from you."

2 THESSALONIANS 3:3 (NIV):

"But the Lord is faithful, and he will strengthen you and protect you from the evil one."

PROVERBS 28:1 (NIV):

"The wicked flee though no one pursues, but the righteous are as bold as a lion."

DEUTERONOMY 28:7 (NIV):

"The Lord will grant that the enemies who rise up against you will be defeated before you. They will come at you from one direction but flee from you in seven."

1 PETER 5:8-9 (NASB):

"Be of sober spirit, be on the alert. Your adversary, the devil, prowls around like a roaring lion, seeking someone to devour. But resist him, firm in your faith, knowing that the same experiences of suffering are being accomplished by your brethren who are in the world."

PSALM 60:12 (NIV):

"With God we will gain the victory, and he will trample down our enemies."

PSALM 91:7 (NIV):

"A thousand may fall at your side, ten thousand at your right hand, but it will not come near you."

PSALM 18:39 (NIV):

"You armed me with strength for battle; you humbled my adversaries before me."

PSALM 91:11-12 (NIV):

"For he will command his angels concerning you to guard you in all your ways; they will lift you up in their hands, so that you will not strike your foot against a stone."

MATTHEW 18:18 (NIV):

"Truly I tell you, whatever you bind on earth will be bound in heaven, and whatever you loose on earth will be loosed in heaven."

ISAIAH 41:10 (NIV):

"So do not fear, for I am with you; do not be dismayed, for I am your God. I will strengthen you and help you; I will uphold you with my righteous right hand."

ISAIAH 43:1-2 (NASB1995):

"But now, thus says the Lord, your Creator, O Jacob, and He who formed you, O Israel, "Do not fear, for I have redeemed you; I have called you by name; you are mine!"

ISAIAH 54:4A (NIV):

"Do not be afraid; you will not be put to shame. Do not fear disgrace; you will not be humiliated."

ISAIAH 54:17 (NIV):

"No weapon forged against you will prevail, and you will refute every tongue that accuses you. This is the heritage of the servants of the Lord, and this is their vindication from me," declares the Lord."

JEREMIAH 1:19 (NIV):

"They will fight against you but will not overcome you, for I am with you and will rescue you," declares the Lord."

2 CHRONICLES 20:15B (NIV):

"This is what the Lord says to you: 'Do not be afraid or discouraged because of this vast army. For the battle is not yours, but God's.'"

1 CORINTHIANS 16:13 (NIV):

"Be on your guard; stand firm in the faith; be courageous; be strong."

PSALM 144:1 (NIV):

"Praise be to the Lord my Rock, who trains my hands for war, my fingers for battle."

2 TIMOTHY 4:18A (NIV):

"The Lord will rescue me from every evil attack and will bring me safely to his heavenly kingdom."

PSALM 44:5 (NIV):

"Through you we push back our enemies; through your name we trample our foes."

REVELATION 12:11 (NIV):

"They triumphed over him by the blood of the Lamb and by the word of their testimony; they did not love their lives so much as to shrink from death."

23

TAKE THE
MOUNTAIN!

The steepest mountain I've ever climbed was in Italy when headed to a monastery at night with a car full of people. The road's incline was straight up the mountain with no guardrails, lights, or signage. It was our son Tom's wedding, and his bride-to-be, Alexis, had dreamed since childhood of being married on a quaint Italian mountainside. The trip there was harrowing. We had quite a fiasco flying into Rome, navigating car rentals, trains, and guests. I rented a car, which is always smaller than promised, to drive the bride and groom and everyone's luggage on the three-hour journey to a tiny Tuscan town.

The bride's mom, aunt, brother, and grandma had to take a train and then a bus. It was my job to pick them up at our destination's bus stop. After accidentally driving in a bus lane when leaving Rome and experiencing a few other road hazards, I made it to Sansepolcro. There was just one more problem. I didn't have enough room to pick them up if anyone else was in the vehicle. I drove over 4,000 feet on the steep, straight incline up the mountain to drop off my son and his bride, then raced back down to town to find the bus station. Their bus was due! I spoke no Italian and couldn't read a sign. The car's GPS system had no clues. I prayed and finally pulled up to a fire station to get help. The man could only point the other way. I went that direction, praying fervently and thinking of the grandma standing in the dark in a strange town. As I prayed, I encountered a bus headed toward me. I made a U-turn in the road and followed that bus straight to the roadside drop-off.

I was never so relieved as when I saw the grandma and crew get off the bus! Because the car was so small, the bride's mom had to crouch behind the driver's seat and hold on to my headrest for fear of life as we climbed straight up the mountain. My warning could not have prepared them for that climb!

Later that night, I discovered my husband's plane was delayed and he would arrive an hour before the wedding the following day! It was a bit mentally challenging, but the only option was to persevere. When all the preparations for the ceremony were finished, I only had a few minutes to prepare myself. In a hurry, I applied dry shampoo to my hair then realized, as the entire bottle dumped on my head, that it was the refill and not the squirt applicator.

I then had a stark, white face and granny hair, dry and white. My dress was the traditional Italian wedding black. White hair, white face, and black clothes—my first Goth look. It was too late. I had to attend as I was.

As Tom and Alexis exchanged their beautiful vows amidst the fall leaves and lovely, misty tuscan mountain view, the presence of the Spirit of God was strong, it flooded all our hearts, and we cried tears of joy. It was overwhelmingly powerful and anointed by God

Himself. As they shared handwritten vows in a tender ceremony, all was forgotten of the hectic scenes beforehand, the pressures, and my own flawed appearance.

The disciples asked Jesus what His coming would be like. Jesus shared His coming would be like a wedding. All the disciples were Galilean and knew their wedding customs. In a Galilean wedding, the father and son would make a covenant with the bride, and her father would make a covenant with their family. To seal their covenant of betrothal, the bride would drink from a cup of wine offered by the groom, known as the cup of joy. They would part, and the groom would go with his father to prepare a place for her in his father's house. During their time of separation, the bride would begin her preparation of making herself ready for her groom's appearance.

Galilean weddings had a humorous, special twist. The groom would appear sometime between the midnight hour and the wee hours of the morning, like a thief in the night. When all the wedding preparations were made, the father would tap his son and say, "Go and get your bride!" Only the father knew the time, but everyone who truly knew the family recognized the season was close.

The groom would go through the streets blowing a shofar as guests grabbed their cloaks and came along to join the wedding party. The groom appeared at her door to get his bride and placed her on a litter (riser) where she was carried to the marriage supper to exchange vows, feast, and celebrate for seven days. Once the doors to the wedding venue were closed, no one else could enter. The guests had to have oil ready for their lamps, watching and waiting for the groom's shofar to blast in the night.

THE DAY IS NEAR WHEN THE FATHER WILL APPEAR TO HIS SON, TAP HIM ON THE SHOULDER, AND SAY, "GO AND GET YOUR BRIDE."

The day is near when the Father will appear to His Son, tap Him on the shoulder, and say, "Go and get your bride."

During the trials of COVID and social upheaval, I grew intensely protective of our church family, our ministry friends and partners, and our family. I wanted to gather the ones I love and care for to a safe place, an island or somewhere far away, to protect them. Then I realized that's how Jesus feels toward us. He even said to Israel how He longed to gather them, but they would not let Him. Jesus's incredible desire for us and to protect us will bring Him back to gather His beloved ones to a place He has prepared for us.

GOD IS CALLING US TO BE SOLDIERS OF THE LIGHT, WITH LOVE AS OUR WEAPON AND THE HOLY SPIRIT AS OUR SOURCE OF POWER AND PROTECTION.

Until the day of the Lord's return, we must live on guard and make the most of our days, for the days are evil. We must put on the full armor of God, of Ephesians 6, and be dressed for war. God is calling us to be soldiers of the light, with love as our weapon and the Holy Spirit as our source of power and protection. We must keep ourselves free from the love of the world and its sin-filled temptations.

God's method of "being alert and staying aware" with peace-filled hearts is prayer.

Be anxious for nothing, but in everything by prayer and supplication, with thanksgiving, let your requests be made known to God; and the peace of God, which surpasses all understanding, will GUARD your hearts and minds through Christ Jesus.

—Philippians 4:6-7 (NKJV)

Keep your heart and mind guarded. Our minds must be renewed to what God says. Our hearts must be sold out to the Kingdom of God. We extensively expose evil in systems so as "not to be ignorant of Satan's schemes" and proactively move to bring God's answers. How do we deal with evil and schemes? We pray fervently. We petition heaven. We make intercession in prayer. God desires to reach people, and we need to build a bridge between them and God. We do this by praying for them and holding evil back so they can hear Him. We demonstrate His good will toward them. We push back the evil that is blinding them by praying. The entire Lord's Prayer is an outline on how to pray and bring heaven into encounters on Earth.

Jesus said to pray like this:

Our Father in heaven, may your name be kept holy. May your Kingdom come soon. May your will be done on earth, as it is in heaven. Give us today the food we need, and forgive us our sins, as we have forgiven those who sin against us. And don't let us yield to temptation, but rescue us from the evil one.

If you forgive those who sin against you, your heavenly Father will forgive you. But if you refuse to forgive others, your Father will not forgive your sins.

—Matthew 6:9-15 (NLT)

We honor Him as holy, our source, keeping His Kingdom foremost in our thoughts and minds. We receive our needs met and believe His Kingdom operates here just as it does in heaven, to be reproduced in the earth. We pray to stay free from temptation and extend His forgiveness toward others and ourselves. Forgiveness is the key to staying free from the enemy's condemning voice and allowing bitterness to consume our soul.

Admittedly, I found myself getting frustrated enough to jump to my feet and yell at the TV a few times over the last years. The injustice just got too much for me! I had to stop, pray, and remind myself that God's justice is inescapable even if it may appear to be delayed for a brief moment in time.

Isaiah 32:5-8 (NKJV) remind us:

> *The foolish person will no longer be called generous. Nor the miser said to be bountiful; for the foolish person will speak foolishness, and his heart will work iniquity: To practice ungodliness, to utter error against the Lord, to keep the hungry unsatisfied, and he will cause the drink of the thirsty to fail. Also the schemes of the schemer are evil; he devises wicked plans to destroy the poor with lying words, even when the needy speaks justice. But a generous man devises generous things, and by generosity he shall stand.*

Did you see that? A generous person will stand! So when evildoers are devising evil plans to harm people, to work injustice, God instructs us to devise generous things. And in this, we will stand! This is how we overcome evil with good!

In March of 2020, two days before Washington, D.C. locked down due to COVID-19, Gary and I flew to D.C. The airport was apocalyptic with very few people, and Pennsylvania Avenue was entirely empty. We walked from building to building and prayed over our nation and government. No TV crews were with us—just us and a phone. That January, God had told me to go. I had originally planned to take 75 women, but due to the challenges, it was just the two of us. But women on guard were praying for us. We made our trek through the foundations of our nation's government, stopping as the Holy Spirit led, and praying against corruption in our nation's capital, at the Department of Justice, the FBI, and interceding for our country to stand in this dark hour.

When we arrived at the Capitol, a strong and urgent prophetic anointing to pray came upon me. I began to bind Satanic powers against the unborn and our nation. I decreed freedom from oppression. It was intense. Then we stood at the Supreme Court and did the same.

I would later learn that Congress was in an emergency session. Nancy Pelosi had arrived to add a tremendous amount for abortion funding and measures to the trillions for COVID relief that were to be passed by emergency order. I believe God had us there to pray fervently to stop this atrocity in prayer, along with others across our nation. It was voted down.

Jeremiah said:

> *"Now the Lord gave me knowledge of it, and I know it; for You showed me their doings. But I was like a docile lamb brought to*

the slaughter; and I did not know that they had devised schemes against me, saying, 'Let us destroy the tree with its fruit, and let us cut him off from the land of the living, that his name may be remembered no more.'"

—Jeremiah 11:18-19 (NKJV)

Jeremiah was feeling the pressure of his enemies' plot to destroy him and God's people. He turned to God to bring justice—and God did!

Lamentations 3:59-60 (NLT) remind us:

You have seen the wrong they have done to me, Lord. Be my judge, and prove me right. You have seen the vengeful plots my enemies have laid against me.

Yes, God has heard! He says He will vindicate you when evil tries to discourage you.

Psalm 37:6-8 (NKJV) promise:

He shall bring forth your righteousness as the light, and your justice as the noonday. Rest in the Lord, and wait patiently for Him; do not fret because of him who prospers in his way, because of the man who brings wicked schemes to pass. Cease from anger, and forsake wrath; do not fret—it only causes harm.

Unbridled anger or fear will not help us, but God will! Our faith is in an unshakable Kingdom. The attacks that try to destroy God's people have always been a springboard to blessings from God. You may ask, "How?"

We grow through pressure! Our ability to use the sword of the Spirit gets sharpened. It tests our allegiance to God, and we find a deeper commitment, which orchestrates a win in the battle for us and produces fear in our enemies. Pressure intensifies our resolve to do something! To take action! To enter the battle all in!

THE ATTACKS THAT TRY TO DESTROY GOD'S PEOPLE HAVE ALWAYS BEEN A SPRINGBOARD TO BLESSINGS FROM GOD.

God's love and compassion for you is rewarded with blessings spiritually, emotionally, and materially. We inherit the Kingdom as we stand and fight alongside our King!

Matthew 5:10-12 (NKJV) say we are blessed, or happy, when we are mistreated.

Blessed are those who are persecuted for righteousness' sake, for theirs is the kingdom of heaven. Blessed are you when they revile and persecute you, and say all kinds of evil against you falsely for My sake. Rejoice and be exceedingly glad, for great is your reward in heaven, for so they persecuted the prophets who were before you.

If we recognize that their insults, attitudes, and evil plots work for us, we can get happy about it instead of fretting in fear or seething in anger. As Paul says in 2 Corinthians 12:10 (NIV):

"That is why, for Christ's sake, I delight in weaknesses, in insults, in hardships, in persecutions, in difficulties. For when I am weak, then I am strong."

Even when it appears as if I have lost something for following Jesus, my all-time favorite reminder that I need to readjust my attitude is in Mark 10:30. Jesus promises that when we give up anything for the Kingdom of God, it's only temporary! He said whoever gives up anything will not *"fail to receive a hundred times as much in this present age: homes, brothers, sisters, mothers, children and fields—along with persecutions—and in the age to come eternal life"* (Mark 10:30, NIV).

Romans 8:35-37 are our guarantee that no matter what attempts to harm us, there is absolutely nothing that can come between God and His great love for us. Our faith works by knowing His love is completely reliable.

> *Who shall separate us from the love of Christ? Shall trouble or hardship or persecution or famine or nakedness or danger or sword? As it is written: "For your sake we face death all day long; we are considered as sheep to be slaughtered." No, in all these things we are more than conquerors through him who loved us.*
> —Romans 8:35-37 (NIV)

Finally, it is that love that always causes us to win the fight, to take hold of what is promised, and to see the victory He promised. Psalm 110:3 (AMP) says, *"Your people will offer themselves willingly [to participate in Your battle] in the day of Your power...."*

Fight Like Heaven!

"FOR WHOSOEVER IS BORN OF GOD OVERCOMETH THE WORLD. AND THIS IS THE VICTORY THAT OVERCOMETH THE WORLD, EVEN OUR FAITH."

(1 JOHN 5:4, KJ21)

ENDNOTES

1   https://www.weforum.org/about/history

2   https://www.weforum.org/about/world-economic-forum

3   Klaus Schwab, "Davos Manifesto 2020: The Universal Purpose of a Company in the Fourth Industrial Revolution," https://www.weforum.org, December 2, 2019

4   https://www.weforum.org/communities/strategic-partnership

5   Klaus Schwab, "Now Is the Time for a 'Great Reset,'" https://www.weforum.org, June 3, 2020

6   "The Great Reset," https://www.weforum.org

7   Ida Auken, World Economic Forum, "Welcome to 2030: I Own Nothing, Have No Privacy and Life Has Never Been Better," https://www.forbes.com, November 10, 2016

8   https://web.archive.org/web/20200919112906/https://twitter.com/wef/status/799632174043561984

9   Klaus Schwab, *The Fourth Industrial Revolution*, 2013, page 25

10   World Economic Forum, "The Fourth Industrial Revolution," https://www.youtube.com, December 17, 2015

11   Juliana Chan and Benjamin Seet, "Where Will Evolution Take Us in the Fourth Industrial Revolution?" https://www.weforum.org, June 29, 2019

12   Dr. Zelenko | Yuval Noah Harari | "Who Is the Anti-God Agenda-Pushing-Leader of 'The Great Reset'?" https://www.zeeemedia.com, March 27, 2022

13 Laura Miller, "Why Has Silicon Valley Embraced a Little-known Israeli Academic?" https://www.slate.com/culture, November 1, 2018

14 Ibid.

15 Dr. Zelenko | Yuval Noah Harari | "Who Is the Anti-God Agenda-Pushing-Leader of 'The Great Reset'?" https://www.zeeeme-dia.com, March 27, 2022

16 Yuval Noah Harari | "We Don't Need to Wait for Jesus Christ to Overcome Death," https://www.battleplan.news, April 28, 2022

17 Dr. Zelenko | Yuval Noah Harari | "Who Is the Anti-God Agenda-Pushing-Leader of 'The Great Reset'?" https://www.zeeeme-dia.com, March 27, 2022

18 Yuval Noah Harari | "We Don't Need to Wait for Jesus Christ to Overcome Death," https://www.battleplan.news, April 28, 2022

19 Dr. Zelenko | Yuval Noah Harari | "Who Is the Anti-God Agenda-Pushing-Leader of 'The Great Reset'?" https://www.zeeeme-dia.com, March 27, 2022

20 Transhumanism | "Klaus Schwab and Dr. Yuval Noah Harari Explain the Great Reset/Transhumanism Agenda," https://rumble.com, February 8, 2022

21 Ibid.

22 Yuval Noah Harari | "We Don't Need to Wait for Jesus Christ to Overcome Death," https://www.battleplan.news, April 28, 2022

23 Transhumanism | "Klaus Schwab and Dr. Yuval Noah Harari Explain the Great Reset/Transhumanism Agenda," https://rumble.com, February 8, 2022

24 Ibid.

25 Yuval Noah Harari | "We Don't Need to Wait for Jesus Christ to Overcome Death," https://www.battleplan.news, April 28, 2022

26 Ibid.

27   Transhumanism | "Klaus Schwab and Dr. Yuval Noah Harari Explain the Great Reset/Transhumanism Agenda," https://rumble.com, February 8, 2022

28   Ibid.

29   Ibid.

30   Dr. Zelenko | Yuval Noah Harari | "Who Is the Anti-God Agenda-Pushing-Leader of 'The Great Reset'?" https://www.zeeemedia.com, March 27, 2022

31   Yuval Noah Harari | "We Don't Need to Wait for Jesus Christ to Overcome Death," https://www.battleplan.news, April 28, 2022

32   Ibid.

33   https://www.younggloballeaders.org/community

34   https://www.weforum.org

35   Nota Akhir Zaman, "Document: Hidden Alliance of Former WEF Young Global Leaders Working in Lockstep," https://www.wikispooks.com, January 27, 2022

36   https://wikispooks.com/wiki/WEF/Young Global Leaders

37   "Unmasked: Klaus Schwab's Traitors—A More Complete List. Meet the Young Global Leaders, Class of 2021. You Don't Know Their Names, but You Will," https://www.dailynewsbreak.com

38   Joss Wynne Evans, "Klaus Schwab's WEF Alumni—A List," https://www.tarableu.com, October 6, 2021

39   https://www.strategic-culture.org/news, November 19, 2021

40   https://www.en.wikipedia.org/wiki/Young_Global_Leaders

41   https://www.younggloballeaders.org/vision-and-mission

42   https://www.weforum.org/about/Klaus-Schwab

43   https://www.britannica.com

44   https:// www.en.wikipedia.com/wiki/shinar#cite

45   K. van der Toorn, P.W. van der Horst, "Nimrod Before and After the Bible," The Harvard Theological Review, 83 *(1): 1–29, esp. 2–4,* January 1990

46   Rev. A. J. B. Vuibert, *An Ancient History: From the Creation to the Fall of the Western Empire in A. D. 476,* pg. 25

47   David Rohl, *Legends: The Genesis of Civilization* (1998) and *The Lost Testament* (2002)

48   https://www.vision.org

49   "Religion and Spirituality: The Hapless Gods of Egypt," https://www.vision.org

50   "The Myth of Osiris and Isis," https://www.worldhistoryedu.com, April 19, 2022

51   "The Hidden Hand of the Order of the Illuminati, Freemasonry and the Occult," https://thestrangerfiction.com, August 24, 2019

52   "Skull and bones, Secret Society, Yale University," https://www.brittanica.com

53   Paul Goldstein and Jeffrey Steinberg, "George Bush, Skull & Bones, and the New World Order," https://www.biliotecapleyades.net.com, April 1991

54   "Skull and Bones or 7 Fast Facts about Yale's Secret Society," https://www.newenglandhistoricalsociety.com

55   "Secret Societies," The History Channel

56   "Who Was Albert Pike?" https://www.threeworldwars.com

57   Albert Pike, *Morals and Dogma of the Ancient and Accepted Scottish Rite of Freemasonry,* 1871

58   https://www.freemasonrywatchdog.org

59   Walter Martin, *Kingdom of the Cults*

60   "Global Celebrities Who Have turned Hindu or Have Been Touched by Sanatana Dharma," https://www.mynation.com

61   https://www/en.wikipedia.com/Rajneesh

62   "Christians Are the Largest Religious Group in 2015," https://
      www.pewresearchcenter.com

63   "The Mathematical Probability Jesus Is Christ," https://www.
      empower.global

64   Alfred Edersheim, *The Life and Times of Jesus the Messiah*,
      1993, chapter 9

65   Walter Martin, *Kingdom of the Cults: The Definitive Work on
      the Subject*

66   Arthur Lyons, *Satan Wants You*, Mysterious Press, 1988

67   "Answers," https://www.billygraham.org, May 18, 2011

68   Manfred Bartel, *The Jesuits History and Legend of the Society of
      Jesus*, 1984

69   Adolf Hitler

70   Hermann Raushnig, Hitler m'a dit, Paris, 1939

71   Breitbart News network

72   "Archbishop Vigano Calls Out Catholic Leaders," https://www.
      thenewamerican.com, February 4, 2022

73   Tom DeWeese, "Agenda 21 to Green New Deal – The War on
      Human Society," https://www.americanpolicy.org, December 14,
      2020

74   Alexander King and Bertrand Schneider, *The First Global Revo-
      lution: A Report by the Council of the Club of Rome*, 1991

75   Dr. Eric T. Karlstrom, Natural Climate Change, "Anthropocentric
      (Man-caused) Global Warming (AGW): Should Fraud, Fiction,
      and Fear Provide the Basis for Public Policy?" https://www.natu-
      ralclimatechange.org

76   Tom DeWeese, "Agenda 21 to Green New Deal – The War on
      Human Society," https://www.americanpolicy.org, December 14,
      2020

77   "United Nations Conference on Environment & Development, Rio de Janeiro, Brazil, 3 to 14 June 1992; Agenda 21," https://sustainabledevelopment.un.org/outcomedocuments/agenda21

78   Tom DeWeese, "Agenda 21 to Green New Deal – The War on Human Society," https://www.americanpolicy.org, December 14, 2020

79   "United Nations Conference on Environment & Development, Rio de Janeiro, Brazil, 3 to 14 June 1992; Agenda 21," https://sustainabledevelopment.un.org/outcomedocuments/agenda21

80   "United Nations: Department of Economic and Social Affairs, Transforming Our World: The 2030 Agenda for Sustainable Development," https://www.sdgs.un.org/2030agenda

81   Tom DeWeese, "The Fraud of Climate Change and the Drive for Control," https://www.americanpolicy.org, February 4, 2021

82   Kyle Morris and Sam Dorman, "Over 63 Million Abortions Have Occurred in the US Since Roe v. Wade Decision in 1973," https://www.news.yahoo.com, May 4, 2022

83   "Abortion Leading Cause of Death," Breitbart, January 2, 2022

84   Alatheia Larsen, "Planned Parenthood's Top 7 Donors Gave Staggering $324 Million in Four Years," https://www.lifesitenews.com, March 3, 2015

85   https://www.catholiccitizens.org

86   "Archbishop Vigano Calls Out Catholic Leaders," https://www.thenewamerican.com, February 4, 2022

87   *The Four Horsemen of the Endgame* documentary, Ken Klein, 2019

88   "Six Essential International Organizations You Need to Know," https://www.world101.cfr.org

89   "Is the UN More Powerful Than the US? We Find Out," https://www.humanitariancareers.org

90   Tom DeWeese, "Agenda 21 to Green New Deal – The War on Human Society," American Policy Center, https://www.ameri-canpolicyorg./2020/12/14/agenda

91   Ibid.

92   September 11, 1990, George Bush Declares "New World Order," Begins Endless Wars, https://www.weblinenews.com, September 10, 2016

93   Brianna Lyman, "Biden: 'There's Going to Be a New World Order," *Daily Caller*, https://www.dailycaller.com, March 21, 2022

94   Arnold Fruchtenbaum, "The Messianic Time Table According to Daniel the Prophet," https://jewsforjesus.org, April 20, 2018

95   "The Four Beasts or Kingdoms from the Book of Daniel," https://www.thewordonendtimes.com

96   "The Beast Kingdoms of Daniel 2 and Daniel 7," https://www.christianitybeliefs.org/revelation-timeline-decoded, August 2, 2015

97   "The Prophecy of Daniel 2," https://www.signs-of-end-times.com

98   Richard F. Ames, "The Coming One-World Government!" https://www.tomorrowsworld.org

99   Sean Busick, "The American and French Revolutions Compared," https://www.theimaginativeconservative.org, 2013

100 Ibid.

101 Paul D. Jagger, "The City, The Crown, and The Royal Family," https://www.cityandlivery.co.uk

102 https://www.rothschildarchive.org

103 https://www.britannica.com/Rothschild family, European family

104 *The Four Horsemen of the Endgame* documentary, Ken Klein, 2019

105 "Traders: The East India Company & Asia,| Royal Museums Greenwich," https://www.rmg.co.uk

106 "British East India Company," https://www.historycrunch.com

107 Brian Duignan, "5 Fast Facts About the East India Company," https://www.britannica.com

108 "Karl Marx was Rothschild's Third Cousin," https://www.christianobserver.com

109 Karl Marx and Fredrich Engels, "Manifesto of the Communist Party," https://www.marxists.org, February 1848

110 David R. Papke, "Karl Marx on Religion," https://www.law.marquette.edu/facultyblog

111 *The Four Horsemen of the Endgame* documentary, Ken Klein, 2019

112 *The Four Horsemen of the Endgame* documentary, Ken Klein, 2019

113 "Timeline of Depopulation Demanded by the British Rothschild's Crime Syndicate – Your Time Should NOT Be Wasted," https://www.concisepolitics.com, February 11, 2018

114 David Menton, "The Religion of Nature: Social Darwinism," *Essays on Origins: Creation vs. Evolution*, revised and reprinted September 23, 2017, https://www.answeringenesis.org/charles-darwin/darwinism/religion-of-nature-social-darwinism

115 *The Four Horsemen of the Endgame* documentary, Ken Klein, 2019

116 "Margaret Sanger on 'Human Weeds' – 'Real Facts About Birth Control'" | Eugenics and Other Evils, https://www.eugenics.com, 1923

117 Brian Clowes, Ph.D., "The Strange World of Margaret Sanger's *Birth Control Review: Part 1*," https://www.hli.org, April 18, 2017

118   *The Four Horsemen of the Endgame* documentary, Ken Klein, 2019

119   Naeim Darzi, "Socialism, Eugenics, and Population Control," https://www.epochtimes.com, March 10, 2009

120   *The Four Horsemen of the Endgame* documentary, Ken Klein, 2019

121   Cecil Rhodes and John Ruskin | Ethio-enemamar Blog, https://www.wordpress.com

122   John Ruskin (1819-1900) (mentored Cecil Rhodes) | https://www.mediachecker.wordpress.com

123   "Rhodes Scholarships and the British Network of Agents in the World | Military Foreign Affairs Policy Journal for Clandestine Services," https://www.veteranstoday.com, April 7, 2022

124   *The Four Horsemen of the Endgame* documentary, Ken Klein, 2019

125   https://www.wikipedia.com/chathamhouse

126   *The Four Horsemen of the Endgame* documentary, Ken Klein, 2019

127   "U.S. National Debt Tops $30 Trillion as Borrowing Surged," https://www.nytimes.com, February 1, 2022

128   Kimberly Amadeo, "US Inflation Rate by Year: 1929-2023," https://www.thebalance.com, March 28, 2022

129   Jeff Neal, "When Nixon Went to China," Harvard Law Today, https://www.today.law.harvard.edu, February 17, 2022

130   "U.S. Relations with China 1949-2022," https:/www.cfr.org

131   Ibid.

132   Ibid.

133   Michelle Nash-Hoff, "It's Time to End China's Most Favored Nation Status," https://www.themadeinamericamovement.com

134   Soo Youn, "40% of Americans Don't Have $400 in the Bank for Emergency Expenses: Federal Reserve," http://www.abcnews. go.com, May 24, 2019

135   Abraham Flexner, "Medical Education in the United States and Canada: A Report to the Carnegie Foundation for the Advancement of Teaching," page 22

136   "The Truth about the Rockefeller Drug Empire," https://www. thelibertybeacon.com, October 7, 2015

137   Ken Adachi, "Forbidden Cures," https://www.educate-yourself. org, August, 2002

138   Martha Rosenberg, "Why Do Few Women Know the Dangers of the Pill?" https://www.theepochtimes.com/c-womens-health, March 16, 2022

139   Mike Gaskins, *In the Name of the Pill*, Copyright 2019

140   Martha Rosenberg, "Why Do Few Woman Know the Dangers of the Pill?" https://www.theepochtimes.com, March 14, 2022

141   Zachary Steiber, "EXCLUSIVE: Fauci says Great Barrington Declaration Reminds Him of AIDS Denialism," https://www. theepochtimes.com, March 16, 2022

142   Abir Ballan, "Question Everything," https://www.theepochtimes. com, July 21, 2021

143   Alice Giordano, "Doctor Honored and Investigated by Same State for Same Work," https://www.theepochtimes.com, March 25, 2022 (updated March 29, 2022)

144   Eva Fu, "Children in China Diagnosed with Leukemia after Vaccine," https://www.theepochtimes.com, March 11, 2022 (updated March 15, 2022)

145   Julian Conradson, "SHOCKING: Millennials Experienced the Worst-Ever Excess Mortality in History—An 84% Increase in Deaths After Vaccine Mandates Introduced," https://www.the-gatewaypundit.com, March 19, 2022

146   Mark Tapscott, "NIH Deleted Info from Wuhan Lab," https:// www.theepochtimes.com, March 30, 2022

147 "Drug Overdose Deaths in the U.S. Top 100,000 Annually," https://www.cdc.gov, November 17, 2021

148 "Overdose Death Rates," https://www.nida.nih.gov/trends-statistics, January, 2022

149 Clay Clark, "The Great Reset: 'Humans Are Hackable Animals, Free Will Is Over?' – Professor Yuval Noah Harari," February 7, 2022

150 Dr. Joseph Mercola, "The Global Takeover Hinges on Pandemics and Transhumanism," https://www.basedunderground.com, April 16, 2022

151 Ibid.

152 Ibid.

153 Jon Jureidini and Leemon B. McHenry, Professor Emeritus, "The Illusion of Evidence Based Medicine," https://www.bmj.com, March 16, 2022

154 Ibid.

155 https://www.nobelprize.org/prizes/medicine/2015/press-release

156 Ronald Reagan, "Abortion and the Conscience of the Nation," https://www.humanlifereview.com

157 https://www.who.int/fact-sheets/detail/abortion, November 25, 2021

158 Mike Landry, "Report Exposes FDA's Purchase of Fetal Heads, Organs Used for 'Humanized Mice' Project," https//www.westernjournal.com, September 20, 2021

159 Dr. Joseph Mercola, "The Global Takeover Hinges on Pandemics and Transhumanism," https://www.basedunderground.com, April 16, 2022

160 https://www.gs.statcounter.com/search-engine-market-share

161 Joe Allen, "Vaxxed by Machines, Tracked by Machines: Humanity to Be Augmented One Cell at a Time," https://joebot.substack.com, March 29, 2022

162 Avery M. Jackson, III, MD, FACS, FAANS, *The GOD Prescription: Our Heavenly Father's Plan for Spiritual, Mental, and Physical Health*, 2018.

163 Sarah Taylor, "Jen Psaki Tells Chris Wallace that Kindergarten Teachers Should Be Able to Talk with Children about Whether They Believe They Are a 'Girl or a Boy,'" https://www.theblaze.com/news, April 21, 2022

164 Abigail Shrier, *Irreversible Damage: The Transgender Craze Seducing Our Daughters,* 2020

165 Abigail Shrier, "How Activist Teachers Recruit Kids," https://www.substack.com

166 https://www.itspronouncedmetrosexual.com/2018/10/the-genderbread-person-v4

167 https://nationalfile.com/wp-content/uploads/2019/10/GenderbreadPersonLGBTQUmbrella.pdf

168 https://transstudent.org/gender

169 Stephanie Kramer, "U.S. Has World's Highest Rate of Children Living in Single-parent Households," https://www.pewresearch.org, December 12, 2019

170 Amanda Barrosi, Kim Parker, and Jesse Bennett, "As Millennials Near 40, They're Approaching Family Life Differently Than Previous Generations," https://www.pewresearch.org, May 27, 2020

171 John Elflein, "Distribution of the 10 Leading Causes of Death Among Teenagers Aged 15-19 Years in the United States in 2019," https://www.statista.com, October 25, 2021

172 Alia Dastagir, "More Young People Are Dying by Suicide, and Experts Aren't Sure Why," https://www.usatoday.com, September 11, 2020

173 "Developmental Competencies and Resilience," https://www. youth.gov/youth-topics

174 Joseph R. John, "The Indoctrination of American Students in Socialism," https://www.sonorannews.com, October 7, 2019

175 Ibid.

176 Jacqueline, "Abigail Adams, Wife of Our Second President, Was a Homeschool Mom," https://www.deeprootsathome.com, October 1, 2018, modified February 8, 2022

177 Jessica Parnell, "Famous Homeschoolers," https://www. homeschoolacademy.com, February 28, 2019

178 Vaneetha Rendall Risner, "Will You Lose Your Faith in College?" https://www.desiringgod.org, August 23, 2018

179 Preston Cooper, "Is College Worth It? A Comprehensive Return on Investment Analysis," https://www.freopp.org, October 19, 2021

180 Melanie Hanson, "Average Cost of College and Tuition," https:// www.educationdata.org, January 27, 2022

181 Melanie Hanson, "Student Loan Forgiveness Statistics," https:// www.educationdata.org, January 1, 2022

182 Caroline Smith, "University vs. Apprenticeship: Which One Is Right for You?" https://www.skillsyouneed.com

183 The Editorial Team of "Nine Commentaries on the Communist Party," "How the Spector of Communism Is Ruling Our World Chapter Five, Part II: Infiltrating the West (UPDATED)," https:// www.theepochtimes.com, June 21, 2018, Updated April 1, 2022

184 Data from the National Vital Statistics System – Series 21, Number, "Divorces and Divorce Rates, United States," https://www. cdc.gov, March 1978

185 W. Cleon Skousen, *The Naked Communist*, Izzard Ink, Salt Lake City, Utah, Copyright 1958

186   Leslie Bray Brewer, "Our Nation's Consecration," https://www.thestokesnews.com, September 27, 2017

187   Leslie Bray Brewer, "Our Nation's Consecration," https://www.thestokesnews.com, September, 2017

188   Charles Spiering, "Donald Trump Visits St. John's Church, Vows to End the Rioting," https://www.breitbart.com, June 1, 2020

189   Karl Gelles, Veronica Bravo, and George Petras, "How Police Pushed Aside Protestors Ahead of Trump's Controversial Church Photo," https://www.usatoday.com, June 5, 2020

190   L. Brent Bozell, Founder and President of the Media Research Group, "BOZELL: The Real Story of Black Lives Matter—Marxist, Anti-Family Radicals," https://www.cnsnews.com, July 1, 2020

191   Tom Kertscher and Amy Sherman, "Ask Politifact: Does Black Lives Matter Aim to Destroy the Nuclear Family?" https://www.politifact.com, August 28, 2020

192   https://www.merriam-webster.com

193   L. Brent Bozell, Founder and President of the Media Research Group, "BOZELL: The Real Story of Black Lives Matter—Marxist, Anti-Family Radicals," https://www.cnsnews.com, July 1, 2020

194   https://www.allianceforreligiousfreedom.com

195   Jesse L. Jackson, Jr., *The Finger of God: From the Lineage of David to the Presidency of the United States*, Archway Publishing, Bloomington, Indiana, 2021

196   Thomas Paine, *Common Sense*, Philadelphia, Pennsylvania, January, 1776

197   Aaron Baer, President of the Center for Christian Virtue (CCV)

198   U.S. Senate: Constitution Day, https://www.senate.gov

199   Alexander Hamilton, "The Federalist No. 33," *The Independent Journal*, January 1788

200   "Overview—Rule of Law," https://www.uscourts.gov

201 Alexis Flynn, "What are Examples of the Rule of Law?" https://www.greedhead.net

202 "The Rule of Law and Transitional Justice in Conflict and Post-Conflict Societies: Report of the Secretary-General," https://www.un.org, 2004

203 Alexander Hamilton, "The Federalist 73," *The Independent Journal*, May 28, 1788

204 28 U. S. C. § 453, Oaths of Justices and Judges, emphasis added

205 5 U. S. C. § 3331, Oath of Office, emphasis added

206 *Declaration of Independence*, July 4, 1776

207 Shobhit Seth, "The World's Top Media Companies," https://investopedia.com, updated April 14, 2022

208 Joseph Johnson, "Global Market Share of Search Engines 2010-2022," https://www.statista.com, March 1, 2022

209 Joe Concha, "Fox News Anchor Addresses Cutting Off Gingrich Linking Soros to Violent Protests," https://www.thehill.com, September 17, 2020

210 Masooma Haq and Jan Jekielek, "Upcoming Platform Truth Social Key Step Toward Restoring Good Governance: CEO Devin Numes," https://www.theepochtimes.com, February 7, 2022

211 Fred Lucas, "Clinton, Trump, and 6 Keys to What's Next in Special Counsel's Spying Probe," https://www.thedailysignal.com, February 23, 2022

212 "Judicial Watch: Records Reveal Tech Operatives Allegedly Used by Hillary Clinton Campaign to Spy on Trump WH Had Contract with Defense Advanced Research Projects Agency," https://www.judicialwatch.org, February 16, 2022

213 "What Is Psychological Warfare?—Definition, Techniques & Examples," https://www.study.com, July 24, 2020

214   "What is Psychological Warfare?—Definition, Techniques & Examples," https://www.study.com, July 24, 2020, updated January 24, 2022

215   OAN Newsroom, "CNN Executive Says Network Spins Truth, Joins Project Veritas," https://www.conservativedailynews.com, February 27, 2022

216   Dan Avery, "Nearly 1 in 10 Teens Identify as Gender-Diverse," https://www.nbcnews.com, May 21, 2021

217   "Key Terms and Concepts in Understanding Gender Diversity and Sexual Orientation Among Students," https://www.apa.org/pi/lgbt/programs/safe-supportive/lgbt/key-terms.pdf

218   "The Trevor Project National Survey on LGBTQ Youth Mental Health," https://www.thetrevorproject.org

219   Lawrence S. Mayer and Paul R. McHugh, "Executive Summary," *Sexuality and Gender Findings from the Biological, Psychological, and Social Sciences, The New Atlantis*, Number 50, Fall 2016, pp. 7-9

220   https://www.lexico.com/en/definition/brainwashing

221   Tarpley Hitt, "New Data from the National Center for Missing and Exploited Children Reveals Facebook had 20.3 Million Reported Incidents of CSAM, While Pornhub Parent MindGeek Had Only 13,000," https://www.thedailybeast.com, February 24, 2021

222   https://www.cdc.gov/suicide/pdf/NCIPC-Suicide-FactSheet.pdf

223   Zak Doffman, "Is TikTok Spying on You for China?" https://www.forbes.com, July 25, 2020

224   Douglas Murray, "TIKTOK TIMEBOMB: China Is 'Evil Empire Harvesting Brits' Data Through TikTok,' Says Mike Pompeo," https://www.thesun.co.uk, July 22, 2020

225   Lorenzo Puertas, "TikTok Users Are Feeding Data to the CCP," https://theepochtimes.com, February 13 2022, Updated February 15, 2022

226 Allum Bokhari, "Red-Handed: Microsoft Created Research Lab to Work on Artificial Intelligence For Chinese Military," http://www.breitbart.com, March 3, 2022

227 Paul Bois, "REPORT: Popular Video Game 'The Last of Us II' Goes Ultra-Woke," https://www.dailywire.com, June 29, 2020

228 Mos Neammance, "Is the Metaverse Dangerous? A Deeper Look into Virtual Groping," https://www.kulturehub.com

229 Kate Kostar, "Louis Vuitton to Release New NFT Collection," https://raritysniper.com/news, April 19, 2022

230 John Ghlionn, "The Metaverse: Zuckerberg's Brave New World," https://www.cointelegraph.com, August 11, 2011

231 Joshua Rhett Miller, "Disney Exec Vows More Gay Characters Amid Huge Inclusivity Push," https://www.nypost.com, March 30, 2022

232 Bailee Hill, "Parents Outraged Over Disney Pushback on Florida Parental Rights: 'Leave the Kids Alone,'" https://www.foxnews.com, March 31, 2022

233 Marguerite Reardon, "Section 230: How It Shields Facebook and Why Congress Wants Changes," https://www.cnet.com, October 6, 2021

234 Kevin Roose, "Epoch Times, Punished by Facebook, Gets a New Megaphone on YouTube," https://www.nytimes.com, February 5, 2020

235 https://www.lexico.com/definition/media

236 Camille Kimberly, "30 Top Conservative News Sites in the U.S.," https://www.drudge-report.net, February 25, 2022

237 Gen Z Conservative, "17 Companies to Buy From and Support," https://www.thebluestateconservative.com, January 27, 2021

238 Gen Z Conservatives, "12 Woke Companies to Avoid," https://www.genzconservative.com, January 18, 2021

239   David Folkenflik, "Another Top CNN Executive Resigns as Warner Media CEO Cites Ethical Lapses," https://www.npr.org, February 16, 2022

240   "'The Chosen"—#1 Crowdfunded Media Project in History—Releases Official Trailer and First Episode for Free', https://www.prnewswire.com, April 16, 2019

241   Tony Kumer, "Children's Ministry Statistics (2019): How Do Kids Come to Christ?" https://www.ministry-to-children.com, February 17, 2022

242   "Religious Youths Are Less Likely to Experiment with Drugs and Alcohol, Baylor Study Finds," https://www.sciencedaily.com, September 8, 2014

243   "Oregon Becomes the First State to Decriminalize Hard Drugs Like Cocaine and Heroin," https://www.cbsnews.com, November 4, 2020

244   Sandra Woien, "Americans Spend $70 Billion on Pets, and That Money Could Do More Good," https://www.theconversation.com, October 15, 2018

245   "National Pet Industry Exceeds Over $100 Billion in Sales for First Time in Industry History," https://www.prnewswire.com, March 24, 2021

246   Emily DeCiccio, "The Pet Business Is Booming as Americans Spend More on Their Animals While They Work From Home," https://www.cnbc.com, December 5, 2020

247   Luke Kenton, "School Accused of Installing Litter Boxes for Students Who Identify as Cats Hits Back After Parents' Outrage," https://www.the-sun.com/news, January 22, 2022